Digital Project Practice for Banking and FinTech

New technology and changes in the regulatory framework have had a significant impact; various new players have emerged, and new business models have evolved. API-based ecosystems have become the new normal and collaboration in the financial and banking industry has reached new levels. *Digital Project Practice for Banking and FinTech* focuses on technology changes in the financial industry and their implications for business practice.

A combination of practical experience in the field as well as academic research, the book explores a wide range of topics in the multifaceted landscape of FinTech. It examines the industry's various dimensions, implications, and potential based on academic research and practice. From project management in the digital era to the regulation and supervision of FinTech companies, the book delves into distinct aspects of this dynamic field, offering valuable insights and practical knowledge. It provides an in-depth overview of various unfolding developments and how to deal with and benefit from them.

The book begins by exploring the unique challenges and opportunities project management presents in the digital era. It examines the evolving role of project management and provides strategies for effectively navigating the complexities of digital transformation initiatives. The book then covers such topics as:

- Financial Technology Canvas, a powerful tool for facilitating effective communication within FinTech teams
- Process automation implementation in the financial sector and related benefits, challenges, and best practices to drive operational efficiency and enhance customer experiences
- Robotic process automation in financial institutions
- Cyptoeconomics and its potential implications for the diffusion of payment technologies
- The efficiency and risk factors associated with digital disruption in the banking sector.

At its core, this book is about real-world practice in the digital banking industry. It is a source of different perspectives and diverse experiences from the global financial and banking industry.

Digital Project Practice for Banking and FinTech

Edited by
Tobias Endress

CRC Press
Taylor & Francis Group
Boca Raton London New York

CRC Press is an imprint of the
Taylor & Francis Group, an **informa** business

Designed cover image: Olena Shkavron

First edition published [2024]
2385 NW Executive Center Drive, Suite 320, Boca Raton FL 33431

and by CRC Press
4 Park Square, Milton Park, Abingdon, Oxon, OX14 4RN

CRC Press is an imprint of Taylor & Francis Group, LLC

© 2024 Taylor & Francis Group, LLC

ISBN: 9781032498065 (hbk)
ISBN: 9781032493657 (pbk)
ISBN: 9781003395560 (ebk)

DOI: 10.1201/9781003395560

Typeset in Garamond
by Newgen Publishing UK

Contents

Preface

Dear Reader,

Welcome to the world of FinTech, where finance and technology converge to reshape how we conduct business, manage our finances, and interact with financial institutions. The Banking and FinTech industry face dramatic changes. The rapid advancement of digital technologies has brought about a paradigm shift in the financial industry. New technology and changes in the regulatory framework have a significant impact, various new players become part of the industry and new business models emerge. API-based ecosystems have become the new normal and collaboration in the industry has reached new levels. All this opens up new opportunities and challenges for both established players and innovative startups. The book at hand is the 3rd volume of the "Digital Project Practice" book series. The previous books, *Digital Project Practice: Managing Innovation and Change,* and *Digital Project Practice for New Work and Industry 4.0* received excellent feedback and reviews. It has become a valuable resource for practitioners as well as academics. This encouraged the co-authors and me to start working on the 3rd volume. This volume is focused on recent technological changes in the financial industry and its implications for business practice. The chapters are based on practical experience in the field as well as the latest academic research on the topic. This book is a comprehensive exploration of a wide range of topics in the multifaceted landscape of FinTech, examining its various dimensions, implications, and potential based on academic research and practical experience in the field. From project management in the digital era to the regulation and supervision of FinTech companies, each chapter delves into a distinct aspect of this dynamic field, offering valuable insights and practical knowledge. This book provides an in-depth overview of various unfolding developments in this business and how to deal with and benefit from them.

Chapter 1: Project Management in the Digital Era
The first chapter sets the stage by exploring the unique challenges and opportunities that project management presents in the digital era. It examines the evolving role of project management and provides strategies for effectively navigating the complexities of digital transformation initiatives.

Chapter 2: Facilitating Communication: The Financial Technology Canvas
Communication is the lifeblood of any successful project. This chapter introduces the Financial Technology Canvas, a powerful tool for facilitating effective communication within FinTech teams. Professionals can use this canvas to align and communicate their goals, streamline processes, and foster collaboration in a rapidly evolving environment.

Chapter 3: FinTech Process Automation
Automation has revolutionized numerous industries, and FinTech is no exception. This chapter explores process automation implementation in the financial sector, discussing the benefits, challenges, and best practices for leveraging this technology to drive operational efficiency and enhance customer experiences.

Chapter 4: Robotic Process Automation in Financial Institutions
Building upon the previous chapter, we delve deeper into the application of Robotic Process Automation (RPA) in financial institutions. By automating repetitive tasks, RPA improves efficiency and frees up human resources for more strategic and value-added activities. This chapter provides insights into adopting and implementing RPA in financial settings.

Chapter 5: Future Cryptoeconomics: Digital Diffusion of PayTech
Cryptocurrencies and Blockchain technology have transformed the landscape of financial transactions. In this chapter, we explore the concept of cryptoeconomics and its potential implications for the diffusion of payment technologies (PayTech) in the future, shedding light on the changing dynamics of financial transactions.

Chapter 6: Cryptocurrencies and FinTech for People in a Hurry
For those seeking a quick understanding of cryptocurrencies and their impact on FinTech, this chapter serves as a concise guide. It provides an overview of the key concepts, benefits, and challenges associated with cryptocurrencies, enabling readers to grasp the essentials in a time-efficient manner.

Chapter 7: Digital Disruption in the Banking Sector: Evaluating Efficiency and Risk
The digitization of banking services has disrupted traditional business models and introduced new risks and opportunities. This chapter evaluates the efficiency and risk factors associated with digital disruption in the banking sector, offering insights into strategic decision-making in the face of rapidly evolving customer expectations and emerging technologies.

Chapter 8: Crowdfunding as a Digital Financing Alternative
Crowdfunding has become a popular alternative financing method for startups and innovative projects. This chapter delves into the intricacies of crowdfunding,

examining different models, strategies for success, and the evolving landscape governing this dynamic form of fundraising.

Chapter 9: Which Signals Promise Success in Crowdfunding? A Simple Guide for Start-Ups
Drawing from empirical research, this chapter provides a practical guide for startups embarking on crowdfunding campaigns. It explores the signals that indicate potential success and offers valuable tips for entrepreneurs seeking to optimize their chances of achieving their funding goals.

Chapter 10: Making Finance Invisible: What Defines Embedded Finance and its Effects on User Experience?
Embedded finance refers to the integration of financial services into non-financial platforms, enabling seamless and frictionless transactions. This chapter explores the concept of embedded finance and its profound impact on user experience, shedding light on the opportunities and challenges presented by this emerging trend.

Chapter 11: The Buy-Now-Pay-Later Ecosystem: New (Algo)Rhythms of Spending and Reframed Relationships
The buy-now-pay-later (BNPL) ecosystem has gained immense popularity, revolutionizing how consumers approach spending and debt. This chapter delves into the algorithms and dynamics of the BNPL model, examining its effects on consumer behavior, financial well-being, and the relationship between merchants and customers.

Chapter 12: Zero Trust in Banking and FinTech
This chapter introduces the Zero Trust Architecture (ZTA) concept and its application in the banking and financial services industry. It highlights the increasing need for collaboration in API-based ecosystems and the potential risks associated with data protection and transaction security. The chapter explains the need for management attention and proper design when implementing Zero Trust in an organization.

Chapter 13: Sustainable Development Goals as Unintended Consequences of Digital Transformation Strategies: Case of Siam Commercial Bank
Digital transformation strategies often have unintended consequences, and this chapter explores the case of the Sustainable Development Goals (SDGs) as a positive outcome resulting from the efforts of a financial institution, SCB in Thailand. Organizations can create lasting positive impacts by aligning digital transformation initiatives with sustainable development.

Chapter 14: Working With, Not Against: An Asian Cooperative Approach in Developing FinTech

This chapter explores the unique cooperative approach to FinTech development in Asia. Asia has been at the forefront of FinTech innovation by fostering collaboration between governments, regulators, financial institutions, and technology companies. This chapter provides insights into the Asian cooperative model and its implications for global FinTech advancement.

Chapter 15: Blockchain for Financial Transactions: An Overview of Application Fields in Payment Transactions and for Securities Services

The rapid evolution of FinTech necessitates robust regulation and supervision frameworks to ensure consumer protection, market stability, and innovation. This final chapter delves into the regulatory challenges and approaches in overseeing FinTech companies, discussing the delicate balance between fostering innovation and managing risk.

The "Digital Project Practice" book series introduces the relevant methods, covers the practical aspect, critically acclaims existing approaches and practices, and shows limitations. In essence, the books cover appropriate methods along with human/social factors. In fact, the human element is one of the running themes in the book series. You can regard it as contributing to the discussion of ongoing business practices and methods. It also aims to nourish and stimulate dialogue in the professional community.

At its core, this book is about real-world practice in the digital banking industry, different perspectives, and diverse experiences from around the world. I hope you enjoy reading it and that it can help you reflect on current practices in your organization.

With best regards,
Dr. Tobias Endress
Lautoka/Fiji Islands, July 1st, 2023

Editor

Tobias Endress is an assistant professor and program director for Business Analytics and Digital Transformation at the Asian Institute of Technology (AIT) | School of Management. He has more than 20 years of professional experience in digital project business and innovation management. His former (non-academic) roles include project manager, product owner and business analyst for leading European and US financial services companies.

He has completed professional training for banking, graduated in Computer Science and Business Administration at VWA Frankfurt/Main, and in Business Economics at Avans+ in Breda (NL). He got a Master's Degree in Leadership in Digital Communication at Berlin University of the Arts (UdK Berlin), as well as a Doctorate in Business Administration at the University of Gloucestershire in Cheltenham (UK). He is also the director of the Startup Grind Chapter in Bangkok.

Contributors

Florian W. Bartholomae is a professor of Economics at Munich Business School, associate professor at the Bundeswehr University Munich, and lecturer at IMC FH Krems.

His research interests include the economics of the information society, industrial organization, regional economics, and trade theory. Regularly, he publishes his research results in reputable journals and presents them at international conferences. Besides, he is the author of several very successful textbooks on economics, including game theory. He holds a degree in Economics from the Ludwig-Maximilians-University. Both his doctorate and his postdoctoral lecture qualification in Economics were completed at the Bundeswehr University, Munich.

Jibran Ahmed Bugvi is a doctoral candidate at the Asian Institute of Technology (AIT) School of Management. He has more than 13 years of professional experience in international banking, online travel, payments, FinTech, dealing with global payment and FinTech providers in every continent and working with innovative companies, start-ups and traditional financial institutions, particularly with regards to services on online digital platforms and embedded finance.

He holds an undergraduate degree in Accounting & Finance from Lahore University of Management Sciences (LUMS), has cleared all levels of global certifications like Chartered Financial Analyst (CFA), Financial Risk Manager (FRM) and Sustainability and Climate Risk (SCR). He has also been a speaker at various forums on payments, FinTech, climate risk.

Kourosh Dadgar is an associate professor of information systems and business analytics at the school of management, University of San Francisco. He has published papers in prestigious journals of *JAIS* (*Journal of the Association for Information Systems*), *IJIM* (*International Journal of Information Management*), *JBE* (*Journal of Business Ethics*) and presented at the flagship IS conferences of ICIS (International Conference on Information Systems) and HICSS (The Hawaii International Conference on System Sciences). He holds a health IT minitrack at the HICSS conference. His main research areas are ICT-enabled self-management and value-sensitive healthcare systems and technologies.

Wesley L. Harris, PhD, NAE is the Charles Stark Draper Professor of Aeronautics and Astronautics, Massachusetts Institute of Technology (MIT). Performed, from 1990 to 1993, as vice president and chief administrative officer of the University of Tennessee Space Institute. From 1985 to 1990 served as dean of the School of Engineering and professor of Mechanical Engineering at the University of Connecticut. From 1972 to 1985, he held several faculty and administrative positions at MIT. Research associated with transonics, aeroacoustics, rarefied gas dynamics, hypersonics, sustainment of capital assets, economic incentives in production of defense systems, and chaos in sickle cell disease. He has worked with industry and governments to design and build joint industry–government–university research programs and centers.

Michael Jacobus is a passionate project manager and expert for digitalization with 10+ years of professional experience in the German banking industry. Currently he is head of the RPA center of excellence as well as expert in process optimization at Helaba, a leading German commercial bank. Prior to that role, he was global senior project manager at Commerzbank AG implementing digital platforms and trade surveillance systems in Asia, Europe and America. He has several years of professional expertise in regulatory sales support for securities and derivatives in medium and large sized enterprises. Besides that, Michael is a certified Scrum Master and has experience in agile consulting and restructuring departmental areas to agile delivery organizations. His academic background is a B.A. from the Berlin School of Economics and Law.

Syed Shurid Khan is a former corporate banker turned professor cum meditation enthusiast. He is currently the director of the International Finance program and an assistant professor of economics at the Asian Institute of Technology (AIT) in Bangkok. His research experiences come from working on local food system modeling and renewable energy policies of the United States during his time as a researcher with the UHERO–Hawaii's top economic think-tank. His research expertise also lies in business strategy and leadership, financial markets, and applied econometrics. He also explores different areas within behavioral economics, particularly how soft skills, for example, hobbies, meditation, and the like, rewire our brains and minds and how they influence the notion of personal liberty as well as professional integrity. During his leisure time, Syed likes to travel and meditate. In recent months, his daughter Suhaa Khan is deciding between a cat and a dog to adopt.

Chris Lobello is a financial markets practitioner and occasional teacher who has worked with several FinTech startups over the past five years. After living and working in Asia for 27 years he and his family have recently relocated to Castle Rock, Colorado, where he teaches, writes, and consults with startup businesses. He holds an EMBA from INSEAD where he has served as a visiting fellow with their Center for Decision Making and Risk Management. He teaches as an adjunct at some of the world's top business schools in Asia, Europe, and North America. He serves on several industry boards and was a member of various FTSE Index advisory committees for 20 years, and is a board member for CQAsia, the Asian branch of the Chicago Quantitative Alliance. He recently took on the additional responsibility of helping to run a traveling circus, serving as CEO of The Venardos Circus.

Volkmar Mrass, is the director of the Institute for Digital Platforms in Administration and Society and professor of Digital Public Administration Management at the University of Applied Sciences, Public Administration and Finance, Ludwigsburg, Germany. Previously, he has, amongst others, held scientific positions at Georg-August-University Göttingen, Germany, and the University of Kassel, Germany. Academic stays abroad amongst others led him to the City University of Hong Kong, China, the Indian Institute of Management, Bangalore, India, the University of St. Gallen, Switzerland, and the Harvard Extension School, United States. He also worked for several years in the corporate world, amongst others more than 14 years for the IT Service Provider of the German Savings Banks Finance Group, Finanz Informatik (and its predecessor companies) in Frankfurt am Main, Germany.

Marc Nathmann, PhD is legal counsel and attorney at law at ING Germany in Frankfurt. There he advises on banking supervisory and capital markets law in the areas of payment transactions and securities.

His research interests include FinTech and AI. He regularly gives lectures on banking, capital markets law and commercial law. He has published articles on topics dealing with the legal classification of innovations and new technologies. After his studies at the University of Münster and the German University of Administrative Sciences in Speyer, he stayed abroad at a major international law firm in Shanghai, China, worked at KPMG, a securities bank and a FinTech consulting firm. He completed his doctorate on the subject of FinTech at the Technical University of Chemnitz.

Nguyen Quynh Phuong, PhD, is currently working at the The Business School, RMIT University, Vietnam as lecturer and at the School of Management and Entrepreneurship, Shiv Nadar University, Delhi NCR, India as assistant professor. She teaches undergraduate, post graduate and executive audiences. Her current research interests are sustainability, Environmental Social Governance (ESG), and business strategy for sustainability. Before becoming an educator, she worked at the International Organisation for Migration, UN Migration in London, United Kingdom, and Ho Chi Minh City, Vietnam.

Jayant Ramanand is a blockchain infrastructure specialist, DeFi operator and partner at Corthos Capital. Originally from Hyderabad, India, Jayant has lived in

Hong Kong since 2018 working full time with blockchain technologies, first with Hex Trust, a regulated Asian custodian and later with MANTRA Finance, building the future of finance. He is currently working with a fund management group to establish a proof-of-stake crypto fund as well as designing a microlending platform to bring the next wave of users into the formal financial system. He holds an MBA from the Chinese University of Hong Kong where he first met Chris while taking several of his courses.

Ruffin Relja is a senior lecturer in Marketing at Gloucestershire Business School, the University of Gloucestershire, UK. His research explores the impact of brands on different aspects of consumers' lives, in particular the formation of consumer relationships with objects and brands. Ruffin's multidisciplinary research interest lies in the broader field of Consumer Culture Theory (CCT), extending to the sustainability of innovations, markets, and consumers.

Martin Schneider, PhD, is responsible for the IT platforms at Helaba, Landesbank Hessen-Thüringen since 2022. Before that he was heading the CI/CD engineers at Commerzbank. Martin is a young leader with a passion for innovation, digitization and cultural change, project management (agile, classic) expertise, and professional experience in the banking and insurance industry. He holds a PhD (Dr. rer. pol.) in Finance from the University of Potsdam and a Master's degree from The London School of Economics and Political Science complemented by international work experience in New York, London, Luxembourg and Moscow.

Jeevesh Sharma, PhD, is working as assistant professor in the Department of Commerce, School of Business and Commerce, Manipal University, Jaipur, India. She holds her PhD (Finance) and Masters (MBA) degree. Additionally, she also holds a Master of Commerce degree. She has gained a total experience of about 8 years in academics, having a specialization in the field of finance courses. Her area of research is corporate social responsibility, corporate governance, and FinTech. She has attended and presented at many prestigious conferences, additionally also attended workshops, and FDP's. Furthermore, she has research publications (all in referred journals) including Scopus and Elsevier publications.

Nirmala Sookharry is the head of Optimizers within Capital Markets Project Management Practice at FIS Global, one of the leading providers of technology solutions for merchants, banks and capital markets firms globally. Nirmala is a versatile and accomplished professional with over 15 years' experience in project and program management roles and process improvement. She is leading a specialist team to drive delivery excellence across capital markets by adopting a new way of working and making full use of the latest disruptive technology.

Having a strong business acumen with extensive FinTech industry knowledge, Nirmala has led several cross-functional projects and multi-product programs for several Tier-1 investment banking sectors. Being a product agnostic project leader, Nirmala has a track record of highly successful engagement across the investment banking sectors. She is a pioneer, a strong believer in working smarter and will never hesitate to challenge the status quo.

Eva Stumpfegger is currently professor of Finance at Munich Business School. During her professional career, she has been very successful in the fields of brokerage, asset management, banking, insurance, and consulting and can build on a comprehensive wealth of experience.

She holds a degree in business administration from Passau University and a Doctorate in Business Administration from the University of Gloucestershire.

Sundar Venkatesh, PhD, School of Management and Entrepreneurship, Shiv Nadar Institution of Eminence, Delhi NCR, India. Dr. Sundar Venkatesh is an educator committed to academic excellence with a philosophy of application-based teaching and research. He has significant experience of working across cultures and is a winner of several outstanding teacher awards.

He is well known for excellence in designing and delivering customized learning solutions for executive and leadership development to large companies across a variety of industries, regionally. Dr. Venkatesh has a track record of significant contributions to academic administration and higher education management in multicultural settings and online teaching. He is the author of several publications including four books, numerous articles in international refereed journals and conferences and case studies based in emerging markets of Asia. He is an experienced supervisor of research at Master's and PhD levels.

Philippa Ward is a reader in Services Marketing at Gloucestershire Business School, University of Gloucestershire, UK and has over 25 years of retail and academic experience. She also has a range of journal and book publications and over 30 doctoral completions. Philippa's research centres on the effects of situational factors on consumers, the psychological and sociological determinants of consumption, and the exploration of value. She is a passionate advocate both of the application of a wider range of methods in marketing research and of transdisciplinarity.

Jarunee Wonglimpiyarat, PhD, ACA, FCCA, CPA, CIA, CFE, CGAP, CFSA, CRMA, FCMA, CGMA, CISA, CISM, CLP, RTTP, is full professor of Technology Management. She graduated from the University of Manchester, UK, and has postdoctoral fellowships at Boston University and Harvard University, USA. She has working experiences at PricewaterhouseCoopers, Standard Chartered Bank, Citibank N.A., Boston Technology Commercialisation Institute, US Securities and

Exchange Commission and serves as visiting professor at Boston University, USA. Dr. Wonglimpiyarat currently works as a research scientist at the Department of Aeronautics and Astronautics, Massachusetts Institute of Technology, USA and Leonardo Research Centre, Imperial College London, UK.

Anita Lifen Zhao is an associate professor in Marketing at the School of Management, Swansea University, UK. She considers herself a mixed-method researcher and is interested in consumerism and sustainable consumption in China, as well as other emerging and developing markets. She also investigates the adoption and usage of online financial services among young consumers. She has published her work in a range of journals, including the *Journal of Business Research*, the *Journal of Marketing Management*, the *Journal of Consumer Behaviour*, the *Service Industries Journal*, and the *International Journal of Bank Marketing*.

Chapter 1

Project Management in the Digital Era

Nirmala Sookharry

Chapter Overview

In this ever-changing, ambiguous, and dynamic landscape, disruptive technologies are reshaping markets at an unprecedented and extraordinary velocity–rendering many traditional business models obsolete. *Project Management is no exception.* The massive ripple effect of disruptive technologies is proving to be a powerful catalyst in accelerating how Project Management practice adapts to new methods to deliver value to their customers and assert their relevance in this highly competitive industry. High performing organizations are already embracing this disruption, reimagining their mission, adopting innovative tools, with a keen eye on bridging the costly gap between strategy design and value delivery. FinTech leaders are already aligning project delivery with organizational strategy and fully understand the urgent need to shift to a digital practice.

As the head of Optimizers at FIS Global, I am at the forefront of strategizing a new operating model to drive operational efficiency. One of our key initiatives is to onboard an innovative Project Management tool to automate manual, repeatable processes which will free up our project managers' capacity and allow them to focus on delivering real business value to their customer base.

DOI: 10.1201/9781003395560-1

1.1 Next Gen Digital Project Management

1.1.1 How will the Project Manager lead in the Digital Age?

The continuous digital shift and emergence of innovative tools have undoubtedly changed the perception of the ideal Project Manager. Project Management has evolved over the past decade from a simple rulebook to embedding a deeper understanding of organizational maturity and business agility. Project Management methodologies and common best practices provided by institutions such as the Project Management Institute (PMI) will need to evolve further to capture the true essence of business agility by adapting to the needs of the disruptive digital world (PMI, n.d.). Traditionally, Project Managers are known to follow a specific project methodology (waterfall, agile or hybrid) to deliver their projects focusing predominantly on the triple constraints: Scope, Cost and Time (Baratta, 2007; PMI, 2021). In today's rapidly evolving and highly competitive environment, organizations need to equip their Project Management Practice with a toolkit to accelerate project delivery to deliver value to their clients, without compromising on project governance and best practices.

The Next Gen Digital Practice will heavily rely on organizations and individuals alike to have a growth mindset, fully embrace a broad spectrum of competencies, adopt a common framework to standardize Project Management approaches and industrialize project administration through automation. Using innovative Project Management software, organizations can complete certain tasks exponentially faster and with far lower error rates than humans can achieve manually which will eventually drive operational efficiency. Tasks that are generally low complexity such as project reporting, risk, and issue management can be easily handled by automation. By freeing up capacity, the Next Gen Project Managers will have more time for strategic, higher-value work and make impactful contribution in leading rather than day to day management of routine tasks.

In the new world, we will see the roles of Project Managers slowly shift into Value Managers within the value delivery landscape—expanding to be those of a strategic advisor, innovator, communicator, big thinker, and leaders. Project Leaders will be in high demand as organizations will recognize that strategy is implemented through projects and programs. As disruptive technology frees them from mundane routines, it will provide more opportunity to innovate and focus on delivering excellence. As Project Leaders take on a more expansive role, training and skill development will become even more crucial. Innovators are responding with formal processes for developing those competencies through internal and external training in data science, collaborative leadership and embracing an innovative mindset.

1.1.2 Developing the Next Generation Project Management Skillsets

Evidently, success relies on a workforce that can manage the impact of new technologies. Project Leaders are essential in tomorrow's changing landscape. According to a report by the Project Management Institute, by 2027 employers will need nearly 88 million people in project related roles and 85% of the jobs that will be available by 2030 have not even been invented yet (PMI, 2017). As organizations continue to recognize the importance of Project Leaders, they will need to make training and development a priority, adopt a formal, documented career path for Project Leaders to retain talent and reduce attrition.

In addition to the core Project Management skillsets that span across leadership, effective communication, negotiation (to mention but a few), the next generation Project Leaders will need to inculcate a new set of skills to strive for in this digital era.

- *Digital awareness*: Project Management practice is evolving past the weekly progress reports in board meetings for stakeholder engagement. It has now become empowered with the use of digital applications, platforms, and dashboards for instant communication and real time progress updates. The Next Gen Project Manager needs to fully grasp new technologies and be capable of using the new age digital tools to manage their project.
- *Innovative mindset*: Do less and achieve more. Project Managers who can think innovatively and find smarter ways to achieve great outcomes will be favored in today's job markets. Skills and experience alone are no longer sufficient. It is now crucial to innovate and get creative to remain relevant.
- *Data driven decision making*: Utilizing and interpreting data to make smart business decisions is at the core of digital project practice. The challenge today is synthesizing and structuring the high volumes of available data to gain useful insights that can move a project forward. The next gen Project Leaders will be using the latest tool to make insightful decisions and will gain a competitive edge.
- *Operating models*: In an effort to keep up with the digital age, organizations are becoming increasingly agile and are finding ways to optimize to maximize efficiencies and are reducing costs while keeping the level and quality of the value they are delivering. The Next Gen Project Manager will be more digitally aware and will have a solid understanding of the changes to operating models happening across different sectors.
- *Business agility*: Mature organizations develop their digital strategy in alignment with their business strategies. Gartner reports that 91% of businesses are engaged in some form of digital transformation initiatives. The Project Management Practice must be integrated in such a way as to deliver business agility objectives. The Next Gen Project Manager will be more aligned with the digital strategies, business agility objectives and digital transformation initiatives.

The evolution of the Project Manager and the next career step will involve an enhancement of skill sets and mindset. Not only Project Managers must become more *Digitally Aware* but they must also understand the *True Essence of Digital Transformation*. Beyond using digital transformation as a token, Project Managers must gain a deep

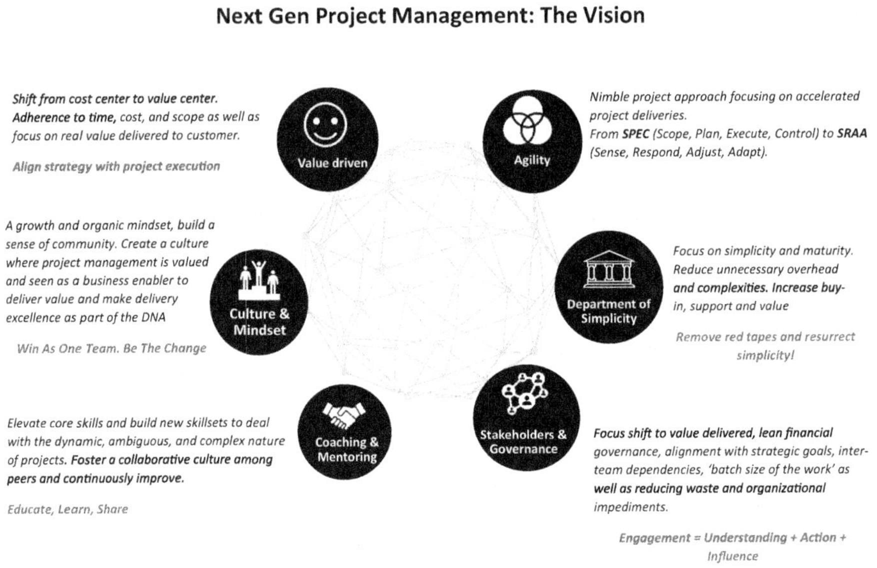

Next Gen Project Management: The Vision

Shift from cost center to value center. **Adherence to time,** cost, and scope as well as focus on real value delivered to customer.

Align strategy with project execution

Value driven

Nimble project approach focusing on accelerated project deliveries. From **SPEC** (Scope, Plan, Execute, Control) to **SRAA** (Sense, Respond, Adjust, Adapt).

Agility

A growth and organic mindset, build a sense of community. Create a culture where project management is valued and seen as a business enabler to deliver value and make delivery excellence as part of the DNA

Win As One Team. Be The Change

Culture & Mindset

Focus on simplicity and maturity. Reduce unnecessary overhead **and complexities. Increase buy-in,** support and value

Remove red tapes and resurrect simplicity!

Department of Simplicity

Elevate core skills and build new skillsets to deal with the dynamic, ambiguous, and complex nature of projects. **Foster a collaborative culture among peers and continuously improve.**

Educate, Learn, Share

Coaching & Mentoring

Stakeholders & Governance

Focus shift to value delivered, lean financial governance, alignment with strategic goals, inter-team dependencies, 'batch size of the work' as **well as reducing waste and organizational impediments.**

Engagement = Understanding + Action + Influence

Figure 1.1   Next Gen Project management: the vision.

understanding of the digital space and the different elements it contains such as the Internet of Things (IoT), Artificial Intelligence (AI), Blockchain, Virtual Reality (VR), Mixed Reality (MR), and Agile Project Management (Jeschke & Endress, 2023).

1.2   Transforming Project Management into Strategic Value Management

Studies show that Project Managers are very well placed to be Value Management leaders (StarAgile, 2019; Thiry, 2019, 2014). The Digital Project Practice will need to repurpose itself and redesign its mission and operation to be more value adding, less bureaucratic, more customer focused, and more in line with agile product management and other modern ways of working. The Next Gen Project Managers will need a growth mindset, evolve traditional delivery metrics and methodologies, and focus on strategic value to play a key role in this transformation. The Next Gen Project Managers will need to be the advocates of newer technologies, having the ability to supervise course correction and being an authority on the technologies themselves.

In today's landscape where disruption is the new normal, organizations need to create a culture of constant change and innovation by encouraging continuous learning and development. Project Leaders must become the change advocates and help others to understand the new technologies in projects, create new processes and cross pollinate learning and development. Organizations must become data powered centers, where leaders rely on data analytics to make informed, actionable decisions.

Finally, the Next Gen Project Manager must become a strategic collaborator and business enabler who will drive strategy delivery and execution. Organizations need to interrupt their status quo to build the future. To remain relevant, the Next Gen Project manager should be a value center not just a cost center.

1.3 How Disruptive Technologies will Transform Project Management

According to research by the Standish Group, approximately $48 trillion are invested in projects every year. Yet only 30% of projects are considered successful. The throw away effort, wasted resources and unrealized benefits of the other 70% are astounding. One main reason why project success rates are so poor is the low level of maturity of technologies available for managing them. Most organizations and Project Leaders are still using spreadsheets, PowerPoint, and other MS Office applications that have not evolved much over the past few decades. These are adequate when you are measuring project success by deliverables and deadlines met, but they fall short in an environment where projects and initiatives are always adapting and continuously changing the business. Although there has been a slight improvement in project portfolio management applications, planning and team collaboration capabilities, automation and "intelligent" features are still lacking.

Change is coming soon, in the next 5 years, at least 75% of project management tasks will be run by AI, powered by big data, machine learning (ML), and natural language processing. When this next generation of tools is widely adopted, there will be radical changes in the Project Management domain.

High performing organizations and Project Leaders that are most prepared for This moment of disruption will stand to reap the most rewards. Nearly every aspect of project management, from planning, reporting to processes and people, will be impacted. Let's take a look at the Top Four.

1.3.1 Better Selection and Prioritization using AI Prediction

The selection and prioritization of projects are a type of prediction often done using pre-defined set of criteria, that is, which projects will bring the most value to the organization? When the correct data is available, AI will be able to detect patterns that cannot be discerned by other means and can vastly exceed human accuracy in making predictions. ML-driven prioritization will eventually result in:

■ Faster identification of launch-ready projects that have the right fundamentals in place

- Selection of projects that have higher chances of success and delivering the highest benefits
- A better BALANCE in the project portfolio and overview of risk in the organization
- Removal of human biases from decision-making.

1.3.2 Enhanced Support for the Project Management Office

Data analytics and automation startups will help organizations streamline and optimize the role of the project management office (PMO). The use of new intelligent tools will radically transform the way PMOs operate and perform with:

- Better monitoring of project progress
- The capability to anticipate potential problems and to address some simple ones automatically
- Automated project setup, preparation, and distribution of project reports
- Compliance monitoring for processes and policies.

1.3.3 Improved, Faster Project Definition, Planning, and Reporting

One of the most developed areas in project management automation is risk management. New applications use big data and ML to help leaders and project managers anticipate risks that might otherwise go unnoticed. These tools can already propose mitigating actions, and soon, they will be able to adjust the plans automatically to avoid certain types of risks.

Similar approaches will soon facilitate project definition, planning, and reporting. These exercises are now time-consuming, repetitive, and mostly manual. ML, natural language processing, and plain text output will lead to:

- Improved project scoping by automating the time-consuming collection and analysis of user stories. These tools will reveal potential problems such as ambiguities, duplicates, omissions, inconsistencies, and complexities.
- Tools to facilitate scheduling processes and draft detailed plans and resource demands.
- Automated reporting will replace today's manually produced reports—which are often weeks old—with real-time data. These tools will also drill deeper than is currently possible, displaying project status, benefits achieved, potential slippage in a clear, objective way.

1.3.4   Virtual Project Assistants

Practically overnight, ChatGPT changed the world's understanding of how AI can analyse massive sets of data and generate novel and immediate insights in plain text. In project management, tools like these will power "bots" and "virtual project assistants."

The virtual project assistant will make full use of historical data and learn from previous time entries, project planning, and the overall context to tailor interactions and smartly capture critical project information. PMOtto is an ML-enabled virtual project assistant that is already in use. A user can ask PMOtto *"Schedule David to install and configure the test server and allocate him full time to complete this task."* The assistant might reply, *"Based on previous similar tasks allocated to David, it seems that he will need two weeks to do the work and not one week as you requested. Can I adjust it?"*

1.4   Now Let's Future Forward to Year 2030 …

1.4.1   Imagine the Future of Project Management in this Real Case Business Scenario

18 June 2030, the CEO of a leading FinTech organization is on her way from London to meet a strategic customer in Philadelphia. After check in at her hotel suite, the day before the big meeting, she takes her smartphone to revisit the client portfolio. Within a few taps, she knows the status of every project and what percentage of expected benefits each one has already delivered. Real time dashboard views of overall status, list of all active risks, key performance indicators are available within a few clicks, as are each team member's morale level and the overall buy-in of critical stakeholders.

She drills down on the "New Product Launch" project which has high strategic significance as it impacts the organization key initiative to successfully launch this product by Q4 2030, with a strong pipeline in Europe and Asian Pacific. A few months earlier, a large competitor had launched a similar product, prompting her company to accelerate its own sustainability rollout. Many AI-driven self-adjustments have already occurred, based on parameters chosen by the project manager and the project team at the initiative's outset. The app informs the CEO of every change that needs her attention—as well as potential risks—and prioritizes decisions that she must make, providing potential mitigation plans to each.

Before making any choices, the CEO calls the Project Manager, who now spends most of his time coaching and supporting the team, maintaining regular conversations with key stakeholders, and cultivating a high-performing culture. A few weeks earlier the project had been slightly behind, and the app recommended that the team should apply agile techniques to speed up one project stream. During the meeting, they simulate possible solutions and agree on a path forward. The project plan is automatically updated, and messages are sent informing affected team members and stakeholders of the changes and a projection of the expected results.

Thanks to new technologies and ways of working, a strategic project that could have drifted out of control—perhaps even to failure—is now again in line to be successful and deliver the expected results.

Back in the present, project management doesn't always move along quite as smoothly, but this future is probably less than a decade away. To get there sooner, innovators and organizations should be investing in project management technology now!

1.5 Summary

The application of artificial intelligence in project management will bring significant benefits, not only in the automation of administrative and low value tasks, but even more important, including AI and other disruptive technologies in your toolbox will help many organizations, its leaders and project managers select, define, and implement projects more successfully.

It's a brutal business reality: Project Management must evolve. No longer inextricably tied to traditional success measures like schedule and budget, this next generation Project Leader must be a strategic enabler—bridging the gap between a company's vision and how that vision comes to life. Not only will this evolution ensure that the organization is ready to make the most of disruptive technologies, but that it can withstand future challenges and capitalize on future opportunities. Higher-performing organizations are leading the way—changing their charters, adjusting approaches, and reinventing processes in ways that allow their organization to thrive in the new age of disruption.

References

Baratta, A. (2007). The value triple constraint: Measuring the effectiveness of the project management paradigm. *PMI Global Congress Proceedings*.

Jeschke, G., & Endress, T. (2023). Industry 4.0–The Impact on Communication and Work Environment. In T. Endress, *Digital Project Practice for New Work and Industry 4.0* (1st ed., pp. 1–15). Auerbach Publications.

PMI. (n.d.). PMI. Retrieved June 11, 2023, from www.pmi.org/

PMI (Ed.). (2021). *The standard for project management and a guide to the project management body of knowledge (PMBOK guide)* (Seventh edition). Project Management Institute, Inc.

PMI. (2017). *Project Management Job Growth and Talent Gap Report*.

StarAgile. (2019). *Earned Value Analysis in Project Management—An Overview*. Staragile. Com.

Thiry, M. (2014). Strategic value management. *PMI Global Congress Proceedings*.

Thiry, M. (2019, October 11). *Making sense of value: What is value?*

Additional Reading

PMI–Thought Leadership series.

Chapter 2

Facilitating Communication: The Financial Technology Canvas

Tobias Endress

Chapter Overview

Financial systems are becoming increasingly complex, and API-based ecosystems, Open Banking, Embedded Finance, and FinTech, have become the backbone of the modern banking system. However, this complexity needs to be managed. It becomes increasingly demanding to get an overview of existing systems, onboard new team members, and systematically plan enhancements. While there are several tools and techniques to describe architecture and systems from a technical perspective, it seems that there are only a few approaches that allow a more holistic perspective, including business models, regulatory requirements, and other relevant aspects. Fragmented documentation and knowledge silos make it difficult to plan strategic enhancements. This chapter aims to introduce a template for developing new financial technology systems and documenting existing ones comprehensively. Whereas the goal is not necessarily to describe all the details, but to bring the central aspects to the point in order to enable all the different stakeholders to participate in the discussion. It can be an important tool for communication, collaboration and to support informed decisions.

DOI: 10.1201/9781003395560-2

2.1 Background, Inspiration, and Context

Financial technology has undergone significant and disruptive changes. The "importance of ecosystems is evident when emerging technologies develop in the FinTech sector and interdependent companies influence the direct development of technology, competencies, and opportunities for new business models in financial services" (Palmié et al., 2020, p. 8). Various new players have become part of the banking ecosystem, building on the concepts of Open Banking and integrating various third-party-providers and technology providers in the banking ecosystem (Schneider, 2023). Actually, it could be regarded as a specific application of Open Innovation (Chesbrough, 2012; Endress, 2023) where a financial organisation doesn't just rely on their internal resources such as their own employees for research and development for innovation. While this approach can be an accelerator for innovation, it also increases the complexity and requires coordination and communication with additional stakeholders (with potentially diverse backgrounds).

The financial system in a commercial bank can be very diverse and might require a robust infrastructure designed to manage various financial operations efficiently. It typically consists of multiple interfaces and software applications that enable seamless interaction between the bank's internal departments, customers, and external partners. The system's primary use cases may include account management, financial transaction processing (PayTech), investment, lending and credit evaluation, risk management, and regulatory compliance (RegTech). The management in

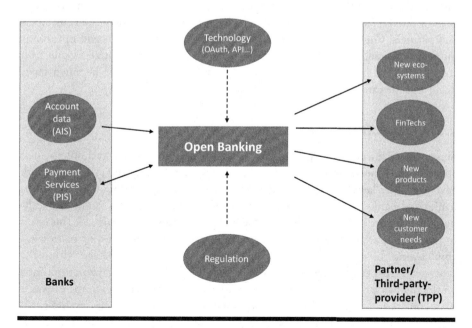

Figure 2.1   Simplified overview of an open banking ecosystem.

this diverse environment requires additional communication efforts and the development of a common language. This chapter suggests a simple approach that gives a quick overview of potentially complex ecosystems. It is somewhat inspired by the Business Model Canvas, which is an established tool to communicate business models as a simple story in the format of a one-pager (Osterwalder et al., 2010). Still, the Financial Technology Canvas is totally different and it is much more focused on the technical aspects and industry specifics like regulation, development (Change the Bank) and operations model (Run the Bank). I've developed this template from practical experience in various banks and financial institutions as well as from experience drawn from teaching financial engineering. The Financial Technology Canvas is intended to serve as a template, overview, and starting point for discussion.

2.2   Key Elements of the Financial Technology Canvas

The Financial Technology Canvas aims to provide an overview of a specific system's most relevant business, technological, and regulatory components. It could be used for a specific technology stack but also–and probably more importantly–to get an overview of the most relevant parts of business use cases with a focus on a specific business objective (see Figure 2.2).

Let's go through the several items of the Financial Technology Canvas step by step. It comprises of several elements on one page. Starting with the key technology, infrastructure, and regulation. In the centre of the canvas is the main objective, and on the left side are opportunities, challenges, and risks next to the ecosystems and partners. On the lower part of the canvas are the development and operations models indicated. The aim is to get the most relevant information at a glance. Of course, the details of the elements might need to be documented in much more detail and the canvas can/should only be a starting point for discussion.

2.2.1   Enabler/Key Technology

Since we are introducing an approach to communicate financial technology, it is apparent that the technology part is crucial to understanding the system at hand. Several enabler/key technologies play a crucial role in the operations of FinTech companies and banks. This item should address questions like, "What is our key technology? Who are our key suppliers? Which key resources do we need? ..." This refers to the general architecture, software used, programming languages, or platforms–emphasising the gatekeeper, partners, and key resources for *your* stake within the ecosystem. This can be seen as the counterpart for the Ecosystem/Partner outlined on the right side of the canvas which refers to external partners. Even if the canvas is to be concise and crisp, don't be tempted to stay at a buzzword level (for example, AI, big data, Blockchain, and smart, data-driven technologies), but describe the crucial core of the system. If you use Blockchain, for example, then you should highlight

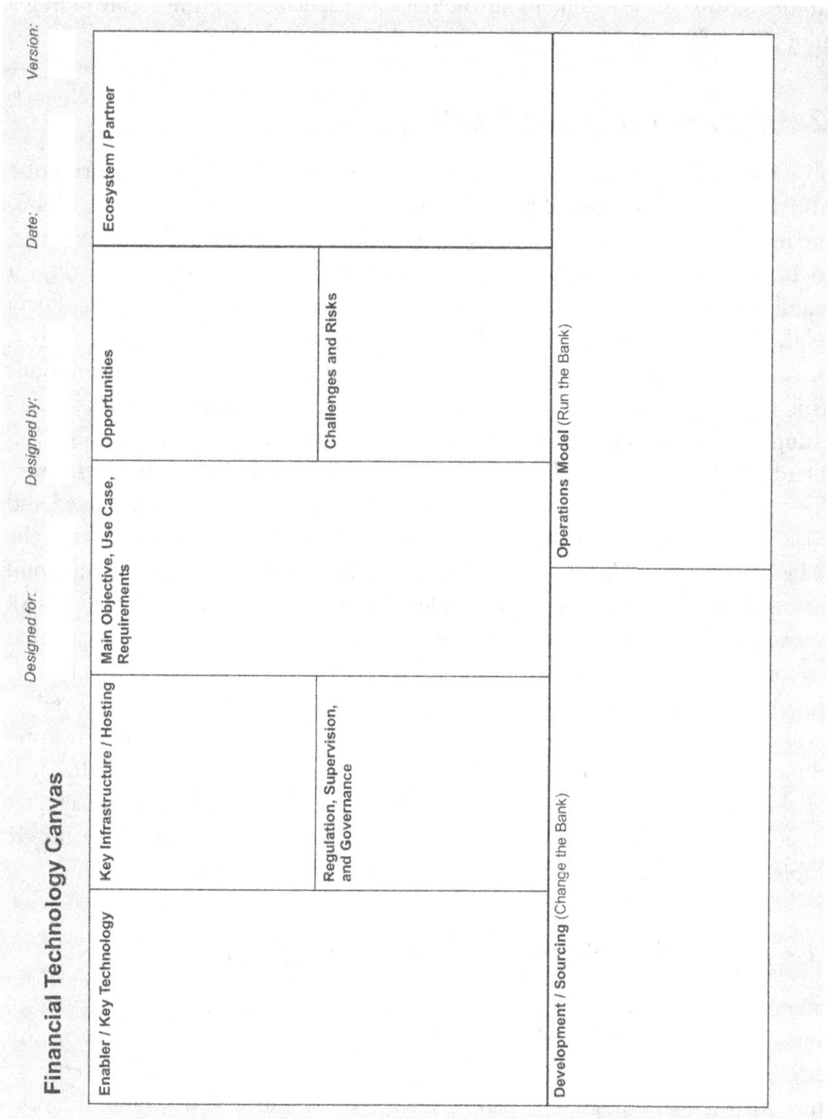

Financial Technology Canvas

Enabler / Key Technology	Key Infrastructure / Hosting	Main Objective, Use Case, Requirements	Opportunities	Ecosystem / Partner
	Regulation, Supervision, and Governance		Challenges and Risks	
Development / Sourcing (Change the Bank)			Operations Model (Run the Bank)	

Designed for:　　Designed by:　　Date:　　Version:

Figure 2.2　Financial technology canvas template (you can find a template to download at www.digital-project-practice.com).

which Blockchain is used (for example, Ethereum, IBM Blockchain, Hyperledger Fabric). Every Blockchain (or other key technology) has specific attributes and certain features (Lawton, 2023; Six et al., 2020). You might also want to highlight if it is dependent on any specific resources, especially when this resource is in high demand or of limited availability. Think about the relevant aspects to communicate aiding a common understanding of the applied technology solutions.

2.2.2 Key Infrastructure/Hosting

The objective of this item is to cover inquiries pertaining to, "What infrastructure is required? In-house or external hosting? Cloud, Co-Location, On-Premise, Web3? Redundancy and access control? Network connectivity (Campus, Direct, Extranet, Leased Line, VPN?) …". Traditionally, the vast majority of corporate hosting of banks and financial institutions were implemented within the infrastructure of data centres that were owned and operated by the organisation itself (Crosby & Curtis, 2021). However, it appears that there is an increasing trend towards cloud solutions as this is typically associated with advantages such as cost savings, enhanced data processing capacity, scalability, and even improved quality of financial services (Hon & Millard, 2018; Yan, 2017). There are significant differences in how the infrastructure is set up and managed, for example, IaaS and PaaS platforms are managed and upgraded by cloud services providers, whereas SaaS platforms are operated from the bank's IT department (Mahalle et al., 2021). Data protection and security of cloud architecture infrastructure continue to challenge organisations (Mahalle et al., 2018). However, it can be argued that a specialised cloud service provider or hyperscaler has more resources and knowledge to tackle these issues as compared to a (small/mid-size) financial services organisation. The location and type of hosting is not only a technical question as it might also have a direct impact on business related features including availability, network latency, and even fairness (Goyal et al., 2022). It should also be stated where the data will be stored and processed, as this may have implications for the governance of the system and what regulatory requirements are applicable (see also item "Regulation, Supervision, and Governance" below).

2.2.3 Regulation, Supervision, and Governance

The financial services industry is a highly regulated environment. The purpose of this item is to tackle queries related to "What are the *key* rules that apply in this context? Is authorization needed? Reporting obligations? What is the governance structure for the technology? …". Some researchers argue that we "must innovate regulatory methods, promote financial pilots, use regulatory technology, and effectively prevent risks brought by opportunities" (Dai, 2021, p. 11) associated with new technology in FinTech and Banking. Having legal advice in the project teams appears to be a necessity (Nathmann, 2020). Furthermore, new standards like ISO 20022 (payment messages) may influence and transform segments of the industry over a period of several years and might outline the roadmap for further developments in the industry. However, in many cases, there are still communication barriers due to the different perspectives and working cultures. Introducing the Financial Technology Canvas might help to overcome some of these frictions in communication and foster a common understanding. It can be argued that a comprehensive regulatory framework provides investment protection (Amstad, 2019; Baker & Robinson, 2021). Some also argue that it can empower financial inclusion (Abubakar & Handayani, 2019). A stable and reasonable development of regulation and appropriate technology (RegTech) might even open an opportunity for the establishment of a new way to design and implement regulation and the idea of "embedded regulation" (Zetzsche et al., 2020). Keep in mind that banking supervision and regulators are important stakeholders in the financial ecosystem. We need not only to ensure adherence to regulatory requirements, but technology might also help to automate reporting and track compliance-related activities. Financial regulators are challenged to respond to the innovation opportunities presented by financial technology. Current rules are not necessarily sufficient or adequate to regulate new business models and new products relating to innovations such as crypto assets or digital financial services. Some regulators have been establishing innovation hubs and regulatory sandboxes to respond to new financial innovations (De Koker et al., 2020).

Data protection and privacy are also relevant in this context. Actually, the paradigm shift from "the company owns the data" to "the client owns the data" can be considered a main driver for Open Banking–although there is apparently still room for improvement to empower the clients (Dorfleitner et al., 2021). The management of client data gets more complex in collaborative environments (API-based ecosystems), and privacy management needs to be taken to a new level (Long et al., 2020; Mahalle et al., 2018; Wang et al., 2020). It might also be helpful to indicate the ecological footprint of the system and its relation to the UN Sustainable Development Goals (SDGs) (Hoang et al., 2022; *Sustainable Development Goals | United Nations Development Programme*, n.d.). Carbon risks, just to name one example, enjoy increasing awareness in and outside of the financial community (Semieniuk et al., 2021). Managing the governance and navigating the regulatory environment are central aspects of the development and operation of financial technology.

2.2.4 *Main Objective, Use Case, Requirements*

This is, for good reason, the most central item on the canvas. It is about the business value, commercialisation, and highlights the main objective of the system. All other items are only there because this is the objective to be achieved/supported. This item aims to provide answers to questions regarding "What value do we deliver to the customer? What is the purpose of the product? What are the core requirements and MVP? …". Still, it is not easy to find a common language that is precise enough but still easy to understand for the diverse stakeholders in this context. Communicating system requirements is a difficult topic and there are various approaches with the aim of facilitating it. Examples are, the Unified Modelling Language, User Requirements Notation (Sharifi et al., 2022), Scaled Agile Framework (SAFe) and banks aim to become more 'agile' (Santhanam & Suresh, 2022). Still, these approaches are mainly focused on internal processes, IT, and software requirements engineering (Farooq et al., 2022) and might not be very useful in describing the business-driven ecosystem, including factors like business value and monetization. However, the business value of a system is crucial in the understanding and strategic planning of the system. The understanding of the system and how the FinTech solution might create value for businesses is a central component (Leong, 2018). Having a clearly stated objective can help to keep a "laser-sharp focus" and avoid "gold plating" (Burke, 2022). Even when the financial system is already implemented and has reached a stage of maturity, it can be helpful to maintain details about a minimum viable product (MVP) as it describes the functional core of the technology from a business perspective. New developments and enhancements should be aware of this functional core to make informed decisions.

2.2.5 Opportunities

The item opportunities are closely related to the business value of the financial system. It describes "unharvested" or potential value that might occur in the context of the described system. The intention of this item is to address questions involving "What opportunities can be identified in context with the system? Which ones have we already addressed? How can we leverage the opportunities? …". Academic literature points out that technologies may help reduce the cost of customer acquisition and servicing, and banks will be much better able to provide easy access to all segments of the population and develop products for disadvantaged people, such as people in remote areas, immigrants and other sensitive groups. Banks are also expected to become more socially responsible on climate change, diversity, health, work-life balance, and so forth. (Murinde et al., 2022). But to emphasise once again, the aim here is not to present some abstract opportunities but to explain specific and tangible possibilities in context with the financial technology presented. While the practice of "Opportunities Management" gets increasing attention in business practice, there is, unfortunately, still only very limited academic research and it seems that best practices need to be established. Opportunities management is often discussed in context with risk management (for example, Alcoat, 2018; Petravi, 2008). Still, it might be helpful to separate these topics as the strategies to leverage this information might be different. Opportunities can be a mighty driving force for innovation and growth. "Banks should pay attention to the current status in inter-organizational factors and notice that innovation would not be realised without appropriate grounds and success should not be expected in a vacuum" (Mousavi et al., 2022, p. 151).

2.2.6   Challenges and Risks

Banks and FinTech organisations are exposed to numerous financial, operational, and environmental risks (Van Greuning & Brajovic Bratanovic, 2020). Risk management is an important task in the organisation. This item is designed to tackle questions that revolve around "What are the core risks related to the development and operations of this financial system? What can be done to mitigate the risks? …". Risk management has always been an important topic for banks and financial institutions. It has gained even more attention and prominence since the global financial crisis, and there has been a vivid discussion and strong focus on how to manage risks and how risks are being identified, measured, and reported in a timely manner (Leo et al., 2019).

Report automation is already a well-established practice in many organisations. It is expected that the risk management domain will apply AI and machine learning techniques to enhance capabilities (Leo et al., 2019). Still, new technology also comes with new challenges and risks. Artificial intelligence, as a recent development, also provides a set of new challenges and risks. "Risk arises from non-representative data, bias inherent in representative data, choice of algorithms, and human decisions, based on their AI interpretations (and whether humans are involved at all once AI has been unleashed). Risk reduction requires a vigilant division of labour between AI and humans for the foreseeable future" (Ashta & Herrmann, 2021).

2.2.7   Ecosystem/Partner

The aim of this item is to provide clarity on questions related to "What is your business ecosystem? What are our main partners? What type of relationship does

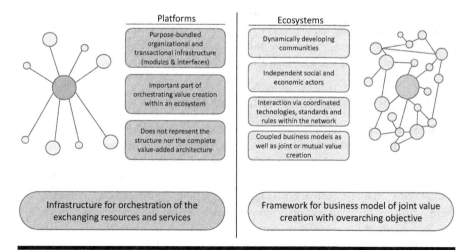

Figure 2.3   Ecosystems developed on platforms.

each of our partners expect us to establish and maintain with them? Which ones have we already established? How are they integrated with the rest of our systems infrastructure? …". An ecosystem represents more than just interaction with partners. It can be considered as the next step in an evolution and represents a social and economic system where various actors interact simultaneously for mutual value creation (see Figure 2.3).

2.2.8 Development/Sourcing (Change the Bank)

The primary objective of this item is to address inquiries regarding "What are the most important costs to create the system and infrastructure? Which Key Resources are most expensive? Make or buy or hybrid? Which Key Activities are most expensive? What is the key know-how? Are there any entry or access barriers or demanding requirements? Do we need licenses? How is the intellectual property (IP) managed? …". It should be indicated whether it is a standard software, the mere use of a platform, or its own development. Over the past three decades, technology has evolved at a rapid pace, with each change having a major impact on banking technology. The evolution has been from the mainframe to client-server, to the use of the internet and now cloud computing. New technologies are arriving daily, eroding business models and shifting the barriers to entry into banking. To remain relevant, the bank must proactively map the future and innovate in business as usual. To meet the challenge, the bank must continuously discover, assess, align, and implement industrialization and innovation drivers in developing and deploying technologies and business models. (Bhatia, 2022b). While clients might expect banks to be stable and maybe even conservative, there is also the expectation to provide state-of-the-art services and keep up with new technology. Large language models (LLM), for example, might change the way of banking and could introduce a new era of conversational banking (Bhatia, 2022a). It can help to establish a culture and a clear structure for embracing ongoing change (often referred to as a "growth mindset"). This helps to build up capacities and the needed mindset to avoid technical debt, and crippling tendencies and can help to embrace 'the next big thing'.

2.2.9 Operations Model (Run the Bank)

The item 'Sourcing and Operations Model' describes how the system is operated in the day-to-day mode, also known as 'Run the Bank' (RTB) activities. This item seeks to cover questions that encompass "What do we need for the ongoing operations? What Service Levels are needed (SLA)? How is service and support organised? How is knowledge management organised? Is ongoing or regular training necessary? Is there a process for changes and improvements? Do we run it ourselves, or do we involve a partner? Do we want to outsource any service or support? …".

Commercial banks traditionally follow a centralised sourcing and operations model. A commercial bank maintains its own dedicated IT infrastructure and employs in-house IT teams responsible for system development, maintenance, and support. The bank's operations involve continuous monitoring, maintenance, and enhancement of the financial system to ensure optimal performance, data security, and compliance with regulatory standards. Additionally, the bank may collaborate with external vendors for specific functionalities like cybersecurity, software updates, or specialised services.

FinTech companies, in contrast, often adopt a hybrid sourcing and operations model, combining in-house capabilities with outsourced services. While core development and strategic functions are usually handled in-house, they may collaborate with technology partners, cloud service providers, or open-source communities for certain components. The operational focus lies on constant innovation, customer support, and service improvement, with dedicated teams ensuring system availability, scalability, and compliance with regulatory frameworks.

Note: The specific interfaces, use cases, and sourcing models may vary depending on the nature of the commercial bank or FinTech company. Many commercial banks aim to adopt FinTech strategies and understand that mastering the technology is a crucial skill. Finding the right balance between the trend to outsource IT services (to save cost and focus on core competencies) and keeping expertise in-house is a management task, one of the most demanding decisions for senior executives.

2.3 Practical Application of the Financial Technology Canvas

The following sections introduce some high-level examples of the challenges of how to describe financial systems in commercial banks and FinTech, including interfaces, use cases, and sourcing and operations models. The challenge is to break down the functionality in technical systems with direct business value.

2.3.1 *Example 1: Commercial Bank Financial System*

Think about a Commercial Bank Financial System like an Online Banking Portal. It allows customers to access their accounts, view balances, initiate transactions, and manage their financial activities. Still, it is not the only way a client can get account information, and initiate payment transactions or investments. Clients also expect a mobile banking app that provides a convenient platform to perform banking operations on their smartphones, including the full range of account information and transactions. This requires various internal interfaces (APIs). Connectivity to the core banking system, which serves as the central hub of the bank's financial operations, storing customer data, managing accounts, and processing transactions, is a necessity and just a first step. Further connectivity might include the connection to a loan origination system. This could extend the functionality and facilitate an online loan application process, including credit evaluation, risk assessment, documentation, and approval. However, this might raise the next requirements, and an interface to the risk management system could be needed to monitor and mitigate various risks associated with the loan, such as credit risk, market risk, and operational risk. Last but not least, we need to consider compliance and regulatory reporting systems. These are supposed to ensure adherence to regulatory requirements, help automate reporting, and track compliance-related activities. While seemingly everything is connected to everything, the Financial Technology Canvas can help to make informed decisions in outlining the core focus of a specific business-driven system outline and its embeddedness in an ecosystem. It can aid in gaining an understanding of sensible boundaries and provides a starting point for further investigation and discussion.

2.3.2   Example 2: FinTech Financial System

FinTech companies tend to leverage advanced technologies to provide innovative financial services. Their financial systems are designed to be agile, scalable, and customer-centric. These systems leverage digital interfaces and cutting-edge analytics to deliver personalised financial solutions, streamline processes, and enhance the overall user experience. Use cases can include digital payments, peer-to-peer lending, robe-advisor, and alternative investment platforms. Blockchain and Smart Contracts may be incorporated for secure and transparent transactions, decentralised identity management, and efficient settlement processes.

Interfaces and use cases often address customer-facing interfaces with mobile apps and web platforms. They offer intuitive interfaces for customers to manage their financial transactions, access investment options, track spending, and receive personalised financial insights.

Some FinTech companies focus on Digital Wallets to enable seamless payments and money transfers through smartphones or other devices, integrating with various payment systems and financial institutions. In many cases, they build on API Integration to facilitate the integration of such services with third-party providers, such as payment gateways, identity verification providers, and credit bureaus, to enable smooth and secure financial transactions. Advanced data analytics and machine learning tools are utilised to analyse customer behaviour, identify patterns, and provide personalised financial recommendations and risk assessments.

2.4   Conclusion

In summary, it can be stated that the interaction in the banking industry is becoming more and more complex. Managing and mastering API-driven ecosystems is a demanding management task. The Financial Technology Canvas can help to get access to get a quick overview due to the one-page design aiming to provide the relevant information at a glance. However, also the creation of the canvas might help to reflect on questions in the context of the systems. It urges the creator to clearly state the main purpose of the system and its key elements. This is not always an easy task and might even foster some controversial discussions within the organisation or with selected partners. It can make different perceptions more transparent and help the different stakeholders to get a holistic picture. In order to have a fruitful discussion, it can help to take different perspectives. The Financial Technology Canvas can support this. Although a product can be managed in all three dimensions (conception, implementation, and commercialisation) simultaneously, conception and implementation are generally completed long before commercialisation. Still, commercialisation is a measure of product management success (Nikola, 2022). Banks and FinTech companies could increase their innovation success through better market orientation, investing resources in exploring customers' explicit and latent needs while eliminating pain points with existing solutions (Mousavi et al., 2022). The Financial Technology Canvas could help to navigate in this demanding context. It comprises key technology, infrastructure, regulation, and places prominently the main business objective. It covers opportunities, challenges, and risks as well as important ecosystem partners. The foundation of the canvas includes CTB and RTB aspects. No change project occurs in a vacuum. We should understand the mechanisms that are in place so that we can build on it. Every business needs to be constantly evolving. This is especially true for an industry like banking which appears to be in a dramatic paradigm shift driven by new technological possibilities.

The Financial Technology Canvas is not a replacement for comprehensive documentation and in-depth requirements. The value is the ease of use and that it helps various stakeholders to engage in the discussion about (technical) ecosystems and their value for the business.

References

Abubakar, L., & Handayani, T. (2019). Strengthening Financial Technology Regulation to Empowerment Financial Inclusive. *Diponegoro Law Review, 4*(2), 274.

Alcoat, A. Z. (2018, November 16). *Risk and Opportunities Management—Apppm*. http://wiki.doing-projects.org/index.php/Risk_and_Opportunities_Management.

Amstad, M. (2019). Regulating FinTech: Objectives, Principles, and Practices. *SSRN Electronic Journal,* Asian Development Bank Institute Working Paper Series 1016, p. 17.

Ashta, A., & Herrmann, H. (2021). Artificial Intelligence and FinTech: An Overview of Opportunities and Risks for Banking, Investments, and Microfinance. *Strategic Change, 30*(3), 211–222.

Baker, D. J., & Robinson, P. H. (Eds.). (2021). *Artificial intelligence and the law: Cybercrime and criminal liability*. Routledge.

Bhatia, M. (2022a). Conversational Banking. In M. Bhatia, *Banking 4.0* (pp. 233–263). Springer Nature Singapore.

Bhatia, M. (2022b). Investing in Alignment of Industrialisation and Innovation Engines. In M. Bhatia, *Banking 4.0* (pp. 41–60). Springer Nature Singapore.

Burke, S. (2022, August 16). Gold Plating in Project Management. *Become a Project Manager.*

Chesbrough, H. (2012). Open Innovation: Where We've Been and Where We're Going. *Research Technology Management, 55*(4), 20–27.

Crosby, C., & Curtis, C. (2021). Hosting or Colocation Data Centers. In H. Geng (Ed.), *Data Center Handbook* (1st ed., pp. 65–75). Wiley.

Dai, W. (2021). Development and Supervision of Robo-Advisors under Digital Financial Inclusion in Complex Systems. *Complexity, 2021*, 1–12.

De Koker, L., Morris, N., & Jaffer, S. (2020). Regulating Financial Services in an Era of Technological Disruption. *Law in Context. A Socio-Legal Journal, 36*(2), 1–24.

Dorfleitner, G., Hornuf, L., & Kreppmeier, J. (2021). Promise Not Fulfilled: FinTech Data Privacy, and the GDPR. *SSRN Electronic Journal,* CESifo Working Paper No. 9359, p. 51.

Endress, T. (2023). Open Innovation Ecosystem in Asia. In T. Endress & Y. F. Badir (Eds.), *Business and Management in Asia: Digital Innovation and Sustainability* (pp. 35–48). Springer Nature Singapore.

Farooq, M. S., Ahmed, M., & Emran, M. (2022). A Survey on Blockchain Acquainted Software Requirements Engineering: Model, Opportunities, Challenges, and Future Directions. *IEEE Access, 10,* 48193–48228.

Goyal, P., Marinos, I., Gupta, E., Bandi, C., Ross, A., & Chandra, R. (2022). Rethinking cloud-hosted financial exchanges for response time fairness. *Proceedings of the 21st ACM Workshop on Hot Topics in Networks,* 108–114.

Hoang, T. G., Nguyen, G. N. T., & Le, D. A. (2022). Developments in Financial Technologies for Achieving the Sustainable Development Goals (SDGs): FinTech and SDGs. In U. Akkucuk (Ed.), *Advances in Environmental Engineering and Green Technologies* (pp. 1–19). IGI Global.

Hon, W. K., & Millard, C. (2018). Banking in the cloud: Part 1–banks' use of cloud services. *Computer Law & Security Review, 34*(1), 4–24.

Lawton, G. (2023, March 3). *Top 9 Blockchain Platforms to Consider in 2023 | TechTarget.* CIO.

Leo, M., Sharma, S., & Maddulety, K. (2019). Machine Learning in Banking Risk Management: A Literature Review. *Risks, 7*(1), 29.

Leong, K. (2018). FinTech (Financial Technology): What is It and How to Use Technologies to Create Business Value in FinTech Way? *International Journal of Innovation, Management and Technology,* 74–78.

Long, G., Tan, Y., Jiang, J., & Zhang, C. (2020). Federated Learning for Open Banking. In Q. Yang, L. Fan, & H. Yu (Eds.), *Federated Learning* (Vol. 12500, pp. 240–254). Springer International Publishing.

Mahalle, A., Yong, J., & Tao, X. (2021). Challenges and Mitigation for Application Deployment over SaaS Platform in Banking and Financial Services Industry. *2021 IEEE 24th International Conference on Computer Supported Cooperative Work in Design (CSCWD),* 288–296.

Mahalle, A., Yong, J., Tao, X., & Shen, J. (2018). Data Privacy and System Security for Banking and Financial Services Industry based on Cloud Computing Infrastructure. *2018 IEEE 22nd International Conference on Computer Supported Cooperative Work in Design (CSCWD),* 407–413.

Mousavi, S. F., Azar, A., & Khodadad, S. H. (2022). Success factors of innovation management in the banking industry using the grounded theory approach. *Journal of Industrial Engineering and Management Studies, 8*(2).

Murinde, V., Rizopoulos, E., & Zachariadis, M. (2022). The impact of the FinTech revolution on the future of banking: Opportunities and risks. *International Review of Financial Analysis, 81*, 102103.

Nathmann, M. (2020). Legal Advice on Innovative Technologies and Business. In T. Endress (Ed.), *Digital Project Practice: Managing Innovation and Change* (pp. 108–142). Tredition.

Nikola, I. (2022). *Product Management of FinTech Projects* [Graduate Thesis, Educons University].

Osterwalder, A., Pigneur, Y., & Clark, T. (2010). *Business model generation: A handbook for visionaries, game changers, and challengers.* Wiley.

Palmié, M., Wincent, J., Parida, V., & Caglar, U. (2020). The evolution of the financial technology ecosystem: An introduction and agenda for future research on disruptive innovations in ecosystems. *Technological Forecasting and Social Change, 151*, 1–11.

Petravi, T. (2008). Project Risks and Opportunities Management. *KSI Transactions, 1*(3), 105–108.

Santhanam, S., & Suresh, M. (2022, August 16). Agile Approach—Study of Project Management Methods in the Banking industry. *Proceedings of the 2nd Indian International Conference on Industrial Engineering and Operations Management.*

Schneider, M. (2023). Open Banking and Digital Ecosystems. In T. Endress, *Digital Project Practice for New Work and Industry 4.0* (1st ed., pp. 169–179). Auerbach Publications.

Semieniuk, G., Campiglio, E., Mercure, J., Volz, U., & Edwards, N. R. (2021). Low-carbon transition risks for finance. *WIREs Climate Change, 12*(1).

Sharifi, S., Amyot, D., Mylopoulos, J., McLaughlin, P., & Feodoroff, R. (2022). Towards Improved Certification of Complex FinTech Systems–A Requirements-based Approach. *2022 IEEE 30th International Requirements Engineering Conference Workshops (REW)*, 205–214.

Six, N., Herbaut, N., & Salinesi, C. (2020). *Which Blockchain to choose? A decision support tool to guide the choice of a Blockchain technology.*

Sustainable Development Goals | United Nations Development Programme. (n.d.). UNDP. Retrieved June 15, 2023, from www.undp.org/sustainable-development-goals

Van Greuning, H., & Brajovic Bratanovic, S. (2020). *Analyzing banking risk: A framework for assessing corporate governance and risk management* (Fourth). World Bank Group.

Wang, H., Ma, S., Dai, H.-N., Imran, M., & Wang, T. (2020). Blockchain-based data privacy management with Nudge theory in open banking. *Future Generation Computer Systems, 110*, 812–823.

Yan, G. (2017). Application of Cloud Computing in Banking: Advantages and Challenges. *Proceedings of the 2017 2nd International Conference on Politics, Economics and Law (ICPEL 2017).* 2017 2nd International Conference on Politics, Economics and Law (ICPEL 2017), Weihai, China.

Zetzsche, D. A., Arner, D. W., & Buckley, R. P. (2020). Decentralized Finance (DeFi). *SSRN Electronic Journal.*

Chapter 3

FinTech Process Automation

Kourosh Dadgar

Chapter Overview

FinTech processes such as ordering, invoicing and billing, and payment, are essential building blocks for any business to provide financial services efficiently and effectively. Multiple stakeholders across the world collaborate in these processes. Process automation simplifies and improves these complex processes by saving time and money and reducing errors. A business process management lifecycle provides a framework to identify, analyze, and improve business processes. The order-to-pay and order-to-cash processes are two most commonly used processes by businesses to deliver products and services to customers and clients. These processes use sensitive identifiable information that needs to be secured and protected and operate in a highly regulated industry that needs to be compliant with a variety of regulations and policies. Alignment between internal and external finTech processes is necessary for the success of process automation and a satisfactory experience for the customers.

3.1 Main/Continuous Text (including Illustrations, Tables, Instructional Elements)

In the post digital revolution, emerging and advanced technologies have fundamentally changed how businesses operate. Organizational processes are chains of activities, resources, and decisions that allow businesses to achieve their immediate, short-term, and long-term goals. Business processes are building blocks of any

DOI: 10.1201/9781003395560-3

organization. Companies are constantly looking for the ways that they can stream-line and make their processes more efficient and effective to save time and money, and to reduce errors. Process improvement is one of the core ideas in the area of business process management (BPM) and it can be achieved by following two broad categories of solutions: organizational restructuring and automation. Organizational restructuring includes structural changes in different parts of the business such as adding new roles and eliminating redundant processes. Automation is the shift from manual and intense cognitive human-based processes to technology-enabled assisted processes. A process may be fully or partially automated depending on the tasks that are performed in the process. The tasks that require human judgment, creativity, and intuition should be partially automated or assisted with technologies such as hiring or admission decisions. The tasks that are laborious, repetitive, and which can be defined based on set of logical rules can be fully automated such as collecting, searching, processing, and analyzing large amounts of complex data with hundreds of attributes. Any change in a process will have an impact on other tasks in the process because process tasks are connected in a chain and a process functions as a whole.

RPA (Robotic Process Automation) is an advanced automation approach where software robots understand and perform tasks and interact with systems and applications beyond simple rule-based automation of the tasks (UiPath, 2023b). With enterprise-wide AI-enabled (artificial intelligence) RPA automation, tasks are not automated in isolation and cognitive human behavior and interactions are automated such as understanding what is on the screen, participating in conversations, completing the necessary keystrokes, and applying machine learning models to make multifaceted decisions. This is one of the main advantages of RPA that allows human actors in a process to focus on critical tasks that cannot be automated and not to spend unnecessary time on identifying and matching automated tasks with others within a broader process chain. Employees will be more productive, satisfied, and engaged. Compared with IT solutions, RPA is easier and faster to implement with a much higher ROI (return on investment) (Lhuer, 2016).

Many organizations have already adopted RPA technologies to streamline their financial processes. McKinsey reports that more than 80% of their clients have been planning, implementing, innovating, or maintaining their RPAs (McCann, 2018). The IRS (Internal Revenue Service) in the United States has adopted robotic pro-cess automation (RPA) within their finance and procurement divisions (UiPath, 2022). Automated processes helped IRS to become agile, manage and process higher numbers of contracts in a much shorter amount of time and with the lowest error rate. They have been able to retrieve and consolidate the necessary data from multiple sources and provide services efficiently for millions of customers and staff. With assistive RPA, IRS employees experience a more satisfying work environment without working on cumbersome long manual finance processes. A large number of companies such as Bilfinger Industrial Services use RPA-enabled robots that auto-mate their order to cash processes. Automated cash to order processes between

Bilfinger and their clients saved the company hundreds of hours of manual data entry and allowed them to process many more orders a day. The time saved for the Bilfinger employees was spent beyond administrative tasks on controlling and improving processes for multiple clients. NTT Communications, a prominent communications carrier with more than 100 offices across 40 countries, has used RPA to automate its procurement processes (UiPath, 2023a). Employees working in the procurement department process and manage hundreds of thousands of contracts and payments every year. With RPA automation, NTT has been able to significantly reduce errors and increase accuracy in the procurement contract and payment processes. Any error in procurement processes significantly delays projects and service delivery. NTT plans to further expand process automation into AI-enabled optical character recognition (OCR) technologies to digitize documents, images and PDFs that are used in those processes into automated editable and searchable files.

3.2 FinTech Processes: Order-to-Pay and Order-to-Cash

Financial technologies are used across a variety of industries to streamline and improve efficiency of payment, order, invoice and many other financial services. Financial services such as order and payment are delivered through an interconnected chain of processes. The customer-facing B2C (business to consumer) processes of order-to-cash allow customers to make orders and payments and helps businesses as sellers to receive orders and collect payments. The B2B (business to business) order-to-pay processes similarly allow businesses as buyers to work with a variety of suppliers, make orders and payments to suppliers for procurement services and receive supplies in exchange (see Figure 3.1). This chapter, for clarity of discussion, mainly focuses on these three important financial services that are central to the success of service-oriented and product-focused businesses.

Ordering, payment, and billing and invoicing processes are the building blocks of order-to-cash and order-to-pay processes, and need further investigation and better understanding prior to any partial or full automation.

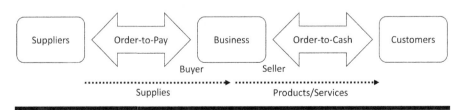

Figure 3.1   Order-to-pay and order-to-cash processes.

3.2.1 Ordering Processes

The ordering process is at the start of the order-to-pay or order-to-cash processes which generates the important data blocks of those processes so that billing, invoicing, and payment processes can build on it. The ordering process should make it easy, efficient, and effective for the customers to order products and services from businesses and businesses to order supplies from suppliers. Any delay, confusion, error, or misalignment in the ordering process will complicate the invoicing and payment processes and make them inefficient and costly. At the time of ordering, all the information needed for the customer or the business to order must be available and all the necessary information needed to track each order should be collected. A reliable, robust, user-friendly, and secure ordering experience will bring in more revenue and customers for businesses and suppliers.

3.2.2 Payment Processes

The advent of internet and digital technologies disrupted payment processes and introduced new transactional possibilities to businesses. The currency used in payments to compensate for the product, service, or work provided is similarly disrupted as new digital technologies gain more presence and usage all around the world. E-payments are the fastest growing form of payment that can be done on portable and desktop devices and computers, and internet-based platforms, and should be versatile, universal, easy to use, reliable, and secure (Lai et al., 2023). Multiple stakeholders are involved in a payment process: businesses, customers and clients, and regulatory bodies. The interests, needs, goals, and concerns of stakeholders must be met in any payment process.

3.2.3 Billing and Invoicing Processes

The order and payment processes are at the beginning and end of the order-to-pay and order-to-cash processes bridged by the billing and invoicing processes. One of the typical costly inefficiencies of the billing process is billing errors that can be challenging and confusing for the customers, hinder payment collection, make the process time consuming, and result in lost sales and markets. An error-free billing process increases customer retention and satisfaction which can significantly add to the value of the customers for the businesses (Tatikonda, 2008). Some typical billing errors are: incorrect prices and charges and customer information, wrong address, and billing duplicates. Billing errors in highly regulated industries are costlier. Hospitals in the U.S. may lose hundreds of thousands of dollars for billing mistakes if they are charged in violation of healthcare regulations and policies such as Medicare codes. Medicare is the biggest payer to hospitals in the U.S. public healthcare system (Connolly, 2001). Medicare insurance claims should be carefully processed to ensure compliance and avoid legal complications and fees. An error-free clean insurance claim is processed and reimbursed much faster without extra costs incurred due to erroneous claims that are paid in a much longer delayed period of time (Painter & Painter, 2016). Accurate data collection from patients and data entry by healthcare personnel are critical to generate clean claims. A convenient billing process has direct impact on patients' satisfaction in using providers' healthcare services and will determine Medicare provider's Medicare reimbursement score for the hospitals (Harris, 2017).

3.3 Automated FinTech Processes

The business process management (BPM) lifecycle provides the steps needed to improve a business process. An effective, successful, and meaningful process automation depends on the identification and analysis steps. Improvements in a business process may include saving time and money, reducing errors, increasing customers' and employees' satisfaction and productivity. The first step is to identify the manageable components (tasks and activities) of a process: things that need to be done to accomplish a goal. Business processes help businesses perform business functions such as ordering, invoicing and billing, and payments in a network of interdependent tasks, resources, decisions. Any change in a process network may have impact on other components of a process and changes do not happen in isolation. This notion is important to plan and implement changes in a process in relation to other process components and the impact that changes might have on them. Collection, access, and use of information is an important factor to ensure that the changes made in a process are based on performance measures, facts, reports, assessments, and continuous measurement of key indicators. Information that is used to improve a process should be accurate, relevant, timely, and verifiable. Poor data quality results in process changes that do not make tangible desired improvements and add to the complexity and effectiveness of a process.

In the analysis step of the BPM lifecycle, based on pre-defined metrics, performance measures, and indicators, improvement areas and process inefficiencies would be investigated and identified. Analysis metrics are decided based on the strategic goals and needs of the business and the goals a process is to accomplish, the business functions that it should perform to make sure a process is effective, achieves the goals, is efficient, works within the constraints of time, cost, quality, and scope. Unnecessary process components, tasks, and resources are removed or replaced and/ or new process components or tasks are introduced. Changes are suggested in the next step to address the issues. These changes may be related to organizational restructuring such as adding new roles, branches, or a hierarchy, or they may be related to partial or complete automation of specific tasks in the process. Process analysis and redesign are collaborative efforts between all of the stakeholders involved in the process and decision makers who may directly or indirectly perform tasks or make decisions in the process or related to it. Process models facilitate communication and collaboration between different stakeholders during the analysis and redesign steps. Once process changes are finalized, they will be implemented and monitored over time to make sure they make improvements in the process otherwise the iterative cycle of identification, analysis, redesign, implementation and monitoring will continue until desired improvements are achieved. Process improvement is a continuous effort as businesses grow, scale, and adapt.

People in processes perform tasks, make decisions, maintain, monitor, and maintain automation and they should be trained, informed, and governed throughout the process automation. Automation brings changes in the processes. Change management is an important factor for the success of automation. Human process components implement, adopt, and adapt to them. Work culture should be open to changes that make it easier to work on daily tasks. The automation change must be an incremental approach. A sudden change forced by organizations on people will not succeed and is not sustainable. Organizations that make strategic changes need to prepare, train, and educate their employees who need to work through those changes. The benefits need to be communicated and concerns need to be addressed–including losing jobs and working more hours because of automation. An accounting employee who has been with an organization for a long time and performed her daily tasks in a certain manner is willing to adopt changes if they make her job easier and her work more efficient. Use of technologies, and interacting and working with them can be stressful and intimidating. Employees resist change if they are not aware of the reasons for the change. Higher management's commitment such as the CFO (chief financial officer) in transition through an effective change is necessary. Employees trust process changes if the management team guarantees continuous support and commits to comply with organization governance guidelines.

FinTech processes perform highly regulated business functions such as ordering, invoicing, and payment that use highly sensitive and personal identifiable information (PII), such as banking data, ID, email, phone numbers, and addresses. These processes involve in many cases multiple stakeholders and multiple platforms and businesses each with their own sets of regulations, policies, rules, and operational and functional standards and criteria which makes the processes complex and confusing. Automation can streamline and simplify these processes so that stakeholders can focus on and invest in the process components and parts that need continuous governance, monitoring, and maintenance. Privacy concerns of the customers and clients and security vulnerabilities must be identified and protected. Security controls in place should restrict access to critical data to individuals or applications with clear objectives, goals and reasons for the data usage. Process automation should not cloud and dismiss accountability. Any data usage should be intentionally discussed, operationally justified, and functionally designed in process automation. These security restrictions should be effective enough to protect data usage of any critical information in an automated process and at the same time stay flexible for growth, scalability, convenience, and innovative technological enhancements.

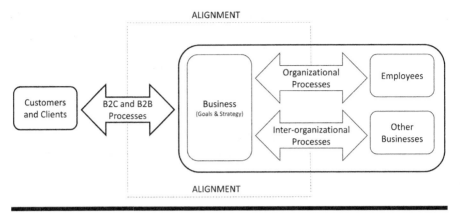

Figure 3.2   Alignment between organizational and B2C/B2B processes.

FinTech processes involve multiple stakeholders and businesses and it is important to ensure their internal and external processes, between businesses, customers, and clients, are strategically and functionally aligned (see Figure 3.2). A basic principle of system integration and migration is to map origin to destination. Process automation should similarly maintain alignments between processes that collaboratively work in a network to deliver products and services to customers and clients by business to business (B2B) or business to consumer (B2C) processes. The order-to-cash process receives orders from customers, bills customers for the costs, collects payments from customers (cash), and delivers products or services to the customers. This multistep process starts from within the organization. Organizational processes decide and manage the initial steps and therefore should be aligned with the later steps in the process. Process automation should not be done in isolation. An effective and efficient automation of one process may not make other processes connected to it as efficient and might even make them more inefficient and difficult to integrate. The order-to-pay process should be similarly aligned with all the internal and external processes that allow a business to order supplies, receive invoices for the costs of the supplies, make payments, and receive the supplies. Procurement is a strategic step in any supply chain and any misalignment, delay, inconsistency in it would be exponentially more severe in the next stages of the supply chain since they depend on how supplies, physical (such as parts) and digital (such as content), are obtained. The alignment between businesses and suppliers helps them better manage their relationships and improve them over time. Procurement automation inherently, if used properly according to the business strategy, goals, and needs, can make businesses become more proactive in how they negotiate terms and prices with the suppliers, more efficient in performing transactional processes, and more predictive about the marker demands, changes, and volatility. The process alignment is not limited to the functional and operational aspects of processes, and infrastructural and architectural standards, and includes legal, policy, and principles, across businesses and industries to ensure compliance between internal, interorganizational, international, and intercontinental processes.

3.3.1 Automated Ordering Processes

Chatbots can replace humans to receive orders and automate the ordering process. Wendy's, the US fast-food chain, will begin using AI-enabled chatbots to receive and process orders from customers (Sirtori-Cortina & Bloomberg, 2023). These robots intelligently recognize employees' and customers' verbal communications. Wendy's goal is to automate ordering process to address the labor shortage and improve customer service and experience. Ordering process is the starting step and gateway that follows by receiving or sending payment, and delivering products and services. This customer-facing steps can benefit from the NLP (natural language processing) and LLM (large language model) technologies and capabilities. Accuracy of these robotic models are important to create a frictionless experience for the customers. Customers' interactions with the ordering system would have many behavioral and cognitive variations because orders are made in different ways in person, using kiosks, drive-thru, using AI assistants such as Apple's Siri or Amazon's Alexa, by phone, email, and other channels of communication. The closer the interactive cognition of the automated ordering systems to the human natural ways of ordering, the more positive will be the experience of the customers.

The most effective automated ordering process integrates the four steps of ordering in one place: search, find, buy and delivery. If any of these steps is done outside a centralized platform, the process becomes confusing and cumbersome. Daimler Trucks North America has launched a single one-stop platform, Excelerator, to streamline the ordering of auto parts and provide a quicker repair turn around for customers which will enhance their experience with the auto services (Ligouri, 2020). In the hospitality industry the ordering experience is central to the success and growth of businesses. An automated omnichannel multi-stakeholder ordering system, similar to NOQ's (NOQ, 2021), allows customers to seamlessly order products and services and vendors to manage orders and order their own supplies to manage guests and customer queues at events. A supply to product process that is consolidated in one platform provides an integrated ordering solution to store order data in one place and gain insights to enhance customer experience.

3.3.2 Automated Payment Processes

Payment systems and protocols vary by industry and country. Some payment systems have higher levels of adoption and penetrate a larger segment of markets such as PayPal in the US. The safe approach to automate a payment system is to adopt a multi-channel multi-standard approach to allow a variety of transactions from different customers and clients with different technological capabilities and resources. Some industry-specific B2B alliances and consortia use single standard payment systems which are not scalable to other industries and are limited to specific use cases. The issues of auditable compliance with governmental regulations and industry standards, privacy of customer and client data, and security of transactions and banking data will remain important and challenging as more international, interorganizational, and cross-platform transactions are pursued.

West Tennessee Healthcare has adopted a physician-payment strategy of the DocTime platform to automate and streamline payments to healthcare providers (Ludi, 2023). The new payment platform automates time-consuming approval steps, removes waiting time for check requests, ensures compliance which is one of the main challenges in healthcare with too many restrictive regulations such as HIPAA[1] (The Health Insurance Portability and Accountability Act) in the US, and provides data-driven insights so that hospitals track their payments over time and identify inconsistencies. An effective payment strategy addresses physicians' needs and hospitals' business goals equally and follows a balanced approach. A flexible automation of payment processes allows manual changes for any reconciliation scenarios and stores transaction records and history and generates reports and documents necessary for future internal and external audits. It is important to plan payment automation that works with the banks since they might detect RPA-enabled transactions as an anomaly and stop them based on their cybersecurity criteria (Fiserv, 2022). Patient-customers prefer flexible payment methods and electronic payments and reports show that a growing number of patients expect their healthcare providers to use more advanced technologies in collecting and processing medical payments (Salucro, 2022).

3.3.3 Automated Billing and Invoicing Processes

Fraud detection is an important factor in a successful and reliable billing processes (Davis, 2003). In any business client relationship, fraudulent bills are the result of failure to record, document and oversee the entire billing process, lack of effective communication with the clients, improperly created bills, or lack of verification procedures embedded in the billing processes. The risks of such failures are higher in automated processes. It is important to design steps into the billing process that can avoid missteps or address fraudulent bills when they happen (Davis, 2003): create an accuracy criteria against which bills can be evaluated to identify fraudulent or overbills and what can be billable, billing should be done incrementally and in regular and frequent steps over time. Automation can make an erroneous billing process more confusing and costlier and it is not the solution to address billing errors. Customer service chatbots with limited interactive options and solutions to problems and errors, and long waiting time in the queue, are frustrating and reduce customer retention. The root cause of the errors in the billing process should be identified and rectified prior to any full or partial automation. Once the root causes of billing errors are identified, a validating rule-based automation that generates bills would reduce errors in the billing process. An automated billing process should facilitate clear and effective communication between the stakeholders of the billing process to avoid future errors. An ongoing training of the staff involved in the billing process and continuous auditable monitoring of their task performance are key to the success of an error-free billing process.

Procore Invoice Management is an example of an automated system designed to streamline the invoicing and billing process for the construction industry (Odell, 2019). The system integrates and stores all the information needed in the invoicing process in one central platform and allows all the stakeholders involved in the process to perform necessary invoicing and billing tasks through the platform. Consolidation and integration of the process information and tasks prevents performing error-prone tasks of invoicing separately done by emails and spreadsheets to manage works, contracts, and budgets and allows stakeholders such as contractors and subcontractors to transparently communicate throughout the process. A consolidated central data repository in the billing process allows patients to access and know about their medical charges, fees in one place whenever they want similar to the DataDirect solution used by Practice Alternatives that allows them to address patients' inquiries about their bills which would have been an impossibly complex and challenging tasks given the many benefit codes that should be used and interpreted in the billing process (Baker, 2018). The data-driven digital platform of DataDirect simplifies complexity of the billing process and creates transparency between the patients and providers. Orientis Gourmet, owner of premium tea brands, automates its invoicing process using cloud services provided by Esker one of the automation and cloud computing pioneers to process thousands of invoices every year (Esker, 2018). The Esker's platform allows Orientis Gourmet to process invoices as soon as they are received in the system and they are able to quickly verify and validate invoices based on their pre-defined criterial and rules. They have developed stronger relationships with suppliers based on trust and transparency at every step of the invoicing process gained through central automation of invoices and have been able to increase job satisfaction for their employees and stay compliant with their industry-specific regulations and policies.

3.4 Summary

Business processes are building blocks of any business entity that are run in a network of resources, tasks, and decisions to perform business functions. The most commonly used Fintech processes are ordering, invoicing and billing, and payments that are used in order-to-cash and order-to-pay processes to deliver and receive products and services. In order-to-cash processes customers order products and services for which they are billed and make payments to the business. In a B2B order-to-pay process a business orders supplies from suppliers and suppliers bill the business for procurements services and receive payments. These processes can be improved, lower cost, time, and errors, by organizational restructuring or automation. Prior to any partial or full process automation and according to BPM lifecycle framework, process components, tasks, decisions, and resources used in a process should be identified and analyzed so that the automation is implemented effectively and applied to the tasks that have issues, are redundant, and need improvements. Process automation should simplify a process and mitigate unnecessary complexity. The tasks that are manual and repetitive and do not require human judgment, intuition, or creativity are good candidates for partial or full automation. In the future, AI-enabled processes may replicate human judgment and creativity such as RPA chatbots that exhibit human-like behaviors and interactions. The tasks in automated processes are data-driven. The quality of data stored, processed, analyzed, and reported in automated processes should be maintained and validated based on clear business strategy, goals, and needs. Any data usage and access by any human actor, system, or application should be documented and tracked in an auditable format and system logs to create accountability, enforce governance, and show compliance. Automated processes have become more distributed between businesses and entities across the world. Such multi-stakeholder distributed processes should be flexible and customizable to be compliant with national and international regulations, policies, rules, and industry standards and best practices. An end to end functional, operational, and technical alignment between internal and external organizational, B2B, and B2C processes that make products and services and deliver to customers and clients ensures efficient, convenient, and successful experience for all stakeholders involved in those processes performing and maintaining process tasks and receiving process outcomes.

Note

1 www.hhs.gov/hipaa/index.html.

References

Baker, K. (2018, September 4). Practice Alternatives Improves Insurance Billing Process with Progress for Greater Transparency and Improved Customer Satisfaction. www.businesswire.com/news/home/20180904005038/en/Practice-Alternatives-Improves-Insurance-Billing-Process-with-Progress-for-Greater-Transparency-and-Improved-Customer-Satisfaction.

Connolly, A. (2001, January 12). Web service streamlines hospital billing process. *Boston Business Journal*, 20(49), 11. Gale General OneFile.

Davis, A. E. (2003). How to Better Manage the Billing Process. *Commercial Law Bulletin*, 18(1), 8–10. HeinOnline.

Esker. (2018, January 9). Orientis Gourmet Automates Its Supplier Invoicing Process with Esker. www.esker.com/company/press-releases/orientis-gourmet-automates-its-supplier-invoicing-process-esker/.

Fiserv. (2022, May 1). Finding solutions to better manage payment process workflows. *Healthcare Financial Management*, 76(4), 44. Gale OneFile: Business.

Harris, R. (2017, November 1). Connect with Patients During the Billing Process: … And raise healthcare reimbursement. *Health Care Collector*, 31(6). Business Insights: Global.

Lai, K.-K., Chen, Y.-L., Kumar, V., Daim, T., Verma, P., Kao, F.-C., & Liu, R. (2023). Mapping technological trajectories and exploring knowledge sources: A case study of E-payment technologies. *Technological Forecasting & Social Change*, 186(Part B). ScienceDirect.

Lhuer, X. (2016, December 6). The next acronym you need to know about: RPA (robotic process automation) | McKinsey [Interview]. www.mckinsey.com/capabilities/mckin sey-digital/our-insights/the-next-acronym-you-need-to-know-about-rpa.

Ligouri, F. (2020, 18). Daimler Trucks North America Launches Excelerator as One-Stop Shop for Online Parts Ordering | Daimler. https://northamerica.daimlertruck.com/ company/newsroom/PressDetail/daimler-trucks-north-america-launches-excelera tor-2020-05-18.

Ludi. (2023, February 8). West Tennessee Healthcare Automates Physician Payment Process with Ludi's DocTime Platform. PR Newswire. Gale in Context: College.

McCann, D. (2018, September 1). The New Digital Workforce: Robotic process automation emerges from the back office to take on core finance tasks. *CFO, The Magazine for Senior Financial Executives*, 34(4). Business Insights: Global.

NOQ. (2021, November 29). Hospitality Tech Startup NOQ Revolutionizes the Ordering Process with Upgraded Versions of Their Management Backend, Mobile Ordering System, and EPOS Offering. ACCESSWIRE News Room. www.accesswire.com/ 675099/Hospitality-Tech-Startup-NOQ-Revolutionizes-the-Ordering-Process-with-Upgraded-Versions-of-Their-Management-Backend-Mobile-Ordering-System-and-EPOS-Offering.

Odell, H. (2019, July 24). Procore Invoice Management Streamlines Construction Billing Process. Procore Corporate Blog. blog.procore.com/procore-invoice-management-streamlines-construction-billing-process/.

Painter, R., & Painter, M. (2016). Today's billing process: Follow these 11 steps. Urology Times, 44(2). Scopus®.

Salucro. (2022, December 13). New Report Shows the Importance of the Billing Process When Patients Evaluate Healthcare Providers. www.businesswire.com/news/home/ 20221213005361/en/New-Report-Shows-the-Importance-of-the-Billing-Process-When-Patients-Evaluate-Healthcare-Providers.

Sirtori-Cortina, D., & Bloomberg. (2023, May 9). Your next Wendy's drive-thru order may be taken by an A.I. chatbot that understands a "milkshake" is actually a "frosty" in the chain's lingo. Fortune. https://fortune.com/2023/05/09/wendys-ai-powered-chat bot-drive-thru-orders/.

Tatikonda, L. U. (2008, January). A Less Costly Billing Process. *Quality Progress*, 41(1), 30–39.

UiPath. (2022, February 1). IRS Implements Robotic Process Automation Technology from UiPath Within Its Finance and Procurement Divisions. Business Wire, Inc. www.uip ath.com/newsroom/rs-implements-rpa-technology-within-its-finance-procurement-divisions.

UiPath. (2023a). Robotic Process Automation Success—NTT. www.uipath.com/resources/ automation-case-studies/ntt-communications.

UiPath. (2023b). What is Robotic Process Automation—RPA Software | UiPath. www.uip ath.com/rpa/robotic-process-automation.

Chapter 4

Robotic Process Automation in Financial Institutions

Michael Jacobus and Martin Schneider

Chapter Overview

Often minimized as a bridging technology, Robotic Process Automation (RPA) offers the opportunity to enter digitization in particular for established Financial Institutions. It enables systems to be connected quickly and inexpensively without the costly and time-consuming connection of native interfaces, which often contradict the IT architectural reorientation. Even if RPA is already established as a technology for digitizing and automating processes, there are several challenges in practice: The organizational and cultural change must internalize in the company and commitment from senior management is essential. Also, the initial implementation and sustainable establishment of a well-directed Target Operating Model (TOM) is a critical key success factor. RPA can thus stand as a cornerstone of digitization in Financial Institutions and establish itself as a recognized standard in the automation and digitization of processes.

DOI: 10.1201/9781003395560-4

4.1 Change and Challenges in Financial Institutions

Financial Institutions are subject to constant change, for example, due to new or changed customer needs, new regulatory requirements, or completely new strategic orientations. As a result, there are always major change projects and processes, products, software, or other setups being adapted and changed in Financial Institutions. At the same time, Financial Institutions want to offer their products and services efficiently, reliably, economically, sustainably and with future viability. Accordingly, there must be stable and capable processes for service delivery, or these must be designed. Many of the processes that are used in Financial Institutions are already digital or partially digitized. Therefore, many different software programs are needed. Software in Financial Institutions has been in use for years and is becoming increasingly outdated. On the one hand, this is because banks were amongst the first companies to use IT products. This means that there are also some programs from the 1970s that run, for example, on mainframe computers that are still in use because no successor products have been developed and the programs still work reliably. These outdated programs are also known as legacy software or legacy programs. On the other hand, there is standard software that is used similar to other companies, but there is also a lot of bank-specific or even institute-specific software that is developed and maintained by in-house developers (bank employees) or external partners. A wide variety of technical requirements are implemented in this individual software that are required for banking operations, employees, customers, or other parties associated with the Financial Institution and developing new software that meets all the specific requirements takes time and money.

4.2 Balancing Costs for IT and Integration with Robotic Process Automation

The profitability assessment analyzes the cost of replacing legacy software with the cost of not replacing it. The result of this evaluation often leads to the decision that the old systems will continue to operate, be changed slightly and not be replaced. However, it is usually expensive to maintain these old systems and to adapt them to new requirements. The decision therefore does not always just mean continuing to operate and change an old system or to introduce a completely new system that meets the new requirements, but there is also the possibility of continuing to operate a legacy program, together with the use of new software. That fulfills the requirement and thus bridges the gap that the legacy software has and both software components are connected and used together (Forrester Research, 2014). For these connections, alternatives are either to develop native interfaces or to use Robotic Process Automation (RPA).

In the often multi-year project phases for the adjustment of legacy software, the banks are faced with the challenge of finding the most efficient solution for each individual situation. The cleanest, but often also the most inefficient solution at this point is the implementation of native interfaces. However, the connection is usually very expensive and time-consuming. In addition, these investments regularly contradict the desired IT architectural reorientation. In addition, practice shows that fewer and fewer developers are proficient in outdated programming languages such as Cobol. However, in order to ensure the piecemeal connection of modern systems and to enable the conversion to a modern IT architecture, RPA is often the optimal interim solution up to the complete replacement of the legacy software (Willcocks et al., 2015).

RPA is a technology that provides software robots to automate digital tasks and processes. RPA Robots are particularly suitable for frequently occurring, repetitive tasks that have to be processed according to fixed rules (ProResult Unternehmensberatung AG, 2023). RPA is often used when the development and introduction of completely new systems is too expensive or time-consuming, or the task that is automated by RPA is not of great duration, but would still take a lot of effort and time for the limited period of time, if it had to be done manually.

Another key driver for the use of RPA is the ongoing focus on optimizing and automating business processes in the banking landscape. Established methods such as Lean Six Sigma aim to reduce waste and variability in processes. By combining it with RPA as a solution for process automation, the advantages of both methods can be multiplied. The desired target dimensions are diverse. Starting with increasing quality or accelerating processes through to ensuring regulatory requirements. However, the most common criterion for developing RPA Robots is still the Return on Investment (Foundry, 2023). The proportional regular fixed costs for the RPA environment, license fees, servers, and the like, are compared together with the one-off investment costs against the savings in the future. Due to the usually low investment and fixed costs, even simple processes can be automated profitably.

A practical example of dual use with RPA is the connection of a modern frontend program to existing legacy software. Up-to-date interfaces are made available to customers or employees. However, the single point of truth remains the stable and established legacy system. In this constellation, RPA ensures communication between the two systems and takes over the input of data in the same way as the employee would have done in the legacy software before the introduction of the modern front end program (Penttinen et al., 2018).

The systems used in Financial Institutions are also often incompatible with one another, so that, for example, users have to make double entries or manually transfer results from one program to the other. In addition to these technical system breaks, there are sometimes also partially manual or even paper-based process steps, which make work in Financial Institutions more difficult. RPA Robots can overcome the technical system breaks because they act like users in the systems and operate the various systems via user interfaces. However, this is automated and therefore error-free, provided that the RPA development has been implemented accordingly.

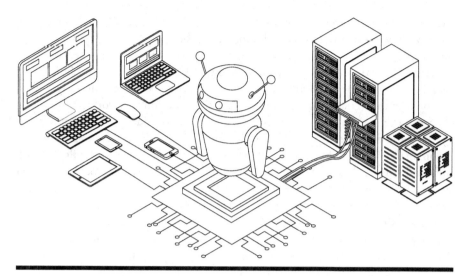

Figure 4.1   The robot in dual use.

RPA Robots are mostly created on no-code or low-code platforms by RPA Developers. Due to the fact that the development environment is based on no-code or low-code, other professional groups can also find an easy way into RPA development and the costs for the development of RPA Robots are therefore lower, as less technically savvy people and therefore significantly more people can do this job (Bygstad, 2015).

RPA development is relatively cheap, can be implemented quickly, can connect a wide variety of new and old systems, and can fully or partially automate a business process that uses various software components, freeing up the workforce for other activities because RPA Robots perform the tasks that were previously performed by real humans (Hofmann et al., 2020). RPA Robots thus support employees and relieve them of–from a human point of view–simple, repetitive, time-consuming activities (Van der Aalst et al., 2018). The employees can therefore concentrate on, for example, creative, more complex or rare tasks and have more time for this.

4.3   Attended and Unattended Robots

RPA Robots can either run as attended or unattended robots. An attended RPA Robot only carries out the automated activities when an employee starts it. This can be the case, for example, when the employee and the RPA Robot share parts of a process sequentially. The employee may also be able to watch the RPA Robot doing the other part of the process, since the RPA Robot is doing the work on the employee's computer. This also makes attended RPA Robots look similar to macros. Often, the robot also uses the employee's unique credentials, including usernames and passwords. With unattended RPA Robots, the robots start without human nudge and employees cannot always see what the RPA Robot is doing. Like other computer systems, this works in a black box and processes the workflow when a technical start signal has come. The scalability of unattended RPA Robots is significantly higher. A robot can theoretically process a task over and over again and work 24/7.

Since attended RPA Robots are comparable to macros and these can be monitored by the individual user of the RPA Robot, there are significantly fewer regulatory requirements for the robot's software documentation. The situation is different with unattended RPA Robots. Like other bank applications, these must be documented in detail.

RPA Robots, whether attended or unattended, can only solve structured problems within clear limits, as described. Nevertheless, the automation potential can be expanded with manageable effort by introducing other established solutions. This includes, for example, Optical Character Recognition (OCR) scanning to digitize paper documents in a process line and make them machine-readable. In addition, unstructured data can be structured using Artificial Intelligence (AI) approaches. A practical example of this is the compliance process for recording employee transactions by listed employees. For this purpose, the paper copy of the trade transaction by other banks is scanned, made readable via OCR, converted into a standard format with an AI tool and finally the data is transferred to the relevant systems with an RPA Robot. But other technologies such as process mining, machine learning and intelligent process automation also come into play where RPA does not offer a solution.

4.4 Target Operating Model for Robotic Process Automation

In order to use RPA as a sustainable opportunity for the digitization and automation of business processes, banks must be able to implement the key success factors. This includes a strong target operation model and the establishment of RPA as a cornerstone in the bank's automation culture (Joseph et al., 2023). A prerequisite for the efficient development and operation of RPA Robots is a functional target operating model, for example, the implementation of a central "Center of Excellence". The required roles and the governance model should be anchored organizationally in the bank's units. The roles and responsibilities in the operating model are precisely defined and their capacities are planned (Willcocks et al., 2015). Guidelines, frameworks and essential processes for the implementation of RPA projects must be coordinated. This includes, for example, the identification and prioritization of processes for automation, but also guidelines for billing, monitoring, reporting or business case tracking. In addition, the technical design must be defined. This includes, for example, defining the functional architecture of the individual RPA Robots as well as the technical components and requirements. A mature and well-coordinated operating model thus serves as the basis for the sustainable scaling of the technology in banks. If the focus is only on the automation potential in certain departments, without significant dependencies on other departments, a divisional operating model is ideal. Here the RPA roles are anchored directly in the department. If, on the other hand, potential is to be leveraged across the entire process landscape of the bank, a central, cross-departmental unit for automation in the bank seems to be the best option (Willcocks et al., 2015). An optimal model for this is the "Center of Excellence" approach (Forrester Research, 2014). The IT department provides the RPA Developers, a process or digitization unit provides the RPA Business Analysts. These two roles work in tandem in the RPA implementation projects. They clarify the requirements of the subject area specialists and implement the RPA Robots as a team.

The RPA Business Analysts are mainly responsible for the process analysis. They provide their optimization know-how for the automation of the process being considered and usually take care of the documentation of the new process. This is usually documented in such a standard way that the RPA Developer can start technical implementation in the next step. In addition, the RPA Business Analysts are often responsible for the documentation of the compliance requirements for RPA Robots.

The RPA Developers are supported by frameworks that allow the structure and architecture of the different RPA Robots to be similar. Templates, standard modules and comprehensive functionalities are developed for a framework and made available to the RPA Developers. As a result, the developers do not have to redevelop these functions and components every time, but can put together their basic functionalities as in a construction kit and only the individual functions for the individual application need to be programmed.

In this target operating model in particular, it is important to implement continuous and targeted process pipelining in order to ensure the long-term profitability of the "Center of Excellence" (Willcocks et al., 2015). Robots are not designed for eternity, as processes are constantly changing and will eventually be replaced. In order to generate sustainable profitability gains, it makes sense to keep an eye on the bank's process map at all times and to maintain contact with the process specialist in the different departments in order to identify new use cases.

References

Bygstad, B. (2015). The coming of lightweight IT. In European Conference on Information Systems (ECIS), Münster. *ECIS 2015 Completed Research Papers*, 1–16. https://doi.org/10.18151/7217282.

Forrester Research. (2014). Building a center of expertise to support robotic automation: Preparing for the life cycle of business change.

Foundry (formerly IDG Communications) (2023). Studie Intelligent Automation 2023.

Hofmann, P., Samp, C., & Urbach, N. (2020). Robotic process automation. *Electronic Markets*, 30, 99–106.

Joseph, L., O'Donnel, B., Le Clair, C., Giron, F. Kalra, A., & Nagel, B. (2023). The 10 Golden Rules Of RPA Success. Forrester. https://reprints2.forrester.com/#/assets/2/661/RES143771/report.

Penttinen, E., Kasslin, H., & Asatiani, A. (2018). How to choose between robotic process automation and Back-end system automation? In Proceedings of the 28th European Conference on Information Systems (ECIS). Portsmouth, UK.

ProResult Unternehmensberatung AG (2023). Robotic Process Automation (RPA) Kompetenz. www.proresult.de/kompetenzen/robotic-process-automation-rpa-kompetenz/.

Van der Aalst, W. M. P., Bichler, M., & Heinzl, A. (2018). Robotic process automation. *Business & Information Systems Engineering*, 60(4), 269–272.

Willcocks, L., Lacity, M., & Craig, A. (2015). The IT function and robotic process automation. The Outsourcing Unit Working Research Paper Series.

Chapter 5

Future Cryptoeconomics: Digital Diffusion of PayTech

Wesley L. Harris and Jarunee Wonglimpiyarat

Chapter Overview

This chapter explores the cryptoeconomics of payment technology (PayTech). It focuses on the complexity of PayTech and the diffusion process. The main contribution of this research study is the development of a new methodology to explore the complexities of innovations. The new methodology of a complexity metric can be applied for analysing the complexity of innovations in various industries. The analyses were performed through seven types of PayTech: (1) ATM/cash cards, (2) credit cards, (3) EFTPOS/debit cards, (4) Internet banking, (5) mobile banking, (6) payment super apps and (7) cryptocurrencies. The findings have shown that ATM/cash cards, credit cards and EFTPOS/debit cards had medium level of complexity whereas Internet banking, mobile banking, payment super apps and cryptocurrencies had low levels of complexity. The power of Internet and Blockchain technologies has facilitated the process of bringing PayTech towards digital diffusion at high speed. The research findings are in line with Rothwell's fifth generation of innovation model–the systems integration and extensive networking model. Given the improving services of PayTech empowered by decentralised Internet Blockchain technologies, PayTech has the potential to disrupt the traditional banking landscape further. The insights from the study can help players in the PayTech industry plan for effective competition in the age of digital transformation.

DOI: 10.1201/9781003395560-5

5.1 Introduction

"Banking is necessary, banks are not."

The above statement has shown the vision of Bill Gates, Former Chairman and Chief Executive of Microsoft, regarding the changing landscape of banking. Traditionally, banks are seen as the vanguard sector in the use of information technology (IT) (Barras, 1986, 1990). Nevertheless, in the future of digitisation, banks may no longer dominate the payments ecosystem. The banking landscape has seen phenomenal changes with the emergence of new players and payment platforms. Payment Technology (PayTech), the new technology concerning fund transfer, is one of the potential technologies to revolutionise the banking landscape. PayTech is a sector of financial technology (FinTech) that can help facilitate the process of cross-border payment. The impact of the global coronavirus (COVID-19) pandemic has already advanced the adoption of digital payments. After COVID-19, it is expected that the rise of FinTech and PayTech will continue to transform or eventually disrupt the banking landscape (Economist Intelligence Unit, 2021).

While there are many research studies in FinTech (Thompson, 2017; Shim and Shin, 2017; Gomber et al., 2017; Wonglimpiyarat, 2018; Iman, 2020 amongst others), there is a dearth of research exploring PayTech, particularly its dimensions of complexity in relation to the diffusion process. Thus, this research study attempts to fill a gap of existing research in PayTech. The term FinTech often refers to the new innovations in the financial services industry empowered by Internet and IT developments. There are 268 Unicorns valued at a total of USD 2.6 trillion (CFTE, 2022).

The objective of this chapter is to explore the cryptoeconomics of PayTech with regard to its complexity level and the diffusion process. The structure of this chapter is organised as follows. Following the introductory section, this chapter has four further sections. Section 2 reviews the theoretical literature on FinTech and PayTech, technology complexity and diffusion, innovation process and disruptive innovation. Section 3 explains the methodology. This research offers a new methodological framework–a complexity metric for analysing the complexity of innovations which can be applied in various industries. Section 4 presents the analyses of findings regarding the cryptoeconomics and diffusion of PayTech. Section 5 concludes the chapter by drawing insightful implications and lessons from the findings.

5.2 Literature Review

5.2.1 FinTech and PayTech

The term 'FinTech' encompasses technology-enabled services and solutions with the use of integrated IT. FinTech offers a new landscape in the digital era of the financial industry. FinTech also provides a platform for banks and non-banks to facilitate cross-network transfers and payment services (Thompson, 2017; Shim and Shin, 2017). FinTech has digitally connected innovations in various industries such as payment and transfers, lending and financing, retail banking, financial management, insurance, markets and exchanges. FinTech helps improve online payment and currency exchanges. It provides an efficient payment platform with lower transaction fees than those of traditional banking transactions.

FinTech covers cryptocurrency such as Bitcoin and Blockchain technologies. Bitcoin and Blockchain technologies reflect the new application of technologies that makes financial service innovations more innovative. Both technologies provide a powerful platform to promote innovation development under the emerging FinTech trend of the global financial service industry (Bank of New York Mellon Corporation, 2015; Kauffman and Ma, 2015; Vranken, 2017; Wonglimpiyarat, 2018; Harris and Wonglimpiyarat, 2019).

Bitcoin was introduced in 2009 by Satoshi Nakamoto. It is an open-source, peer-to-peer (P2P) currency based on the decentralised digital payment system providing online payment solutions. The Bitcoin system allows users to transact directly without needing any financial intermediaries. The Bitcoin system organises transactions by grouping them into blocks and then connecting these blocks based on Blockchain technology. Blockchain technology is a kind of distributed database management system. The information and communications technology (ICT)-driven capacity under the Blockchain technology allows payment clearing and settlement, authenticity verification and the recording of asset ownership. The financial applications of Blockchain technology are, for example, lending, currency exchange and remittances as well as P2P transfers. The non-financial applications of Blockchain technology are, for example, real estate, diamond mining, gold and silver trading, digital content distribution, hospital, trading of stocks, buying and selling innovations through a series of smart contracts (Naveed et al., 2017; Sikorski et al., 2017; Falwadiya and Dhingra, 2022).

Payment Technology (PayTech) is a subsector of FinTech focused on fund transfer and payment transactions. It is the new technology that can improve the efficiency of cross-border payment. PayTech includes card payment, mobile money, digital payment, cryptocurrency and the Internet-of-Things (IoT) as well as other payment-oriented services. The payment gateway of PayTech can be based on the power of Blockchain technology. PayTech has the potential to bring about the disintermediation potential of the banking industry (Raikos, 2019; Polasik et al., 2020).

Figure 5.1 portrays the functions of Blockchain technology. When transactions involving digital currency exchange are initiated over the Internet, the financial and non-financial information is encrypted and stored in the Blockchain. These transactions are securely processed via P2P networks consisting of computer nodes. All transactions are executed instantaneously under the Blockchain system. The successful transactions are then written into the Blockchain through the mining process. These transaction records are updated in real time using the block hashing algorithms. The Blockchain registry (electronic ledgers) is stored as a block in the server node whereby each node has the same copies of the ledger. The blocks are then linked cryptographically together to form a linear chain. The smart contracts written on the Blockchain cannot be altered unless there is a private key to unlock the

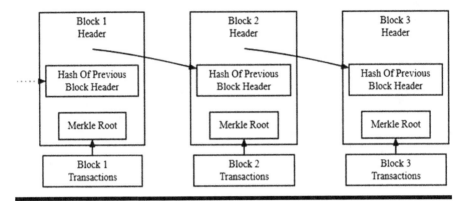

Figure 5.1 Blockchain technology functions.
Source: www.infosecinstitute.com.

address. These properties have virtually eliminated the possibility of counterfeits and frauds (Tapscott and Tapscott, 2016; Naveed et al., 2017; Alabi, 2017; Falwadiya and Dhingra, 2022).

5.2.2 Technology Complexity and Diffusion

The definition of 'complexity' in the Cambridge Dictionary describes it as the combined effects of different factors. Although much literature refers to complexity in a number of ways such as product complexity, technological complexity, organizational complexity, project complexity; the point is the same: components integrated together cause difficulties in transformation into successful products/ processes (Hobday, 1998; Hobday et al., 2000; Russell and Smorodinskaya, 2018; Ruoslahti, 2020).

The literature review on complexity deals with the elements concerning novel technologies and technical systems (Hughes, 1988) or complex products and systems (CoPS) (Hobday, 1998; Hobday et al., 2000). CoPS are high cost, engineering-intensive goods that tend to need collaborative networks among suppliers to turn research initiatives into commercial products. Complexity can affect knowledge processing in the innovation process. The degree of complexities can also affect the process of innovation diffusion (Wonglimpiyarat, 2005: Russell and Smorodinskaya, 2018; Ruoslahti, 2020).

The process of technology diffusion is generally represented by the S-curves. Vernon (1966)'s Product Life Cycle (PLC) is a classical model explaining the development as a pattern of product substitution (the S-curve pattern). Rogers (1962, 1995, 2003) argued that the innovation development process comprises of the stages of problem definition, research (basic and applied), development, commercialisation, adoption and diffusion, and consequences. Vargo, Akaka and Wieland (2020) explored the process of diffusion in a wider perspective: service-ecosystems. They

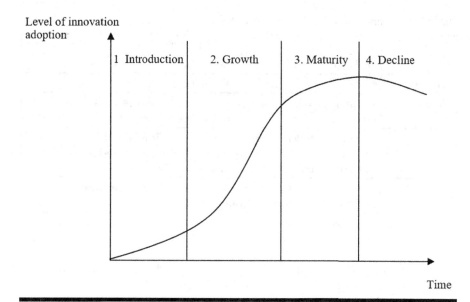

Figure 5.2   The innovation life cycle.
Source: Twiss (1995).

analysed technological and market aspects as well as the roles of different actors/
institutions in the service-centered systems.

Figure 5.2 exhibits the stages along the innovation life cycle: introduction,
growth, maturity and decline. The innovation life cycle provides a basis to understand the process of commercialisation or diffusion of technology products and services. The introduction stage represents the period of uncertainties which requires
problem-solving activities to make a saleable product or useable process. The growth
stage reflects the situation where uncertainties are reduced. This can be seen by the
accelerating rate of innovation adoption after a period of relatively slow growth (the
introduction stage). The maturity and decline stages reflect the diffusion of innovation or commercialisation of innovation (Twiss, 1995).

5.2.3   Innovation Process and Disruptive Innovation

The innovation process can be influenced by the factors of the technology push
(Schumpeter, 1939, 1967), demand pull (Schmookler, 1962) or their interaction
(Freeman, 1982) as triggers of innovations. Rothwell (1992) argued that there are
five generations of models related to the innovation process (Table 5.1). In the first
and second generations, innovation can be seen as a result of a simple linear sequen-
tial process of technology push in the 1960s and the need pull in the 1970s. The
framework of the innovation process has moved to a more pragmatic concept of
integrated model in the 1980s and the systems integration and extensive networking

Table 5.1 Generations of Innovation Models

Generation	Key features
First	*Technology push*: simple linear sequential process
Second	*Need pull*: simple linear sequential process
Third	*Coupling model*: recognizing interaction between different elements and feedback loops between them
Fourth	*Integrated model*: integration within the firm, upstream with key suppliers and downstream with demanding and active customers, emphasis on linkages and alliances
Fifth	*Systems integration and extensive networking model*: flexible and customised response, continuous innovation

Source: Rothwell (1992).

model from the 1990s onwards. Rothwell (1992) defined the fifth generation as the networking model to avoid failure of innovation diffusion.

Christensen (1997) introduced the concept of disruptive innovation describing the way a new entrant displaces incumbent businesses. According to him, a disruptive innovation can create a new market and value network, and eventually disrupt an existing market and value network. The new disruptive innovation steadily improves in a performance–less complex, cheaper, smaller, or more convenient than those established in the mainstream market. Christensen (1997) argued that a disruptive innovation is a product or service designed for a new group of customers. For example, downloadable digital media disrupts the CD and DVD market, the personal computers disrupt the minicomputers, workstations and word processors market, digital photography disrupts the chemical photography market, cellular phones disrupt fixed line telephony, and so forth.

The concept of disruptive innovation can be linked to the literature on discontinuous innovation. The Schumpeterian view of 'creative destruction' emphasises the discontinuity of economic development. The process of creative destruction brings about the economic growth whereas the emergence of new product/ process innovations does not grow out of the old ones but eliminates them (Schumpeter, 1939, 1967; Abernathy and Clark, 1985; Tushman and Anderson, 1987). Similar to the Schumpeterian view of economic development, disruptive innovation can bring to market a very different value proposition and new business model. The disruptive innovation generally has a short product life cycle and the potential to overtake the existing market leaders (Christensen, 1997).

5.3   Research Methodology

While there are many research studies in financial technology (FinTech) (Thompson, 2017; Shim and Shin, 2017; Gomber et al., 2017; Wonglimpiyarat, 2018; Iman,

2020 amongst others), there is a dearth of research exploring payment technology (PayTech) particularly the dimensions of complexity in relation to the process of diffusion. Therefore, this study attempts to fill a gap in this neglected area with a focus on exploring the cryptoeconomics of PayTech–complexity and the diffusion of PayTech.

Table 5.2   Metric for Ranking the Complexity of Innovation

	Variables	*Level of complexities (1 = lowest, 5 = highest)*				
		1	*2*	*3*	*4*	*5*
	Development stage					
1	Scientific or technological difficulties in the task of development					
2	Network coordination or system interface for the implementation of innovation					
3	The capital investment of innovation					
4	Patent protection (legal instruments)					
	Delivery stage					
5	Product/service distribution					
6	Standardization					
	Marketing stage					
7	Understanding customer demand					
8	The existence of competing revenue streams					
9	Marketing activities relative to innovation					
10	Market uncertainties					

Source: The authors' design.

Table 5.3 Analysis of the Complexity Level

Level of complexity	Scores range
1 Lowest	0–10
2 Low	11–20
3 Medium	21–30
4 High	31–40
5 Highest	41–50

Source: The authors' design.

This research develops a new methodology–a complexity metric (Table 5.2) for analysing the complexities of PayTech along the innovation process. The metric can be applied to any products, processes or service innovations in various industries. In analysing the complexity of PayTech, the innovation process consists of three stages: (i) the development stage, (ii) the delivery stage and (iii) the marketing stage (Table 5.2). The development stage covers the period from the development of the innovation to the deliverable stage, namely, the technology works. The delivery stage covers the period from the delivery of innovation to its market launch. The marketing stage covers the period after entering into the marketplace where a focus is on capturing a market share. A complexity metric reflects an implicit assumption that each complexity variable in each stage of innovation is equally influential in determining complexity at the stage level and overall level.

This research employs a case study methodology (Eisenhardt, 1989; Yin, 2013) to explore seven types of PayTech: (1) the automatic teller machine (ATM)/cash cards, (2) credit cards, (3) electronic fund transfer at the point-of-sale (EFTPOS)/debit cards, (4) Internet banking, (5) mobile banking, (6) payment super applications (or payment super apps) (Ali Pay, LINE Pay, Google Pay, Grab Pay, WeChatPay, Apple Pay) and (7) cryptocurrencies (BitCoin, Ethereum, Litecoin, Dodgecoin, Tether, Ripple, Shiba Inu). The ranking of complexities was carried out by professionals and experts in the FinTech industry including FinTech start-ups, researchers and professors in the field in the UK. The rankings and 30 in-depth interviews were facilitated by the use of a semi-structured questionnaire. The analyses regarding the complexity level are based on the score range shown in Table 5.3. Then, the interview data were triangulated by the use of secondary data to achieve the research validity. The sum of all complexity scores can be used to provide insights into the level of complexity and the process of PayTech diffusion.

5.4 Analyses of Findings: Cryptoeconomics and the Digital Diffusion of PayTech

Figure 5.3 portrays the banking landscape in a global context. It shows the development of the banking landscape and financial innovations since its inception in the

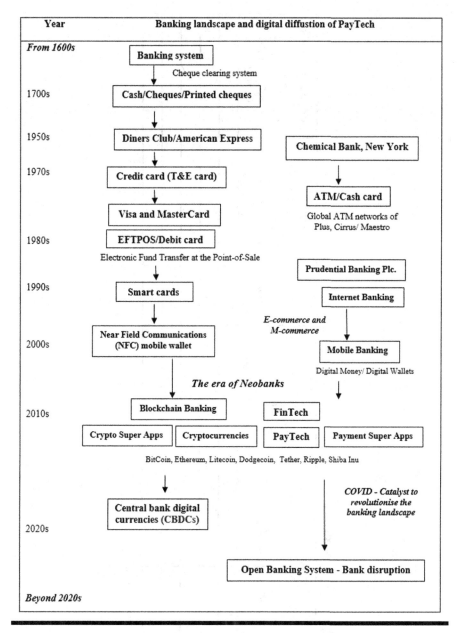

Figure 5.3   Banking landscape and digital diffusion of PayTech.

Source: The authors' design.

Table 5.4 Analyses of Complexity–PayTech

Complexity level	ATM/Cash cards	Credit cards	Electronic Fund Transfer at the Point-of-Sale (EFTPOS)/ Debit cards	Internet banking	Mobile banking	Payment Super Apps (Ali Pay, LINE Pay, Google Pay, Grab Pay, WeChatPay, Apple Pay)	Cryptocurrencies (BitCoin, Ethereum, Litecoin, Dodgecoin, Tether, Ripple, Shiba Inu)
1 Lowest							
2 Low	X			X	X	X	X
3 Medium		X	X				
4 High							
5 Highest							

Source: The author's design.

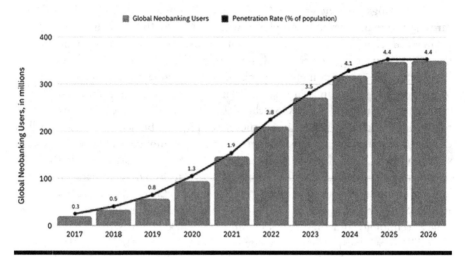

Figure 5.4   Global neobanking users.

Source: Statista, Neobanking Report 2023.

1600s until the present day and into the future. The payment technology (PayTech) began with the introduction of cash/cheques/printed cheques in the 17th century, followed by credit cards in the 1960s, ATM/cash cards in the 1970s, EFTPOS/debit cards in the 1980s, Internet banking/digital money in the 1990s, cryptocurrencies in the 2000s as well as Payment Super Apps and Crypto Super Apps in the 2010s. The outbreak of the global coronavirus (COVID-19) pandemic in 2019 had served as a catalyst in digitally transforming the landscape of the banking industry. Many countries had initiated cross-border sandboxes to support PayTech diffusion. Today, PayTech can be seen as the latest technology having the potential to disrupt the banking landscape further as users are able to transact directly without needing any bank intermediaries.

Figure 5.4 also shows the era of neobanks from the 2010s onwards. It reveals the future trend of neobanks competing to encroach upon the banking landscape. Figure 5.4 exhibits the increasing numbers of neobanking users globally from the years 2017–2026. Currently, there are more than 200 neobanks in the world with approximately 210 million neobank users.

The analyses of complexities with regard to PayTech along the innovation process were performed by using a complexity metric devised in Section 5.3. Table 5.4 shows the analyses of complexities for seven types of PayTech: (1) ATM/cash cards, (2) credit cards, (3) EFTPOS/debit cards, (4) Internet banking, (5) mobile banking, (6) payment super apps (Ali Pay, LINE Pay, Google Pay, Grab Pay, WeChatPay, Apple Pay) and (7) cryptocurrencies (BitCoin, Ethereum, Litecoin, Dodgecoin, Tether, Ripple, Shiba Inu).

The findings have shown that ATM/cash cards, credit cards and EFTPOS/debit cards had a medium level of complexity whereas Internet banking, mobile banking, payment super apps and cryptocurrencies had a low level of complexity. Considering the complexity along the process of innovation, ATM/cash cards, credit cards and EFTPOS/debit cards are highly capitalised in the payment infrastructure in order to provide the service on a large scale. That is to say, the complexity of ATM/cash cards, credit cards and EFTPOS/debit cards lies in the high capital investments required for brick-and-mortar infrastructure or physical branch networks as well as clearing and settlement systems. For Internet banking, mobile banking and payment super apps (Ali Pay, LINE Pay, Google Pay, Grab Pay, WeChatPay, Apple Pay), the payment services are based on the power of Internet technology. Similarly, the digital innovation of cryptocurrencies (BitCoin, Ethereum, Litecoin, Dodgecoin, Tether, Ripple, Shiba Inu) is driven by the power of Blockchain technology (the distributed ledger technology and the process of mining). Blockchain-based cryptocurrencies offer P2P network capability to provide real-time payment platforms and systems.

In the cases of ATM/cash cards, credit cards, EFTPOS/debit cards, Internet banking and mobile banking, banks function as financial intermediaries for payment transactions. However, in the cases of cryptocurrencies, the mining algorithms function as a digital intermediary to facilitate secure payment transactions. There is state/federal legislation regulating the PayTech system operation of ATM/cash cards, credit cards, EFTPOS/debit cards, Internet banking and mobile banking. However, payment super apps and cryptocurrencies do not require government involvement or state regulation to support the process of digital diffusion. Furthermore, the diffusion of ATM/cash cards, credit cards, and EFTPOS/debit cards largely depends on physical networks of electronic payment systems, ATMs, retail outlets and point-of-sale (POS) terminals to provide an automation of fund transfer with market-wide operations. Internet banking and mobile banking services are based on a web-based platform and banking software to provide online payment transactions without physical branches. In the cases of payment super apps and cryptocurrencies, the digital diffusion is based on P2P platforms empowered by Internet and Blockchain technologies.

Figure 5.5 maps the complexity level of PayTech to the process of diffusion. The X-axis shows the level of complexity ranging from 1 (lowest) to 5 (highest) (Table 5.3). ATM/cash cards and credit cards had a medium level of complexity and took 23 years to achieve commercialisation/diffusion. EFTPOS/debit cards had a medium level of complexity and took 17 years to achieve commercialisation/diffusion. Internet banking had a low level of complexity and took 5 years to achieve commercialisation/diffusion. Mobile banking also had a low level of complexity and took 8 years to achieve commercialisation/diffusion. Payment super apps (Ali Pay, LINE Pay, Google Pay, Grab Pay, WeChatPay, Apple Pay) and cryptocurrencies (BitCoin, Ethereum, Litecoin, Dodgecoin, Tether, Ripple, Shiba Inu) took around 1 year to achieve a level of digital diffusion. It is argued that the power of Blockchain-based PayTech has shortened the process of achieving digital diffusion. Nevertheless,

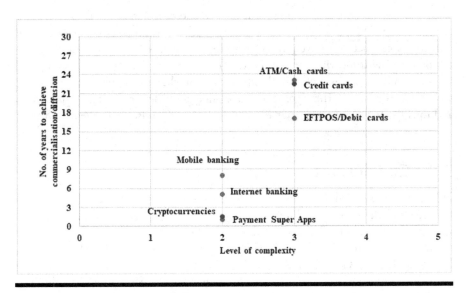

Figure 5.5   Complexity and diffusion of PayTech.

Source: The authors' design.

the findings do not show that complexity is a factor influencing the time taken to achieve commercialisation/diffusion.

The findings are in line with Rothwell (1992)'s fifth generation of innovation model (Table 5.1) arguing the needs for networking to avoid the failure of innovation diffusion. The diffusion process of PayTech needs the systems integration and extensive networking model as argued by Rothwell (1992). The analyses have shown that the diffusion of ATM/cash cards, credit cards, and EFTPOS/debit cards needs extensive networks based on brick-and-mortar infrastructure. The diffusion of Internet banking and mobile banking is based on internet connection monitoring software connecting remote users to cloud-based platforms. The digital diffusion of payment super apps (Ali Pay, LINE Pay, Google Pay, Grab Pay, WeChatPay, Apple Pay) is also driven by Internet technology as the service innovations are based on mobile web applications. The digital diffusion of cryptocurrencies (BitCoin, Ethereum, Litecoin, Dodgecoin, Tether, Ripple, Shiba Inu) is based on Blockchain networks and extensive mining software.

As can be seen from Figure 5.3, Non-banks have now encroached on traditional financial services industry. Arguably, the banking landscape is moving towards disruption as cheques are being replaced by online payments; conventional lending is being replaced by P2P lending platforms; bank credit cards are being replaced by payment gateway solutions from non-banks such as Apple, Amazon, Google, Paytm, WeChat, Alipay. Currently, brick-and-mortar banks are being replaced by neobanks such as Revolut, Monzo, Statrys, N26, Current, Chime, and Cleo. The future of cryptoeconomics would see the growth and diffusion of PayTech take place at high speed. The power of Internet and Blockchain technology would help new non-banks compete effectively in offering better services (customised services) to customers. The improving services of PayTech at a low cost (via using computer software empowered by a decentralised Internet Blockchain) would take customers away from the banks. The algorithms have gradually disintermediated banks' roles and thus PayTech may completely disrupt the banking landscape in the near future.

5.5   Conclusions

This chapter explored the cryptoeconomics with a focus on the complexity of PayTech and the process of diffusion. The analyses were performed through seven types of PayTech: (1) ATM/cash cards, (2) credit cards, (3) EFTPOS/debit cards, (4) Internet banking, (5) mobile banking, (6) payment super apps (Ali Pay, LINE Pay, Google Pay, Grab Pay, WeChatPay, Apple Pay) and (7) cryptocurrencies (BitCoin, Ethereum, Litecoin, Dodgecoin, Tether, Ripple, Shiba Inu). The findings have shown that ATM/cash cards, credit cards and EFTPOS/debit cards had a medium level of complexity whereas Internet banking, mobile banking, payment super apps and cryptocurrencies had a low level of complexity. It is argued that the power of Internet and blockchain technologies has facilitated the process of bringing PayTech–towards commercialisation/diffusion at high speed.

The research findings are in line with Rothwell (1992)'s fifth generation of innovation model–the systems integration and extensive networking model. ATM/cash cards, credit cards, EFTPOS/debit cards are based on networks of brick-and-mortar branches. Internet banking, mobile banking and payment super apps are based on the Internet technology connecting remote users to cloud-based platforms as well as mobile web applications. Cryptocurrencies are based on blockchain networks and extensive mining software. The improving services of PayTech empowered by decentralised Internet blockchain technologies have already taken customers away from the banks. As a consequence, the future of cryptoeconomics would see the potential of PayTech completely disrupting the banking landscape.

This research study contributes to theory and a contribution to practice as follows.

(i) Contribution to theory

The main theoretical contribution of this research study is the development of a new methodology for analysing the complexity of innovation–a complexity metric–which can be applied to various innovations in different industries. The research findings can help strengthen the body of knowledge in PayTech, particularly the linkages between the complexity of innovation and the process of diffusion.

(ii)   Contribution to practice

The findings reveal that the decentralised Internet Blockchain technologies have empowered the digital diffusion of PayTech in recent years. The process of bank disintermediation is taking place as the algorithms become an online intermediary. The lessons and insights from the study can help industry players plan for effective competition in the age of digital transformation. Given the potential of technologies in bank disintermediation, conventional banks need to be prepared by launching a new business model in response to the imminent disruption.

References

Abernathy, W. J., and Clark, K. B. (1985), 'Innovation: Mapping the winds of creative destruction', *Research Policy*, Vol. 14(1), pp. 3–22.

Alabi, K. (2017), 'Digital Blockchain networks appear to be following Metcalfe's Law', *Electronic Commerce Research and Applications*, Vol. 24, pp. 23–29.

Bank of New York Mellon Corporation (2015), *Innovation in Payments: The Future is FinTech*, Bank of New York Mellon Corporation, USA.

Barras, R. (1986) 'Towards a theory of innovation in services', *Research Policy*, Vol. 15, pp. 161–173.

Barras, R. (1990) 'Interactive innovation in financial and business services: the vanguard of the service revolution', *Research Policy*, Vol. 19, pp. 215–237.

CFTE. (2022). Ranking of Largest Fintech Companies in 2022 [Full List]. CFTE. https://courses.cfte.education/ranking-of-largest-fintech-companies/.

Christensen, C. M. (1997), *The Innovator's Dilemma*, Harvard Business School Press, Boston, M.A.

Economist Intelligence Unit (2021), *Going digital: Payments in the post-Covid world*, The Economist Intelligence Unit, London.

Eisenhardt, K. M. (1989), 'Building Theories from Case Study research', *Academy of Management Review*, Vol. 14(4), pp. 532–550.

Falwadiya, H. and Dhingra, S. (2022), 'Blockchain technology adoption in government organizations: a systematic literature review', *Journal of Global Operations and Strategic Sourcing*, Vol. 15 No. 3, pp. 473–501.

Freeman, C. (1982), 'Schumpeter or Schmookler?', in C. Freeman, J. Clark and L. Soete (eds.), *Unemployment and Technical Innovation*, Pinter, London.

Gomber, P., Koch, J. A., and Siering, M. (2017), 'Digital Finance and FinTech: Current research and future research directions', *Journal of Business Economics*, Vol. 87(5), pp. 537–580.

Harris, W.L., and Wonglimpiyarat, J. (2019), 'Blockchain Platform and Future Bank Competition', *Foresight Journal*, Vol. 21(6), pp. 625–639.

Hobday, M. (1998), 'Product complexity, innovation and industrial organisation', *Research Policy*, Vol. 26(6), pp. 689–710.

Hobday, M., Rush, H., and Tidd, J. (2000), 'Innovation in Complex Products and Systems', *Research Policy*, Vol. 29(7–8), pp. 793–804.

Hughes, T. (1988), *The Development of Large Technical Systems*, Campus, Boulder.

Iman, N. (2020), 'The rise and rise of financial technology: The good, the bad, and the verdict', *Cogent Business and Management*, Vol. 7, pp. 1–17.

Kauffman, R. J., and Ma, D. (2015), 'Contemporary research on payments and cards in the global FinTech revolution', *Electronic Commerce Research and Applications*, Vol. 14(5), pp. 261–264.

Naveed, K., Watanabe, C., and Neittaanmaki, P. (2017), 'Co-evolution between streaming and live music leads a way to the sustainable growth of music industry e Lessons from the US experiences', *Technology in Society*, Vol. 50, pp. 1–19.

Polasik, M., Huterska, A., Iftikhar, R., and Mikula, S. (2020), 'The impact of Payment Services Directive 2 on the PayTech sector development in Europe', *Journal of Economic Behavior and Organization*, Vol. 178, pp. 385–401.

Raikos, G. (2019), PayTech and Blockchain: *Adjusting for Security and Risk*. In: T. Chishti, T. Craddock and R. Courtneidge (Eds.), *The PayTech Book: The Payment Technology Handbook for Investors, Entrepreneurs and FinTech Visionaries*, John Wiley & Sons, Chichester.

Rogers, E. (1962), *Diffusion of Innovations*, The Free Press, New York.

Rogers, E. (1995), *Diffusion of Innovations*, The Free Press, New York.

Rogers, E. (2003), *Diffusion of Innovations*, The Free Press, New York.

Rothwell, R. (1992), 'Successful Industrial Innovation: Critical Success Factors for 1990s', *R&D Management*, Vol. 22(3), pp. 221–239.

Ruoslahti, H. (2020), 'Complexity in project co-creation of knowledge for innovation', *Journal of Innovation & Knowledge*, Vol. 5(4), pp. 228–235.

Russell, M. G., and Smorodinskaya, N. V. (2018), 'Leveraging complexity for ecosystemic innovation', *Technological Forecasting and Social Change*, Vol. 136, pp. 114–131.

Schmookler, J. (1962), Economic Sources of Inventive Activity. In: N. Rosenberg (Ed.), *The Economics of Technological Change*, Penguin Books, Harmondsworth.

Schumpeter, J. A. (1939), *Business cycles: A Theoretical, Historical and Statistical Analysis of the Capitalist Process*, 2 vols., McGraw-Hill, New York.

Schumpeter, J. A. (1967), *The Theory of Economic Development*, 5th edn., Oxford University Press, New York.

Shim, Y., and Shin, D. H. (2017), 'Analyzing China's Fintech Industry from the Perspective of Actor–Network Theory', *Telecommunications Policy*, Vol. 40(2–3), pp. 168–181.

Sikorski, J. J., Haughton, J., and Kraft, M. (2017), 'Blockchain technology in the chemical industry: Machine-to-machine electricity market', *Applied Energy*, Vol. 195, pp. 234–246.

Tapscott, D., and Tapscott, A. (2016), *Blockchain Revolution: How the technology behind Bitcoin is changing money*, Business, and the World, Portfolio, New York.

Thompson, B. S. (2017), 'Can Financial Technology Innovate Benefit Distribution in Payments for Ecosystem Services and REDD+?', *Ecological Economics*, Vol. 139, pp. 150–157.

Tushman, M., and Anderson, P. (1987), Technological discontinuities and organization environments. In: A. Pettigrew (Ed.), *The Management of Strategic Change*, Blackwell, Oxford.

Twiss, B. (1995), *Managing Technological Innovation*, Pitman Publishing, London.

Vargo, S. L., Akaka, M. A., and Wieland, H. (2020), 'Rethinking the process of diffusion in innovation: A service-ecosystems and institutional perspective', *Journal of Business Research*, Vol. 116, pp. 526–534.

Vernon, R. (1966), 'International Investment and International Trade in the Product Cycle', *Quarterly Journal of Economics*, Vol. 80(2), pp. 190–207.

Vranken, H. (2017), 'Sustainability of Bitcoin and Blockchains', *Current Opinion in Environmental Sustainability*, Vol. 28, pp. 1–9.

Wonglimpiyarat, J. (2005), 'Does complexity affect the speed of innovation?', *Technovation*, Vol. 25, pp. 865–882.

Wonglimpiyarat, J. (2018). 'Challenges and dynamics of FinTech crowd funding: An innovation system approach', *Journal of High Technology Management Research*, Vol. 29(1), 98–108.

Yin, R. K. (2013), *Case Study Research: Design and Methods*, Sage Publications, London.

Chapter 6

Cryptocurrencies and FinTech for People in a Hurry

Syed Shurid Khan

Chapter Overview

Cryptocurrencies are at the forefront of today's FinTech sector and have gained considerable popularity among both seasoned investors and ordinary retail enthusiasts alike. The expectation is that people will sometime soon ditch any national currency, such as the US Dollar, the Euro, or the Yuan for a more universal form of exchange, such as Bitcoin for transactions across national borders. The present paper attempts to highlight some of the caveats in such feelings towards the future of finance. It also summarizes the brief but rich history of the crypto world and discusses some of the myths surrounding cryptocurrencies and Blockchain technology, and questions their validity. While Blockchain technology's potential in many industries, including the financial sector is promising and might be a possible game-changer–the potential danger of misinterpretation and abuse does exist, nonetheless. In the present paper, the basics of cryptocurrencies and FinTech are revisited and attempts have been made to help see them in the light of basic economic principles behind how money works. The thought experiments, literature review, and critical analysis presented in the present paper indicate that investing in cryptocurrencies needs to be considered with better value judgment, and with relatively more caution both in the sense of investment justification and also in the light of general ethics. Because investing in something that promises a high return with low to no risk (like many crypto assets do), might very well be a red flag about a Ponzi scheme or purely a gamble, which

 DOI: 10.1201/9781003395560-6

are not only potentially illegal but might also damage the general confidence in the financial system if left unchecked.

6.1 Introduction

Cryptocurrencies offer promises – decentralization, transparency, privacy, financial inclusion, and the like – the unique selling points that are yet to be properly weighed against the many misconceptions and abuses that come with them (Trozze et al., 2022). The media and the scientific community analyze and discuss their technicality and their investment prospects, however a basic discussion and understanding of their contribution to the economy and to society are still missing. All in all, the existing literature also does not provide sufficient evidence of the many extraordinary claims that the crypto world makes and lures investors with. Claims such as their credibility as a universal currency, their low investment risks, ability to provide investor security, and associated ethics – are some of the topics that are discussed in the following sections.

An asset market that is unregulated and lacks investor protection, is prone to scams, frauds, market manipulation, and illegal activities. Early and large investors often benefit disproportionately from the capital gains and this may lead to the proliferation of unethical speculation efforts, and also may harm small investors through large price volatility, consequently creating wealth inequality (Kamps et al., 2022). In addition, the mining process and associated energy consumption lead to substantial negative externality on the environment (Badea et al., 2021). These are some major ethical concerns that also need to be weighed in to fully understand the market.

6.2 A Brief History of Crypto and Blockchain

The idea behind today's cryptocurrencies and Blockchain, the key technology behind all of them, has a considerably rich history of development. Despite the widespread belief that the concept of a digital currency (the first one being Bitcoin) is an invention of a mysterious and perhaps fictitious person Satoshi Nakamoto (see Nakamoto, 2008), in fact an American cryptographer David Chaum introduced the concept of electronic cash (eCash) in 1990 (see Chaum and Naor, 1990). Chaum and Noar (1990) first aimed to allow digital transactions with anonymity and privacy through their eCash project. In 2008, Satoshi Nakamoto proposed the principles of a decentralized digital currency in a published whitepaper titled "Bitcoin: A Peer-to-Peer Electronic Cash System," and subsequently the Bitcoin network was launched on 3rd January, 2009. From the beginning, Bitcoin gained traction among cypherpunks[1] and tech enthusiasts. However, the usage of the currency was limited to primarily speculative trading, and some online purchases of illegal items on the dark web (Grabowski, 2019).

It was not until 2013 that cryptocurrency, at that time mainly Bitcoin, gained widespread attention, and interest from the media and subsequent price surges. As a result, many more similar digital currencies were introduced in the market, aptly named "altcoins," namely, alternative coins, such as Ethereum, Litecoin, Ripple, and the like. In 2017, startups and projects started to mushroom, issuing their own tokens (a process known as ICOs[2]) to raise funds – primarily using the Ethereum platform. However, the unregulated nature of Initial Coin Offerings (ICOs) and the prevalence of scams and fraudulent projects led to concerns from regulators worldwide (Fisch, 2019).

Blockchain technology, which is the backbone of cryptocurrencies, was also gaining traction outside digital currencies, as developers started exploring other

Figure 6.1 A digital gold rush? The craze for cryptocurrencies today closely resembles the Gold Rush in the mid-1800s.

Image Source: AI-generated by author on Dall-E 2.

potential applications. For instance, an alternative decentralized domain registration system called Namecoin was created in 2011 (see Kalodner et al., 2015). Financial institutions found various advanced applications of Blockchain technology. Global major banks came together to create the R3 consortium to explore the potential of the technology in the financial sector. Not only the financial sector but other industries including the technology sector started to realize the potential of Blockchain. For example, in 2016, IBM created its own Blockchain platform to provide various enterprise and network solutions. It is to be noted here that although cryptocurrencies were a driving force behind Blockchain's popularity to explode, it is not the only or even primary usage. While Blockchain provides a decentralized ledger system that is known for its transparency and audibility, cryptocurrency markets themselves have not been free from fraud and market manipulation. The collapse of the crypto exchange FTX in November 2022 and the subsequent revelation of mishandling of ledgers and customer funds, alleged fraudulent monetary transactions related to the crypto exchange, and the like, are a testimonial to the fact that dealing with cryptocurrencies is sometimes not necessarily safe and legal, just because they are based on Blockchain technology (Jalan and Matkovskyy, 2023).

6.3 The Basic Functions of Money – Especially Liquidity

Do cryptocurrencies meet the basic conditions to be called money? We call it cryptocurrency – however, it does not do all functions that Macroeconomics 101 textbooks tell us that money should do (see Ammous, 2018; Graham, 1940; Jevons, 1989). Cryptocurrencies are vastly illiquid, partly due to their limited reach in the current economic system (Wei, 2018). The recent volatility in the values of cryptocurrencies perhaps distinguishes them the most from other traditional currencies, such as the USD. While exchange rates of currencies across the globe fluctuate to some degree vis-à-vis the USD, the price fluctuations of cryptocurrencies has been extraordinary, particularly during the pandemic as well as in the post-pandemic era of the Russian invasion of Ukraine. In March 2020, when the global pandemic was officially declared and lockdowns were in place, cryptocurrencies lost much of their value, for example, Bitcoin lost almost 50% of its value at the time along with the whole crypto market crashing. Here digital currencies violate the three main functions of money. First, they did not seem to act as a server as well as a "store of value." For example, if a farmer wanted to sell his or her harvest for Bitcoins before March 2020, so that he or she could use the Bitcoins for next year's farming – the farmer would find production twice as expensive. This would suddenly make agriculture or any sector for that matter no longer viable for someone who stored values in the form of Bitcoins, instead of a regular currency. Secondly, for the same reason as mentioned above – cryptocurrencies cannot perform as a good "unit of account" – money's second function. If Apple Inc. decided before the pandemic that an iPhone's list price would be one-tenth of a Bitcoin (one thousand dollars roughly at that time), can they continue to offer the same price just one month later when the pandemic is declared and subsequently the cryptocurrency market crashes? Therefore, cryptocurrencies do not seem to function well as a unit of account either. Third and finally, to operate as a good "medium of exchange", another major function of money – cryptos need to be widely accepted and remain liquid at all times. However, it is still far-fetched to expect that cryptocurrencies will be accepted anywhere in the market just like a dollar bill any time soon. Regulatory challenges, lack of infrastructure, slow customer adoption, volatility, and the like, are some of the major obstacles blocking cryptocurrencies from being a good medium of exchange.

6.4   Will Cryptocurrencies Eliminate Inflation?

A prevalent discussion point in favor of cryptocurrencies is that the new kind of currency will not be affected by excess money printing, and therefore inflation will no longer remain an investment risk factor. The rationale behind this conclusion was that Bitcoin, the most widely used cryptocurrency for example, is limited in quantity to roughly 23 million coins. Limited supply ensures against devaluation of the currency through printing or mining, such as in the case of a government printing fiat money and thus causing inflation (Panda at al., 2023). Each Bitcoin was valued at USD 20 000 as of 30 April, 2023. If no new Bitcoin can be mined[3], there is no inflation in the value of the coin. However, there has been always drastic volatility in the value of all kinds of cryptocurrencies (Katsiampa, 2017; Agyei et al., 2022; Wei et al., 2023).

The major rationale behind the claim that cryptocurrencies will help fight inflation is that they are limited in supply. For example, Bitcoin is set at twenty-one million coins as its upper limit – a scarcity that is a fundamental characteristic of the coin built into its design. A process known as "halving" cuts half the reward for mining Bitcoins approximately every four years – and this will make the supply reach its maximum by the middle of the next century (around 2140 AD). However, just because something is in limited supply, it is not guaranteed to not get devalued. Let us do a thought experiment to understand why this claim linking limited supply and inflation is flawed. Suppose we are in the late 1990s and for some reason, the world leaders decide that dial-up modems can no longer be manufactured without government permission so that the governments can maintain a fixed total supply of the devices (for whatever reason, just for the sake of the thought experiment). Does that guarantee that the limited supply of dial-up modems makes them very pricey? Most probably no, because soon in the mid-2000s, newer and better ways of internet accessibility emerge in the tech world. Everybody now will have other choices, such as switching to Broadband/Optical Fiber connectivity instead of old-style dial-up

Figure 6.2 The government conducts monetary policies by adjusting the money supply to steer the economy in the right direction. Image Source: AI-generated by author on Tome.app.

modems that used to use the land-phone lines. The point here is that just because a cryptocurrency is in limited supply, it does not mean that its value will not fall. The value of any asset, including cryptocurrencies is affected by many factors, such as investor sentiment, change in regulations, technological advancement, and availability of substitutes, and so forth. As a result, cryptocurrencies in general might face inflation, namely, they can afford fewer goods and services after regulation is in place. Finally, technological advancement may lead to the creation of newer and better versions of digital currencies which might also make the existing currencies, Bitcoin, Ethereum, and the like, fall in price. For instance, while Bitcoin is capped at only 21 million coins, investor demand might easily be diverted to other similar assets currently existing in the market or the new ones that might come to the market soon. Hence, although governments might print money and may cause inflation, cryptocurrencies might still fare much worse than fiat currency with respect to inflation as an investment concern.

6.5 Currency or Commodity

Another major claim circulating in the FinTech sphere is that cryptocurrencies will eventually replace traditional currencies. It should not be forgotten that the governments and the central banks do not only print money but are also responsible for managing economies. Having control over money circulation is crucial to their execution of monetary policies (Claeys et al., 2018). Therefore, the governments are unlikely to relinquish their control over the money being circulated in the economy and let digital currencies dictate the economy in the near future. The lack of stability, accountability, and regulation poses a serious obstacle to widespread adoption of cryptos as a primary form of currency (see Hsu et al., 2023). Therefore, a key question is whether investors really see cryptocurrencies as a functioning true currency, or just as a commodity or security (such as gold or stock), in which they can do speculative trading. If investors are not crystal clear on this beforehand, any mental process involving analysis of investment in them shall be vastly flawed.

6.6 History Repeats Itself – Ponzi and Gambling

Ponzi Schemes have been a recurring phenomenon across the history of modern finance. They existed even before the person, Ponzi, whom the scheme is named after, came onto the scene and made this kind of financial pyramid scheme vastly visible and notorious. However, under the nose of mainstream finance, Ponzi schemes have been a regular fixture in the system. In a Ponzi scheme, existing investors are paid returns from only fresh funds collected from new subscribers, and the process goes on for a long time, generating seemingly unlimited cashflow for the original creators of the scheme and promising abnormally high returns and low risks for retail investors until the whole scheme eventually collapses when no new subscriber can be found or the regulators intervene. After the collapse of the world's second-largest cryptocurrency exchange FTX, the operating style of the exchange has been alleged to be very similar to a Ponzi scheme. The founder and CEO of FTX, Sam Bankman-Fried or SBF had been transferring customer funds to FTX's sister company Alameda Research, without the knowledge of the FTX customers – the currently ongoing civil suit alleges that FTX used "false representation and deceptive conduct."

Many other cryptocurrencies and crypto-based proprietary tokens have also failed to deliver the promises that come with Blockchain technology. Instead, they mostly attempted to proliferate riding on the same prevalent factors that help a

Ponzi scheme (see Andrade and Nowall, 2023). Therefore, someone needs to be aware of the common red flags, such as signs of excessive greed among the general investors, the promises of high returns with low to no risk, people investing without a basic understanding of finance, social pressure, word-of-mouth referrals, and regulatory oversight, etc.

6.7 Concluding Remarks: The Future of FinTech

As new technologies have emerged, the financial sector has always revamped itself and progressed at the same pace. Hence it is very likely that Blockchain technology has the potential to enrich FinTech. Digital payment solutions, peer-to-peer (P2P) transfers, mobile wallets, and QR code transactions have made our lives easier and have led to a much broader financial inclusion. FinTech also allows the financial sector to use algorithms, and AI-based platforms to make many financial processes and management faster, more efficient, and accessible. Cryptocurrencies, such as Bitcoin and Ethereum are at the forefront of FinTech advancement in the twenty-first century. However, general caution and financial literacy are warranted when it comes to investing in an asset. Careful judgment, following basic investment principles, and ethical considerations never fail to protect the economic system.

Looking at the history is important to understand the future of FinTech or the financial system in general. In 1997-98, the Asian financial crisis was caused by currency pegs and speculative attacks when many Asian countries had pegged their currencies to the USD. Speculative investment in technology companies lead to the Dot-com Bubble which burst at the very beginning of the current millennium (2000-2002). Speculative real-estate investments, the subprime mortgage crisis, and subsequent housing loan defaults caused the 2008 Financial Crisis. The one thing that was common to all these global financial crises is the expectation of "quick profits."

In the post-pandemic world, the outlook of the global economy today seems to be very grim in the eyes of many thought leaders, and global business leaders. A possible recession is looming round the corner when Russia and Ukraine are at war, and when the US and China are no longer very good friends. Tech companies, including, Facebook, Microsoft, and Google have been regularly conducting layoffs, the US Federal Reserve has been hiking key interest rates to control inflation, and other central banks across the globe are on their toes to maintain a healthy level of foreign reserve, and so forth.

Our financial sector today faces the same challenges as the ones they had throughout history. Financial technology or FinTech improved the sector in terms of efficiency and accessibility, but the economic principles and financial fundamentals beneath the surface have always remained the same. General financial literacy among retail investors, ethical and moral understanding, and regulatory control are some of the key features that are the gold standard. No matter how advanced we are in FinTech and technology in other sectors, human behavior plays the most important role in our economy and society. Hence, even after we have Blockchain technology in the financial sector – Economics 101 and Finance 101 will always remain the most relevant principles underpinning any economic progress and financial prosperity.

Notes

1 Cypherpunk: someone who advocates social and political change through the use of strong cryptography and privacy-enhancing technologies; an active movement that exists since at least the late 1980s.
2 A new cryptocurrency project or Blockchain platform may raise funds by issuing their own tokens or coins to investors in exchange for major cryptos like Bitcoin or Ethereum. This process is known as Initial Coin Offering (ICO), which is similar to an Initial Public Offering (IPO) in traditional finance. See Fisch (2019) for more details.
3 Mining is the term used to describe the process of creating new crypto coins. More details can be found in this article https://cointelegraph.com/learn/how-to-mine-bitc oin-a-beginners-guide-to-mine-btc.

References

Agyei, S. K., Adam, A. M., Bossman, A., Asiamah, O., Owusu Junior, P., Asafo-Adjei, R., & Asafo-Adjei, E. (2022). Does volatility in cryptocurrencies drive the interconnectedness between the cryptocurrencies market? Insights from wavelets. *Cogent Economics & Finance*, 10(1), 2061682.

Ammous, S. (2018). Can cryptocurrencies fulfil the functions of money?. *The Quarterly Review of Economics and Finance*, 70, 38–51.

Andrade, M., & Newall, P. W. (2023). Cryptocurrencies as Gamblified Financial Assets and Cryptocasinos: Novel Risks for a Public Health Approach to Gambling. *Risks*, 11, 49.

Badea, L., & Mungiu-Pupăzan, M. C. (2021). The economic and environmental impact of bitcoin. *IEEE Access*, 9, 48091–48104.

Chaum, D., Fiat, A., & Naor, M. (1990). Untraceable electronic cash. In Advances in Cryptology—CRYPTO'88: Proceedings 8 (pp. 319–327). Springer New York.

Claeys, G., Demertzis, M., & Efstathiou, K. (2018). Cryptocurrencies and monetary policy (No. 2018/10). Bruegel Policy Contribution.

Fisch, C. (2019). Initial coin offerings (ICOs) to finance new ventures. *Journal of Business Venturing*, 34(1), 1–22.

Grabowski, M. (2019). Cryptocurrencies: A primer on digital money. Routledge.

Graham, F. D. (1940). The primary functions of money and their consummation in monetary policy. *American Economic Review*, 30(1), 1–16.

Hsu, P. P., Chen, Y. H. C., & Wang, C. H. (2023). Currency or commodity competition? Bitcoin price trends in the post-pandemic era. *International Journal of Applied Economics, Finance and Accounting*, 15(2), 61–70.

Jalan, A., & Matkovskyy, R. (2023). Systemic risks in the cryptocurrency market: Evidence from the FTX collapse. *Finance Research Letters*, 53, 103670.

Jevons, W. S. (1989). Money and the Mechanism of Exchange. In General Equilibrium Models of Monetary Economies (pp. 55–65). Academic Press.

Kalodner, H. A., Carlsten, M., Ellenbogen, P. M., Bonneau, J., & Narayanan, A. (2015, June). An Empirical Study of Namecoin and Lessons for Decentralized Namespace Design. In *WEIS* (Vol. 1, No. 1, pp. 1–23).

Kamps, J., Trozze, A., & Kleinberg, B. (2022). Cryptocurrencies:: Boons and curses for fraud prevention. In *A Fresh Look at Fraud* (pp. 192–219). Routledge.

Katsiampa, P. (2017). Volatility estimation for Bitcoin: A comparison of GARCH models. *Economics Letters*, 158, 3–6.

Manne, R. (2011). The Cypherpunk Revolutionary Robert Manne on Julian Assange. *Monthly, The*, (Mar 2011), 16–35.

Nakamoto, S. (2008). Bitcoin: A peer-to-peer electronic cash system. *Decentralized Business Review*, 21260.

Panda, S. K., Sathya, A. R., & Das, S. (2023). Bitcoin: Beginning of the Cryptocurrency Era. In *Recent Advances in Blockchain Technology: Real-World Applications* (pp. 25–58). Cham: Springer International Publishing.

Trozze, A., Kamps, J., Akartuna, E. A., Hetzel, F. J., Kleinberg, B., Davies, T., & Johnson, S. D. (2022). Cryptocurrencies and future financial crime. *Crime Science*, 11, 1–35.

Wei, W. C. (2018). Liquidity and market efficiency in cryptocurrencies. *Economics Letters*, 168, 21–24.

Wei, Y., Wang, Y., Lucey, B. M., & Vigne, S. A. (2023). Cryptocurrency uncertainty and volatility forecasting of precious metal futures markets. *Journal of Commodity Markets*, 29, 100305.

Chapter 7

Digital Disruption in Banking Sector: Evaluating Efficiency and Risk

Jeevesh Sharma

Chapter Overview

The integration of digital technology into various business processes, organizational endeavors, and business models is referred to as digital transformation or the digitalization of enterprises. Digitalization had a significant impact on the banking sector, leading to increased convenience, efficiency, and innovation. However, it has also increased competition and disrupted traditional business models. The digital disruption has remarkably influenced the banking sector in recent years. The digital transformation of the banking industry is being fuelled by several factors, including cost savings, improved client experience, greater operating efficiency, and optimization of the entire business process. This disruption has been driven by advances in technology, changing consumer behavior, and increased competition. The motive of this chapter is to evaluate the scenario of digital transformation in the banking industry. Through reviewing prior literature, it can be concluded that to a large extent, the digital revolution in financial services has changed the functioning of the banking sector. Although it has provided various methods and techniques to make our lives easy, an addition to it has also given birth to various fraudulent cases. There are some risks while performing digital banking such as identity theft, phishing, cybercrime,

DOI: 10.1201/9781003395560-7

fraud, and the like. This chapter also analyzes the various strategies related to over-coming or techniques to deal with the risks associated with digital disruption in the banking sector. Additionally, this chapter assesses the influence of digital transformation in financial services with reference to the banking system. The foundation of a digital bank is its platform, which enables banks to provide consumers with cutting-edge digital goods and services and because of the influence of this, consumer protection issues are more prominent.

7.1   Introduction

Digital transformation in financial services has given birth to a new revolution in the financial market and institutions. On a large scale, this has replaced the functioning of conventional financing with various technologies and given rise to digital eco-system in the financial market (Scardovi, 2017; Pashkov & Pelykh, 2020). Among financial institutions the banking sector has witnessed a major transformation in the operation of the banking ecosystem. From the opening of an account to the trans-ferring of money across the world everything is influenced by technological advance-ment. Numerous techniques and instruments have been developed in the digital banking system. Online banking, e-banking, M-banking (Mobile-banking), debit cards, and credit cards are the techniques and instruments to perform E-banking transactions.

The banking industry is transitioning away from a reliance on branch offices in favor of information technology (IT), big data, and highly qualified personnel. Prior to this transformation, banks and markets were already intertwined, with an increasing proportion of intermediate operations adopting a market-based strategy. In their primary activities, such as payment and advice services, digitally advancing intermediaries have increased competition for banks. Both the uptake of various new digital technologies and the expansion of the client base linked to them have grown greatly (Vives, 2019). In fact, the fundamental shift is already being brought about by digital industry disruption, leaving incumbents with potentially out-of-date legacy systems and over-extended branch networks to keep up with the service standards that new competitors can provide. Customers nowadays need services to be open and user-friendly. This chapter evaluates the threat posed by digital banking in the context of a long succession of financial and technological advances in the banking industry.

The objective of this chapter is to evaluate the scenario of digital transformation in the banking sector, resulting in increases in efficiency in banking operations or financial functioning and the risks associated with it. This chapter also analyzes the various strategies related to overcoming, or techniques to deal with, the risks associated with digital disruption in the banking sector. To achieve this objective it reviews prior literature related to the chapter theme. Additionally, this chapter also uses various published materials such as institutional reports, database reports, and numerous information available on several web links such as blogs, news reports, OECD, Deloitte, Statista, and so forth.

The chapter presents both the positive and negative aspects of digital technology or digital transformation in the banking sector. Through reviewing prior literature, it can be concluded that to a large extent, the digital transformation in financial services has changed the functioning of financial institutions. Although it has provided various methods and techniques to make our life easy, in addition it has also given birth to various fraudulent cases. There are some risks while performing digital banking such as identity theft, phishing, cybercrime, fraud, and the like. Further, this chapter also presents strategies to overcome these problems such as integrated security, awareness programs in society, the installation of antivirus software in the systems, promoting double authentication, and techniques of machine learning and data analytics.

The remainder of this chapter is structured as follows. The influence of digital transformation on banking operations and how it impacts the banking industry is discussed as numerous past works on this topic are presented in section 7.1. Sections 7.2 and 7.3 outline the digital transformation in financial services. The digital disruption in the banking industry is covered in sections 7.4 and 7.5, and the risk related to this disruption in the banking ecosystem is covered in sections 7.6 and 7.7. Section 7.8 describes the numerous methods to avoid this disruption. Section 7.9 deals with some facts and figures related to the disruption of digital banking globally and in the Indian context. Lastly, section 7.10 presents the conclusion of the chapter.

7.1.1 The Objectives of this Chapter

■ To evaluate the efficiency and risk associated with digital transformation in the banking industry
■ To assess digital disruption in the banking sector.

7.2 Literature Review

This chapter's objective is to examine the impact of digital transformation on the financial industry. In order to investigate this, the chapter has provided a comprehensive analysis of the negative and positive effects of digital transformation on the financial industry. In light of this, the significance of digital transformation in financial services and institutions prior to identifying the main causes of digital disruption in banking is given.

7.3 Digital Transformation in Financial Services and Banking

Enterprise Resource Planning (ERP) is one example of a classic technology that has been improved by the application of modern IT, such as analytics, mobile computing, social media, or smart embedded devices, to allow significant business gains (Westerman et al., 2014). The digitalization of financial services makes feasible a new perspective feasible on how banking services are offered and delivered to customers. Technology has influenced the evolution of business relationships within companies (Werth et al., 2020). As a result of these developments, products are redesigned, marketing strategies, production, and methods of service delivery through supply chains are modified, and structural autonomy is increased, amongst other modifications (Abdulquadri et al., 2021).

Considering this Figure 7.1 presents the implication of digital transformation in major avenues of financial services. As a consequence of the emergence of information and communication technology, digitalization has emerged as a new phenomenon. The year 2008 marked the debut of the active boom in the FinTech industry, and the economic sector was among the first to witness its impact (Omarini, 2017). As a result of the economic crisis, financial institutions were compelled to seek out novel methods to reduce expenses without sacrificing service quality. Through automation and personalization, digital transformation in financial services can help businesses attain client retention, customer satisfaction, and business sustainability. The digital finance cube and its dimensions framework classify digital finance, digital investments, digital money, digital payments, digital insurance, and digital financial advising as digital finance services (Gomber et al., 2018; Ozili, 2018). The

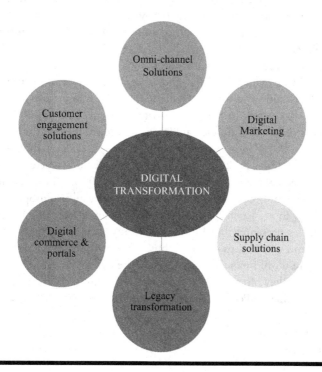

Figure 7.1   Digital transformation in the financial services.

conventional business models of retail banks are severely impacted by the emergence of digital innovators in the financial services industry (Feyen et al., 2021; Abdulquadri et al., 2021). They have historically created value by merging several industries, including lending, investment, and transactions, which, in the long-term. meet the diverse financial needs of their consumers (Werth et al., 2020).

What is the meaning of digital transformation in banking? The primary objective, according to financial and banking reports, is digital innovation (Cuesta et al., 2015). Realistically, it signifies a paradigm transition involving offline and manual processes being replaced by web-based and electronic offerings (Omarini, 2017; Cuesta et al., 2015; Khanchel, 2019). When banking officials realized about digital wallets and other innovations for the first time, they were astonished. Several different and unique digital projects were implemented by them to make banking operations easier and more effective. Digital transformation in banking is now focused on customer experience, platform-based applications, integrated digital systems, Artificial Intelligence (AI) infrastructure, and, most importantly, the emergence and propagation of Blockchain technologies. FinTech as well as large non-bank technology firms in e-retailing, media, and other industries, could take advantage of this variation in the banking industry's business model (Feyen et al., 2021; Breidbach et al., 2020). With the emergence of technologies in the functions of banks it has opened the door for cyber-crimes too. These cyber attackers have the opportunity to weaken the protective advisory influence that banks have on their clients thanks to technological advancements and changes in consumer behavior.

According to Skinner, technological innovation is primarily responsible for the rise of digital banking (Skinner, 2014, p.93). When information is digitized and transmitted through various channels, such as the internet, mobile devices, automated teller machines (ATMs), and other technologically driven pathways, digital banking is said to be able to facilitate financial transactions and other types of transactions. According to Statista's report, between 2021 and 2024, people are predicted to use online and mobile banking more and more, with the biggest market being in Asia. In 2020, more than 805 million people will use online banking in the Far East and China. By 2024, this number is expected to be close to a billion. Asia was the biggest market for online banking in 2020, but the countries with the highest percentage of people using online banking were all in Europe. South Korea came in sixth, with a 74 percent usage rate. Banks are attempting to capitalize on the opportunities presented by the market through the digital transformation of banking. Without a doubt, the banking business has undergone a significant transformation as a result of financial technologies. The best chance for banks to develop and improve how they offer financial services is for them to embrace innovation and adopt new technologies. People can do advanced digital self-service tasks including:

- self-recordkeeping
- remote account opening with the aid of the most recent banking technologies
- buying insurance

- starting a loan
- various other activities.

Post-2015, the path to digital transformation had become more difficult due to the availability of risk mitigation instruments. With the emergence of venture capital funding, FinTech disruptions, mobile wallets, chatbots, personalised banking and conversational banking, traditional banks encountered a great deal of resistance. As the banking and finance sector advanced towards the start of 2020, banks and financial institutions were striving to achieve digital transformation in banking. The following are the key technologies that are used in the digital transformation of banking:

In the quest for digitalization, banks are using various technologies in the banking process to attain a smooth flow of work for customers and for bank management also (Cuesta e al., 2015; Abuhasan & Moreb, 2021). Digitalization is altering the norms of multiple sectors via possible disruptions of business models, resulting in the emergence of a significantly more complex and dynamic ecosystem for growth and innovation (Iansiti and Levien, 2004). The digital network has sparked the rapid growth of emerging technologies including social media, cloud computing, analytics and big data, wearable devices, 3D printing, and autonomous intelligent machines.

In the last few years, digital change has had a big effect on the banking industry. This change has been caused by improvements in technology, changes in how people act, and more competition. Below are some of the ways that technological advancement has altered the banking industry:

1. Mobile Banking: The proliferation of smartphones and mobile apps has resulted in the expansion of mobile banking. Customers may now access their accounts, conduct transactions, and manage their funds at any time and from any location. This has boosted client convenience and flexibility while also reducing the necessity for physical branches.

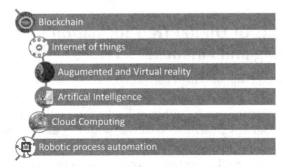

Figure 7.2   Digital banking technologies.

2. Online Banking: Online banking has grown in popularity as an acceptable substitute for conventional banking. Customers are able to login to their accounts, check their statements, and make transactions online. This has also resulted in the elimination of some physical branches, lowering the costs connected with their maintenance.

3. Digital Payments: Customers are increasingly turning to digital payment methods such as PayPal, Venmo, and Apple Pay to complete their financial transactions. This has resulted in a decrease in the use of cash and cheques, in addition to making it possible for transactions to be completed more quickly and with more efficiency.

4. Artificial Intelligence (AI): In the financial industry, artificial intelligence is being utilized to enhance customer service, detect fraudulent activity, and automate procedures. Because of this, we have seen improvements in both efficiency and accuracy, in addition to cost savings.

5. Blockchain: The banking sector started using Blockchain technology to enhance safety measures, save operational expenses, and boost levels of transparency. It could revolutionize the way in which banks carry out their business and communicate with one another.

6. Cloud computing: Advances in data storage and transmission enable data and software aggregation in specialized 'cloud' locations. This has a significant impact on the banking value chain. Data and software can now be kept with a third party rather than in-house. Smaller businesses can benefit from cheaper costs provided by cloud provider professionals' economies of scale.

The banking industry as a whole has been significantly impacted by the rise of digital disruption, which has ultimately led to improved levels of convenience, efficiency, and innovation. However, technology has also led to an increase in competitiveness and has shaken up established methods of conducting business. Banks that can adjust to these shifts and are willing to embrace digital transformation will be in a stronger position to achieve success in the years to come.

7.4 Benefits of Digital Transformation in Banking and Financial Services

Due to digitalization, the banking operation has improved a lot, and the efficiency of the banking system has increased. Digital transformation helped in reducing costs and simplifying the process. It has made the functioning of banking easy and convenient for both customers and bankers. With the use of devices and smart applications, a customer may access his bank account and perform transactions from anywhere and at any time. It saves the customers money and time because they don't have to visit a bank or wait in lines to get their work done. There is no doubt that it has improved convenience and customer service.

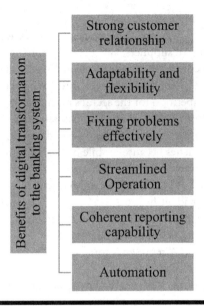

Figure 7.3   Benefit of digital transformation to the banking system.

The following figure shows some benefits that show how the digital transformation benefitted the banking system:

One of the most noteworthy developments in the finance sector is the widespread adoption of digital banking over traditional banking methods. The banking industry has undergone a digital transformation to know how banks and other financial institutions understand, engage with, and meet the demands of their consumers. To be more exact, an effective digital transformation starts with knowing digital client behavior, preferences, choices, likes, dislikes, and stated and unstated expectations. Therefore, improving customer experience, smooth administrative processes, and strong management are the key components that contribute to the successful implementation of digital transformation in banking and financial services.

This section emphasises the positive aspect of digital transformation in financial services and banking. As earlier stated, technology on the one hand brings efficiency but on the other hand, it comes along with various serious issues also. The following section explains the negative aspect of digital transformation in the banking sector, which can be called "Digital Disruption".

7.5   Digital Disruption in Banking

Chris Skinner defines digitalization for the financial industry as follows: "Banking is no longer money banking but data banking, and saving the data storage is more essential than ever" (Skinner, 2014, pp. 11, 14). This digital change may make the financial system more efficient and help more people get access to money through innovation, a wider range of suppliers, and a more competitive system. Additionally, market expansion will result from this disruption. This disruption will place pressure on the profit margins of incumbents, possibly inducing them to take on more risk, and it will stimulate competition for the sector's revenues. As a result of digitalization in the banking sector the existence of physical bank branches is vanishing (Koskinen & Manninen, 2019). The relevance of branch-based banking has passed. Rarely do customers visit bank branches because mobile banking technology is replacing them as the primary point of interaction with bank customers (Balkan, 2021). Customers are frequently compelled to visit banks solely to disclose, for example, ID proof for the purpose of customer identification (KYC) regulations. If these rules change or banks do not need these proofs or documents, the frequency of visiting a bank may drop even more (Graupner & Maedche, 2015).

The following Figure 7.4 represents some of the technological disruptions that are shaping the banking sector.

Analysts in the banking business have encountered new nomenclature over the last three years: P2P, crypto-currencies, Blockchain decentralised ledger technology, robo-advisors, chatbots, big data, millennials, sandbox. FinTech, or the application of digital technology to finance, is upending the financial industry. PayPal, Venmo, M-Pesa, ApplePay, and Alipay are just a few of the new payment methods that have emerged. TransferWise and WorldRemit compete

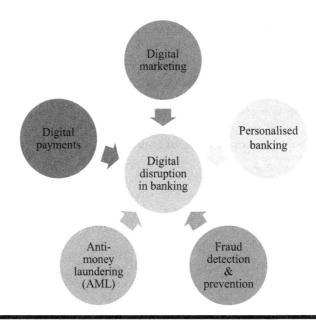

Figure 7.4   Digital disruption in the banking sector.

for international transfers and remittances with incumbents Western Union and MoneyGram (Dermine, 2017).

7.6 Factors Disrupting the Banking Sector

Understanding the primary elements driving the impact of digital technology on banking markets is critical. The following are some of the primary drivers of digital disruption in the banking business.

The above-mentioned factors which are fostering disruption in the banking industry through technological advancements. Figure 7.5 demonstrated the percentage of disruptors in the banking sector. Among these factors, customers' expectations mark high disruption. Resultant digital banking customers' expectations are very high because all the physical activities related to banking are eliminated through E-banking and M-banking. These have given rise to cyber fraud also, and to resolve this, proper compliance is the primary requirement. Similarly, factors like Blockchain, AI, FinTech, and BigTech, and the like, are also contributors.

In recent years, digital banking, which refers to the provision of banking services via digital channels such as mobile applications, websites, and online platforms, has become more prevalent. These disruptors have influenced the banking system on a large scale in terms of security, compliance, customer retention, and having strong networks.

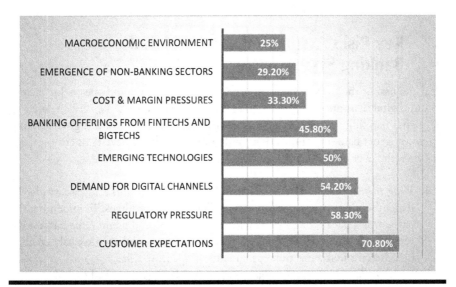

Figure 7.5   Major factors disrupting the banking sector.

Security and Fraud: Ensuring the security of consumer data and protecting against fraud is one of the primary challenges of digital banking. As banking services migrate to digital platforms, cybercriminals continue to develop sophisticated exploit techniques. To mitigate these risks, banks must employ robust security measures, such as encryption, multi-factor authentication, and real-time fraud detection systems.

Compliance: Digital banking operations are subject to a variety of legal obligations, such as safeguarding information confidentiality, Anti-Money Laundering (AML), and Know Your Customer (KYC) regulations. To make certain that their digital financial transactions comply with these rules and regulations, banks must invest in sophisticated regulatory frameworks and systems. Keeping up to date with altering regulatory landscapes can be difficult, especially in a world of technology that is swiftly evolving.

Digital banking requires the development and maintenance of solid technological platforms. It involves deploying scalable cloud-based solutions and ensuring high system accessibility and reliability. Integration of numerous online media and outside services, such as payment processors or personal finance management tools, can be challenging and requires collaboration and compatibility.

Customer retention requires quick and effective service to consumers. Customers can seek assistance more conveniently when various channels of support are available, such as chatbots, live chat, email, or phone support. Continuous interactions, such as notifications, alerts, and account-related updates, keeps customers notified and interested. Due to the entrance of digital disruptors, there are many risks which are associated with digital banking systems.

7.7 Key Risks Associated with a Digital Banking System

After discussing the core challenges, digital transformation, and the major factors behind digital disruption in the banking sector, there are some key risks related to the digital banking system. Figure 7.6 depicts some key risks in a digital banking system. Internet banking, applications and usage of multiple devices opens the door for cybercrimes or cyberattacks.

1. *Weak identity*: Nowadays individuals have many accounts and passwords. To remember these passwords can be a challenge for individuals. To remember the passwords a person often prefers to set short, easy, and memorable passwords. Here is the mistake that happens—easy and short passwords are easily cracked by cybercriminals, and they gain an advantage from this.
2. *Social media*: The current scenario is that people like to show off their daily lives in front of the digital world. Social media is the platform where individuals

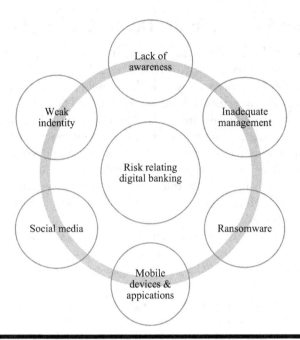

Figure 7.6   Key risk related to the digital banking system.

update their live status and many other things. This is also a major driver of cyber fraud cases.

3. *Inadequate management*: Proper management of personal data is also very important for the person who operates banking on a digital platform. The banks share all related documents by mail to the account holder, although they are protected with a password, still there is a chance of leakage of data.

4. *Lack of awareness*: While performing on a digital platform the individuals are so relaxed that they ignore some of the information that flashes on applications or on devices. Warning messages from the bank are unread by individuals most of the time. Banks are sharing all the preventive measures to be taken in a timely fashion whilst undertaking transactions through mobile banking and e-Banking but these are never read by the individuals. So, these are points that are lacking from the customer side.

5. *Ransomware*: Ransomware is the most common internet security issue. Ransomware is distributed through a variety of methods, including bogus e-mails, web pages, and downloads. Double extortion refers to ransomware that uses both data export and file encryption. If the hackers' demands fail to be fulfilled, they threaten to reveal stolen data with double extortion ransomware.

6. *Multiple devices*: The use of multiple devices also leads to the stealing of sensitive data.

7.8   Cyber Security in the Digital Banking System

Digitalization in the economy has converted conventional financial services into digital financial services. It enables individuals to connect with the global environment. Through the web world, the individual can do anything from very small to very large things in their daily life. They are not only doing shopping on the net but also might also be performing international financial transactions such as transferring money, booking essentials, and so forth. The increasing number of internet users has opened the door to cybercrimes. To save people from the above-mentioned risk cyber security is the saviour. Hence, cyber security plays a vital role in the banking ecosystem. Cyber security represents a range of technologies that help to protect devices from cyber-attacks or cybercrimes.

Cyber security is needed in the banking ecosystem, as nowadays individuals are performing almost all of their financial transactions on the cloud. So, there is an extensive chance of financial losses through phishing, identity threats, malware, spoofing, loss of personal data, fraudulent accesses, and so forth. Figure 7.7 presents the various threats related to digital banking. Cybercrimes not only affect individuals but also affect the bank. Banks must prioritize cybersecurity because data breaches might undermine public confidence in the industry. For banks, it may lead to serious issues. Due to the implementation of cyber security measures, confidential data pertaining to account holders is shielded from prying eyes and kept safe within e-banking platforms. If the protection of this information were ever to be weakened, then it may lead to fraud as well as other problems.

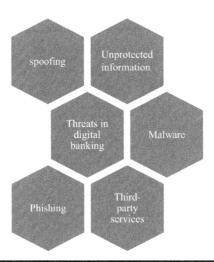

Figure 7.7   Threats for cybersecurity in digital banking.

1. *Unprotected data*: Unprotected data means information that is stored in banks' systems but has no encryption, making it easy for hackers to utilize the data to cause problems for the bank. To avoid this type of activity from occurring, the data should be protected.
2. *Malware*: All transactions are performed through devices. For this reason, al devices must be protected by anti-malware software. In devices various sensitive data is stored. If devices had malware, it would harm an individual's data.
3. *Third-party services*: Numerous banking organizations use third-party services to improve their customer service. However, inadequate cybersecurity could harm the bank who engaged these outside workers.
4. *Spoofing*: This method entails sending text messages to the victims posing as their bank to get the details needed for fraudulent activity, or other crime.
5. *Phishing*: Phishing is the fraudulent use of digital platforms to steal confidential data such as credit card details. Online banking scams evolve. They pretend to be legitimate and steal your login information.

7.9 Strategies to Overcome Digital Disruption in the Banking Sector

To address these threats there are many ways to overcome the various issues. Figure 7.8 has presented some of the major strategies to save ourselves.

1. *Integrated security*: To offer a complete security solution for the organization, an integrated network security strategy considers the proliferation of various assaults as well as diverse endpoint device types. As the Banking, Financial

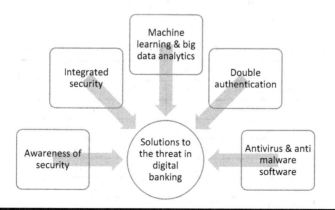

Figure 7.8   Five key solutions in the digital banking system.

Services, and Insurance (BFSI) sector is highly regulated and stores the sensitive information of their clients on the web/internet there is a need to protect the data so that it cannot be stolen by fraudulent individuals.

2. *Awareness of security*: With the increasing number of cybercrimes, individuals must be aware of the importance of security. As most of the financial transactions are performed on the net or web so there can be the possibility of cyber fraud. Therefore, one must not share anything with random callers and must inform banks if anything suspicious happens without delay.

3. *Antivirus software*: There are many viruses that may enter your devices. So, the Trojan virus is the most dangerous virus which accesses your device by making its clone.

4. *Double authentication*: Most of the digital transactions are performed by electronic devices like mobiles, laptops, PCs, and so forth, and everyone has certain login credentials to operate any apps and devices. Amongst these, passwords are a crucial part that must be protected by double security. They cannot be shared by anyone, even family and friends. The passwords must be updated within a certain time frame, and they must be double authenticated.

5. *Machine learning and data analytics*: Machine learning systems can identify fraudulent activity by filtering through enormous amounts of data using multiple techniques. Banks are able to monitor transactions, track client behaviour, and record information for additional compliance and regulatory systems to assist in the reduction of total regulatory risk.

7.10   Data on Digital Disruption in Banking across the World and India

Based on a report published by Global Economic Crime, cyber-crime has shown unprecedented growth and is now the most reported type of commercial crime.

Table 7.1   Bank Frauds in India from 2014 to 2022

Bank Frauds in India	
Years	Amount (in cr.)
2013–14	10170
2014–15	19455
2015–16	18699
2016–17	23934
2017–18	41168
2018–19	71534
2019–20	185468
2021–22	138442

Cyber criminals are always innovating new techniques of assault and data breaching to keep up with the ever-increasing digitalization of the world. Hackers and organized criminals have been unrelenting in their attacks on banks in India. It was seen in a recent Canara Bank incident in which hackers intended to block a portion of the bank's e-payments and defaced the bank's website by inserting a malicious page. The table below presents the total number of banking fraud in India. For the first time in the year 2021–2022, the number of cases decreased compared to other years. Internet banking and the usage of cards are the major reason behind cyber fraud. Although there was a trend of increasing cyber fraud in the banking sector from 2014 to 2020. According to the RBI report 9103 bank fraud incidents were reported in FY 2022. The total value of bank fraud dropped from 1,38 trillion to 604 billion rupees. Table 7.1 summarizes the bank frauds that happened in India from 2014–2022, which shows that financial losses have been increasing over these eight years.

By 2026, the market for global digital banking platforms is projected to be worth $9 billion, growing at a CAGR of 16% throughout that time. The rising significance of the digital client experience, a shorter replacement cycle, and better security and reliability are the factors propelling the growth of the global market for digital banking platforms.

7.11   Conclusion

Digitization in the financial services in the digital ecosystem demonstrates the number of technologies used in financial transactions. Although digital transformation blew the traditional financial services and promoted the digitalization of it in some instances digital transformation raised some negative issues among customers and financial institutions. This chapter has evaluated the threat posed by digital banking in the context of a long succession of financial and technological advances in the banking industry. The purpose of this chapter was to investigate the adoption of technology in the banking industry in addition to the digital disruption occurring in the financial services industry. The digital disruption of the banking industry is anticipated to improve both productivity and customer service overall. This will be accomplished by eliminating inconsistencies in information (via the use of big data, AI/ML technology, and Blockchain technology), providing a user interface that is more appealing to users and providing a higher quality of service, and eventually replacing outdated technology. As a result, the banking industry will move towards a paradigm that is centred on platforms and customers.

References

Abdulquadri, A., Mogaji, E., Kieu, T. A., & Nguyen, N. P. (2021). Digital transformation in financial services provision: A Nigerian perspective to the adoption of chatbot.

Journal of Enterprising Communities: People and Places in the Global Economy, *15*(2), 258–281.

Abuhasan, F., & Moreb, M. (2021, July). The Impact of the Digital Transformation on Customer Experience in Palestine Banks. In *2021 International Conference on Information Technology (ICIT)* (pp. 43–48). IEEE.

Balkan, B. (2021). Impacts of Digitalization on Banks and Banking. *The Impact of Artificial Intelligence on Governance, Economics and Finance, Volume I*, 33–50.

Breidbach, C. F., Keating, B. W., & Lim, C. (2020). Fintech: research directions to explore the digital transformation of financial service systems. *Journal of Service Theory and Practice*, *30*(1), 79–102.

Cuesta, C., Ruesta, M., Tuesta, D., & Urbiola, P. (2015). The digital transformation of the banking industry. *BBVA chapter*, *1*, 1–10.

Dermine, J. (2017). Digital disruption and bank lending. *European Economy*, (2), 63–76.

Feyen, E., Frost, J., Gambacorta, L., Natarajan, H., & Saal, M. (2021). Fintech and the digital transformation of financial services: implications for market structure and public policy. *BIS Chapters*. Bank for International Settlements, number 117.

Gomber, P., Kauffman, R. J., Parker, C., & Weber, B. W. (2018). On the FinTech revolution: Interpreting the forces of innovation, disruption, and transformation in financial services. *Journal of Management Information Systems*, *35*(1), 220–265.

Graupner, E., & Maedche, A. (2015). Process digitisation in retail banking: An empirical examination of process virtualization theory. *International Journal of Electronic Business*, *12*(4), 364–379.

Iansiti, M., & Levien, R. (2004). Keystones and dominators: Framing operating and technology strategy in a business ecosystem. *Harvard Business School, Boston*, *3*, 1–82.

Khanchel, H. (2019). The impact of digital transformation on banking. *Journal of Business Administration Chapter*, *8*(2), 20–29.

Koskinen, K., & Manninen, O. (2019). The impact of digitalisation on bank profitability.

Omarini, A. (2017). The digital transformation in banking and the role of FinTechs in the new financial intermediation scenario. MPRA Paper 85228, University Library of Munich, Germany.

Ozili, P. K. (2018). Impact of digital finance on financial inclusion and stability. *Borsa Istanbul Review*, *18*(4), 329–340.

Pashkov, P., & Pelykh, V. (2020). Digital transformation of financial services on the basis of trust. *Economic and Social Development: Book of Proceedings*, 375–383. Retrieved from: https://enterslice.com/learning/cybersecurity-in-digital-banking-threats-challenges-and-solution/.

Saha, M. (Dec 2021). Private banks seeing jump in number of online frauds: RBI report. Retrieved from: www.business-standard.com/article/finance/private-banks-seeing-jump-in-number-of-online-frauds-rbi-report-121123000047_1.html.

Scardovi, C. (2017). *Digital transformation in financial services* (Vol. 236). Cham: Springer International Publishing.

Shaji, A. M. (2020). Cybersecurity in Digital Banking: Threats, Challenges and Solution, *Enterslice*. https://enterslice.com/learning/cybersecurity-in-digital-banking-threats-challenges-and-solution/.

Skinner, C. (2014). Dijital bankacılık. *Istanbul: BKM bankalararası kart merkezi, 653*.

Statista (July 2022). Number of bank fraud cases across India between from financial year 2009 to 2022. Retrieved from: www.statista.com/statistics/1012729/india-number-of-bank-fraud-cases/.

Statista (May 2022). Most important factors disrupting banking sector according to senior banking executives worldwide in 2018. Retrieved from: www.statista.com/statistics/946835/disrupting-factors-global-banking-sector/.

Statista (May 2023). Number of active online banking users worldwide in 2020 with forecasts from 2021 to 2024, by region. Retrieved from: www.statista.com/statistics/1228757/online-banking-users-worldwide/.

Vives, X. (2019). Digital disruption in banking. *Annual Review of Financial Economics, 11,* 243–272.

Werth, O., Schwarzbach, C., Rodríguez Cardona, D., Breitner, M. H., & Graf von der Schulenburg, J. M. (2020). Influencing factors for the digital transformation in the financial services sector. *Zeitschrift für die gesamte Versicherungswissenschaft, 109*(2), 155–179.

Westerman, G., Bonnet, D., & McAfee, A. (2014). *Leading digital: Turning technology into business transformation.* Harvard Business Press.

Chapter 8

Crowdfunding as a Digital Financing Alternative

Volkmar Mrass

Chapter Overview

Crowdfunding is an alternative, novel form of digital financing that has the potential to alter how companies and individuals organize the collection of their financial resources. Even though more traditional ways of financing still dominate and will do so in the foreseeable future, crowdfunding nevertheless 'democratized' the financing process in parts, opening up opportunities for individuals and companies who formerly did not have proper access to financial resources. Besides these and other benefits, crowdfunding also entails several risks, especially that the value promised cannot be delivered. Established financial institutions such as banks should nevertheless harness this novel form of financing by complementing their services accordingly. Banks who accompany their customers in their crowdfunding journey can not only offer them an added value, but also might gain additional insights which they can harness for other customer relationships and their own market strategies.

8.1 Crowdfunding: An Innovative Financing Instrument

Crowdfunding constitutes one form of crowdsourcing, a term coined by Jeff Howe in 2006 (Howe, 2006). Crowdsourcing builds on and is one variant of the digital

 DOI: 10.1201/9781003395560-8

platform economy (Mrass & Peters, 2019) and has the potential to change the way that companies and other organizations are working currently (Mrass et al., 2018). Similar to crowdsourcing as a whole, there are also several classifications of crowdfunding. Haas et al. (2014) provide an empirical taxonomy of crowdfunding intermediaries where they cluster 127 of such intermediaries in three generic archetypes, distinguishable by their value proposition: altruism, hedonism, and for profit. The authors aim to improve the understanding of crowdfunding by showing how crowdfunding intermediaries manage financial intermediation and digitally transform exchange relations between capital-giving and–seeking agents in two-sided online markets (Haas et al., 2014). Beaulieu et al. (2015) identify three main stakeholder groups in the crowdfunding ecosystem: *website providers* who deliver the technology backbone that allows founders to expose their project to a large number of potential backers and facilitate communication between the founder and backers, *founders* defined as individuals or teams who post their idea on a crowdfunding website to receive funding, and *backers* who contribute money and in addition often also play a role in testing the market and providing judgment about what is a good idea and whether a concept is worth pursuing. Beaulieu et al. (2015) also distinguish six different forms of crowdfunding business models: private equity, royalty, microfinance, peer-to-peer lending, rewards, and donation. Each of these six crowdfunding business models are introduced below (Beaulieu et al., 2015) to provide a basis for a common understanding:

1. Private equity crowdfunding: involves the founder exchanging an ownership interest in the firm in return for a backer's contribution; backers are entitled to future dividends and a share in the proceeds if the company is sold.
2. Royalty crowdfunding: involves the founder agreeing to share the profits from the project with backers; projects are usually not on-going businesses but discreet products such as a record album, a music tour, or a mobile app.
3. Microfinancing crowdfunding: is often used by founders in rural and under-developed areas who have little access to banking products to buy farming supplies (seeds, fertilizer, livestock), or goods to re-sell.
4. Peer-to-peer lending: supports personal loans and small business loans; individuals lend to other individuals, bypassing banks as mediators. Backers, in exchange for their contribution, receive their principal back, plus interest.
5. Rewards crowdfunding: is used when founders have an idea for a project or an ongoing business; for their contributions, founders give backers a copy of the product or a memento from the project (for example, a coffee mug, t-shirt, recognition).
6. Donation crowdfunding: entails founders relying on the social good that the project can provide (for example, funding journalism or scientific research); backers are not given additional incentives other than a "thanks" from the founder.

Crowdfunding is a growing technology-enabled process that was seen to have the potential to disrupt the capital market space (Beaulieu et al., 2015). The fact that potential contributors can be reached digitally via the Internet all over the world via an open call is one reason that makes crowdfunding as a financing alternative attractive. Crowdfunding is processed by using digital platforms–crowdfunding platforms–such as Kickstarter (see: www.kickstarter.com) or Indiegogo (see: www.indiegogo.com) who get a fee for their services. The funding campaigns themselves are often accompanied by social media activities on channels such as Facebook, LinkedIn, Twitter, and more.

Crowdfunding got significant worldwide attention amongst others when the then candidate as US president, Barack Obama, used this instrument to finance his election campaign in 2008. It illustrated to everyone that many rather small amounts of money from altogether 3 950 000 donors could still add up to a strong contribution. On the whole, Obama was able to collect 750 million US dollars for his election campaign–and was even able to save 30 million US dollars which he did not spend (Spiegel.de, 2008).

8.2 Why Banks Should Harness Crowdfunding

Angel, VC Funds and Banks are groups who more traditionally fulfill the role of providing capital to founders and often determine as gatekeepers who will receive funding and who will not (Beaulieu et al., 2015). In contrast to this, crowdfunding is a novel technology-enabled innovation that significantly changes the institutionalized process of raising capital by founders and has been referred to as the 'democratization of entrepreneurial funding'; it remains open what impact crowdfunding might have in the long term on these traditional financing entities (ibid.). Given that crowdfunding constitutes an alternative digital financing model that potentially allows to circumvent traditional financing approaches, financial services providers such as banks initially might look at crowdfunding with mixed feelings. There have even been fears that this novel form of financing might ultimately completely replace banks as financing institutions. At least for now, these fears seem to be greatly exaggerated. On the contrary, banks might even be able to complement their services by partnering with crowdfunding platforms, therefore offering their customers additional financing opportunities, especially for innovative and rather unconventional products and projects.

One famous successful example for crowdfunding (here: microfinancing crowdfunding, as it is called nowadays) comes from the banking sector itself, even years before the term "crowdfunding" was coined: it is the famous case of the Grameen Bank in Bangladesh, founded by Muhammad Yunus, who later received the Nobel Peace Prize in 2006 together with this bank. The goal of this approach was to provide micro credits to low-income people in Bangladesh, mainly women, who could not provide securities. Groups from the respective communities in villages guaranteed for these credits and the close relationships among these groups ensured that the credits were paid back. This approach turned out to be effective regarding its aim to mitigate poverty.

In accordance with this successful example of microfinancing crowdfunding, it is in general important to think about possible motivations of the backers to align with their interests. Beaulieu et al. (2015) posit that in exchange for their contributions, backers can receive extrinsic rewards such as a return on their investment (for example, a copy of a product) and intrinsic rewards (for example, a "warm glow" or the feeling of being a part of something desirable). From my point of view, banks should embrace crowdfunding as an additional and complementary financing alternative for their clients. Such as banks often function as intermediaries for insurance products, for example, from a group they are belonging to (for example, the German Savings Banks who also include and recommend products from the insurance companies of their group), banks could also partner with certain crowdfunding platforms to be able to serve their clients whose needs might be accommodated best by such financial solutions. Besides the fact that banks can prove themselves as "full financial services providers" who can offer access to different financing options, they might also be able to benefit from this step themselves in another way: by accompanying their customers in their crowdfunding journey, they might also be able to estimate if a market for the respective endeavor or product exists. Banks could then use these insights for the consulting of other customers and their own general market strategies.

8.3   Benefits and Risks

As emphasized above, crowdfunding is an innovative alternative financing instrument. It is sometimes even portrayed as a pure and full alternative for or even instead of bank financing/bank funding. One main benefit of this novel form of funding: even though the amount given by a backer can be small in relation to the overall funding needs, if many individuals donate a small amount, large sums of money can be raised quickly and efficiently (Beaulieu et al., 2015). In addition to contributing financially, individuals can also help by spreading awareness through social media, which can build up a crowd of interested parties willing to invest (ibid.). A rather fast access to financial resources, a high number of potential backers who can be reached digitally and easily via the Internet, the spread of non-payment risks, and many more, are potential benefits.

However, crowdfunding as a novel form of financing is no panacea and can—depending on the respective situation—be inappropriate. It is important to note that, while a large number of backers can add to a high amount of money even if the contributions themselves are rather small, it can at the same time also be rather arduous to coordinate this large number of backers and appropriately and continuously communicate with them. Another risk may be that products that aim at being funded via crowdfunding platforms might infringe patent rights of other companies. A third risk, maybe the most well-known from practice, is that founders and their respective companies turn out not to have the necessary experience and skills to "deliver" what they aimed to deliver. Or at least do not deliver in full. Below, there are two such examples:

1. One of the best-known and most successful crowdfunding projects regarding the amount of money raised so far–and at the same time unfortunately unsuccessful regarding the final production of the product and distribution to all of its backers (The Verge, 2019)–was the "coolest cooler": a portable cooler that included lifestyle elements such as a waterproof Bluetooth speaker, bottle openers, LED lights, USB charger and other features, aiming at bringing blended drinks, music and fun to outdoor activities (see: Kickstarter, 2018). 62 642 supporters contributed 13 285 226 US-Dollars within 52 days (ibid.). The project exemplarily shows the risks of crowdfunding: Even though the funding campaign itself was very successful and attracted a large number of enthusiastic backers, the company behind the campaign was finally only able to deliver its product to about two-thirds of the people who ordered it, leaving about 20 000 backers without their desired product and having to shut down the company after about five years (The Verge, 2019).

2. Another such example turned out to be even worse. Not only did the respective founder and their company not seem to have the necessary experience and skills to "deliver" what they aimed to deliver, but also, the money raised via crowdfunding seems not to have been used as was communicated in advance to the backers. This was the case of a crowdfunding campaign on Indiegogo for a smartwatch which by far exceeded the initial campaign goal of 100 000 US dollars, receiving 1.5 Million US dollars. Nevertheless, the company did not really "deliver" on that promise and a co-founder of the company who was meant to produce this smartwatch was even alleged to have used the money to buy a new Ferrari and expensive designer clothes (The New York Observer, 2014).

Even though the examples mentioned above are not the rule and crowdfunding platforms such as Kickstarter and Indiegogo as intermediaries have made several attempts to not only make their backers aware of such risks, but also to take measures to mitigate such risks: "Traditional" financial institutions such as banks might also, besides the many benefits, risk some unintended consequences if such cases happen. One unintended consequence could be a damage of their reputation if they have accompanied their customer in their crowdfunding journey and have recommended them crowdfunding as an appropriate instrument for their purposes. Nevertheless, these are possible consequences that are not distinctive for crowdfunding alone, but can also occur with more traditional financing approaches. If banks are aware of both the benefits and the risks of crowdfunding and are open and transparent regarding recommending them to their customers, crowdfunding can be an attractive digital financial alternative that should also be harnessed by banks, according to the old saying: "if you cannot defend your competitor, embrace him".

8.4 Conclusion

Crowdfunding is a novel digital financing alternative that offers significant benefits, but which, like other financing instruments, also entails risks. Especially for entrepreneurs and innovative and/or rather unconventional endeavors, it can be a very attractive digital financing alternative, sometimes the only one for such target groups. Beaulieu et al. (2015) posit that structures such as venture capital and debt funding become restructured as these older routines and ways of doing business do not support the entrepreneurial economy which demands a higher number of innovative ideas to be financed, at lower costs. Whereas many innovative ideas had no funding outlets, crowdfunding is restructuring the capital markets and allowing lower barriers and increased access to funding (Beaulieu et al., 2015). Until today, crowdfunding has shown its impressive potential, but is still far from really replacing rather traditional forms of financing. Nevertheless, crowdfunding seems to be heading towards a digital financing alternative that can provide significant value not only for niche markets, but has also the potential to develop into a valuable, in parts possibly complementing, financing instrument of a financing-mix that includes several financial instruments.

References

Beaulieu, T., Sarker, S [Suprateek], & Sarker, S [Saonee] (2015). A Conceptual Framework for Understanding Crowdfunding. *Communications of the Association for Information Systems (CAIS)*, *37*(1).

Haas, P., Blohm, I., & Leimeister, J. M. (2014). An Empirical Taxonomy of Crowdfunding Intermediaries. *Proceedings of the International Conference on Information Systems (ICIS) 2014*.

Howe, J. (2006). The Rise of Crowdsourcing. *Wired Magazine*, *14*(6), 176–183. www.wired.com/2006/06/crowds/.

Kickstarter (March 12th, 2018). COOLEST COOLER: 21st Century Cooler that's Actually Cooler, www.kickstarter.com/projects/ryangrepper/coolest-cooler-21st-century-cooler-thats-actually (last time accessed on June 30th, 2023).

Mrass, V., & Peters, C. (2019). Digitale Wertschöpfung durch Crowd Services: Neue Formen des Kundensupports am Beispiel Mila und Swisscom. In S. Robra-Bissantz & C. Lattemann (Eds.), *Edition HMD. Digital Customer Experience: Mit digitalen Diensten Kunden gewinnen und halten* (pp. 271–282). Springer Fachmedien Wiesbaden.

Mrass, V., Peters, C., & Leimeister, J. M. (2018). Managing Complex Work Systems via Crowdworking Platforms: How Intel and Hyve Explore Future Technological Innovations. *51st Hawaii International Conference on System Sciences (HICSS), Waikoloa, USA, Doctoral Consortium.*

Spiegel.de (December 5th, 2008): Spendenrekord: Obama sammelte 750 Millionen Dollar, www.spiegel.de/politik/ausland/spendenrekord-obama-sammelte-750-millionen-dol lar-a-594742.html (last time accessed on June 30th, 2023).

The New York Observer (August 21st, 2014): Indiegogo's 'Scampaign' Problem: Latest Crowdfunded Smartwatch Is Total Garbage, https://observer.com/2014/08/indiego gos-scampaign-problem-latest-crowdfunded-smartwatch-is-total-garbage/ (last time accessed on June 30th, 2023).

The Verge (December 9th, 2019): Crowdfunding disaster Coolest Cooler is shutting down and blaming tariffs for its downfall, www.theverge.com/2019/12/9/21003445/cool est-cooler-update-business-tariffs-kickstarter (last time accessed on June 30th, 2023).

Chapter 9

Which Signals Promise Success in Crowdfunding?: A Simple Guide for Start-Ups

Florian W. Bartholomae and Eva Stumpfegger

Chapter Overview

Equity crowdfunding is the online offering of shares in private companies to small investors through dedicated platforms. Since this is a high-risk financing project for both sides, the investor(s) and the investee, it is in the interest of the company to reduce relevant information asymmetries to increase the success of its crowdinvesting campaign. In the context of the signaling theory, this chapter discusses factors which fulfil this function (specifically, former external funding, business angel backing, accelerator participation, winning grants, and maturity of the company), and factors that may have positive, negative, or no effect on the success (like retained equity and intellectual property rights). The rationale behind each factor is explored, thus providing guidance to start-up companies considering equity crowdfunding.

9.1   Introduction

For a very long time, due to their complexity and many entry barriers, traditional markets allowed only experienced investors to invest in venture capital or angel

DOI: 10.1201/9781003395560-9

funding. However, during financial innovations and increasing technical possibilities, crowdfunding has become increasingly popular for entrepreneurs to finance their ventures by addressing small investors (Vismara, 2021). As an increasing number of more or less reputable and profitable companies make use of this fundraising option, small investors have become more careful in their choices. At the same time, however, the market also has become more attractive for traditional investors who use this mechanism to make their investments (Meyskens & Bird, 2015, Block et al., 2018).

Crowdfunding subsumes a range of activities, which is why it "is an umbrella term used to describe an increasingly widespread form of fundraising, typically via the Internet, whereby groups of people pool money, usually (very) small individual contributions, to support a particular goal" (Ahlers, 2015, p. 955). The success of this type of fundraising is manifested above all by the quick expansion of the worldwide crowdfunding industry: In 2020, the market size for equity-based crowdfunding has reached USD 4.41 billion around the world (Statista Research Department, 2020). This significant market allows smaller firms, individuals, and non-profit organizations to achieve their ambitions thanks to disruptive FinTech trends like platform-based equity crowdfunding, which have been driven by the digitalization of entrepreneurship financing (Iurchenko, 2019). To do this, they can choose from a large number of providers that offer platforms to connect investors and companies. To name a few of the most famous that operate worldwide: Kickstarter, Indiegogo, SyndicateRoom, Crowdcube, Seedrs, Seedinvest, EquityNet and so forth.

Equity crowdfunding, which is a profit-sharing model that facilitates selling securities, has been regarded as being more complex than other forms of crowdfunding (Hossain & Oparaocha, 2017). It is because the platforms need to conduct extensive due diligence, and investors would like to know the entrepreneurs and their businesses better to make their investment decision (Cumming & Dai, 2010; Vismara, 2018a). By taking advantage of web 2.0, equity crowdfunding offers an online marketplace for entrepreneurs to raise money not only from their personal network such as family and friends but also a vast number of potential investors. Unlike traditional business angels and venture capital financing, equity crowdfunding provides almost anyone with an opportunity to fund the business that they believe will succeed which can lead to a "democratization" of entrepreneurial financing, albeit an early study in this area came up with rather mixed results (Cumming et al., 2021). Meanwhile, investors can claim financial returns through the investment they made via equity crowdfunding. The whole model is beneficial for thousands of companies, especially start-ups and scale-ups to nurture their businesses. Consequently, equity crowdfunding is becoming increasingly popular as an alternative financing method among small businesses and start-ups.

Although more and more start-ups have successfully funded their businesses through equity crowdfunding, quite a few entrepreneurs fail to raise their desired amount. As equity crowdfunding provides "market feedback" to entrepreneurs, it allows overconfident entrepreneurs to learn before making production and pricing decisions (Miglo, 2021). Many of them are introducing their business idea to the public for the first time. However, instead of being encouraged by the community, rational entrepreneurs may lose trust in their business plans, resulting in some damage to their reputation. Thus, it is critical for entrepreneurs to launch a successful campaign on the first try. This not only assists business owners in obtaining the required funds, but also motivates them to completely realize their full potential. Consequently, it is critical to identify relevant factors that may influence the outcome of online equity crowdfunding pitches.

9.2 Signaling Theory and Crowdfunding

Crowdfunding has attracted great interest in academia and generated many studies and different approaches (for example, Mollick, 2014; Bruton et al., 2015; Short et al., 2017; Block et al., 2018; Mazzocchini & Lucarelli, 2023). Most studies aim to find out what makes a project successful and leads to its funding. In our analysis we want to focus on what can be learnt from signaling theory, which has been applied by several studies (for example, Huang et al., 2022). To understand how to approach this problem in this framework, let us first present a brief abstract description of the situation to understand relevant aspects of our further analysis.

A fundamental factor in the investor-investee partnership is the information asymmetry that exists between them. Thus, the situation corresponds to the classic principal-agent relationship. The agent is the party that has all the relevant information, in this case this characterizes the investee/entrepreneur. The principal, on the other hand, has little to no information, but is the party that acts as patron. Specifically, this is the investor who entrusts his/her money to the investment recipient in the hope that the recipient will use it profitably for him/her. Both parties, of course, have a self-interest: the principal wants to make a high profit, namely, either the highest possible return for a fixed capital investment or the lowest possible capital investment for a given payoff. The agent, on the other hand, also wants to maximize his/her utility and prefers, in general, to spend the lowest possible effort to achieve the given goal. Hence, there is a conflict of interest, which in extreme cases can lead to failure. In the considered situation, this means that no investment is made. At the beginning of the contractual relationship, the investee is under an obligation to deliver, namely, the investee must convince the investor of his/her qualities by showing, for example, that the business idea is promising; the investee has the necessary know-how; the investee is committed; the investee works hard to fulfil the investor's requirements, and so forth. This is the core of the signaling theory (Spence, 1973, 2002): The listed aspects represent so-called signals that the agent can send out to reduce the information asymmetry, as the investee provides the investor with information that helps him/her to better assess the project.

However, not every aspect is equally suitable as a signal (for example, Yasar et al., 2020): a signal is only credible if it is not too cheap and not too expensive. Consider

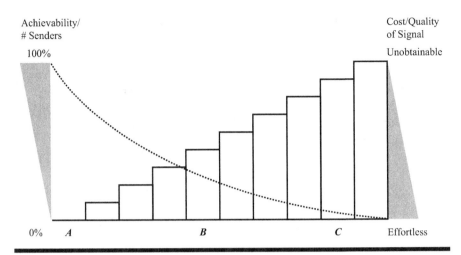

Figure 9.1 Quality of signal and achievability.

Source: Authors' own elaboration.

the following situation as an example. A project requires some basic programming skills, which can be proven by a certificate. There are three programming courses on offer: Course A certifies participation; Course B additionally requires completion of a challenging exam; or Course C, which includes a comprehensive introduction to advanced programming applying several programming languages. This results in a trade-off which is depicted in Figure 9.1: the higher the costs of the signal (bars), the less senders can emit it (dotted curve), namely, course A has low costs and, thus, is achievable by many, while course C has significantly higher costs that are not bearable by many.

Which of these signals makes sense? As course A can be successfully completed by almost anyone with enough time, this signal has no value to the principal. Course C, on the other hand, has the highest requirements, which only the fewest will be able to pass, and are not even necessary for a basic project; in addition, participants of this course would certainly demand much more than the budget for a simple programming project is offering. Course B on the other hand fulfils both requirements: It has a hurdle that not everyone can overcome and thus enables positive selection, and it is not too demanding, so the hurdle can also be overcome by those relevant for the project.

Furthermore, the payment demands also correspond most closely to the budget of the project. In summary, the quintessence is that what matters is what signal is reasonable when rating a crowdfunding project so that it is not too cheap, but nevertheless within the means of the investees.

Besides, crowdfunding also features a special characteristic: there is one agent who wants to convince many principals (small investors) and therefore must send out signals that have to be perceived well enough by as many potential investors as possible

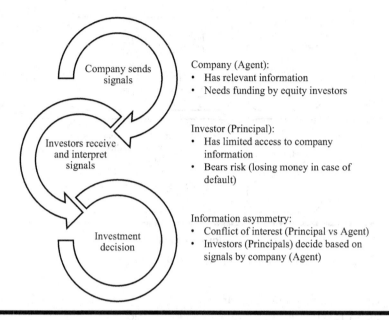

Figure 9.2   Signaling process in crowdfunding
Source: Authors' own elaboration.

(Courtney et al., 2017; Vismara, 2018a). Figure 9.2 depicts the process of companies (agents) sending out signals that are used for investment decisions by investors (agents).

In addition, the principals are operating in a high-risk environment and must accept high levels of uncertainty, as potential returns may only be realized in the distant future (Mazzocchini & Lucarelli, 2023).

The objective now is to identify the signals provided by the investee that increase the probability of funding and can thus be considered success factors.

9.3   Main Success Factors

Literature has identified an abundance of influencing factors. In the following, we analyse and discuss the six most relevant and significant characteristics of a campaign that can act as credible signals: former external financing, business angel backing and accelerator participation, grants, retained equity, intellectual property rights, and maturity of the company. Figure 9.3 summarizes existing research findings on the direction of signals. Most signals have a positive impact, whilst some signals are not entirely clear and require further analysis of the company's business model.

1. Former external financing: Early funding from personal and social media networks sends a positive signal to investors and increases the success in

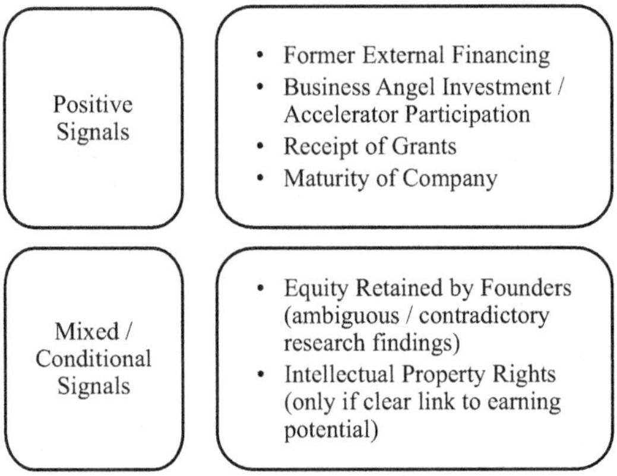

Figure 9.3 Direction of signals in equity crowdfunding.

Source: Authors' own elaboration based on literature review.

equity crowdfunding (Lukkarinen et al., 2016). On the one hand, networks play a role in achieving target funding, as direct access and personal contact with potential investors increases the likelihood of funding. Crowdfunding investors may reasonably assume that network investors have access to better information and therefore perceive previous external financing as a positive signal. In addition, earlier financing shows that the company was able to convince investors of the idea and it has been pursuing the business idea for some time and is passionate about it. Thus, the signal also shows a lasting commitment.

2. Business angel backing and accelerator participation: Business angels have professional knowledge and are experienced in investing in companies at an early stage. They usually bear extremely high risks and expect high returns. Therefore, they are believed to be better at identifying high quality projects than small crowd investors. As most investors on equity crowdfunding platforms are unaccredited investors who lack experience, they tend to follow leading investors such as business angels, accelerators, or the investors with large contributions (Elitzur & Gavious, 2003; Ralcheva & Roosenboom, 2016, 2020; Vismara, 2018b; Signori & Vismara, 2018; Du et al., 2022). Similarly, accelerator programs also offer professional and financial support to start-up companies. Accelerator participation therefore also increases the probability of succeeding in equity crowdfunding (Ralcheva & Roosenboom, 2020).

This third-party involvement is likely to be recognized by investors and reduces their concerns of the future development of the company, which in turn enhances the probability of equity crowdfunding success. This suggests that business angel involvement has a positive impact on the likelihood of fully funded pitches.

3. Grants: External financing may also come from grants (usually offered by the government). Unlike business angel financing, grants are intended to accelerate innovation and foster entrepreneurship of ventures. Winning grants is extremely helpful to start-ups if bank loans, or alternative funding are not available. In addition, grants offer opportunities for conducting further research and development to continue realizing their ideas, especially for companies with advanced technology. Many high-tech companies, such as Apple or Arcis Biotechnology, were lacking early-stage financing and receiving grants allowed them to continue their business.

   As grant applications go through a thorough and structured screening system by an expert jury, being awarded a grant also certifies the quality of the firm (Lerner, 2000). The highly competitive, time consuming and costly screening process discourages low-quality companies from application (Ralcheva & Roosenboom, 2016) fulfilling all requirements for a credible signal. Consequently, winning a grant sends a clear positive signal to investors and reduces information asymmetry, thus encouraging investors to fund the equity crowdfunding campaign.

4. Retained equity: Retained equity shares can be considered as a signal to measure whether entrepreneurs have confidence in their businesses. The rationale behind retained equity is that it is usually costly to retain a large number of shares. If business owners do not expect substantial future cash flows, they would rather offer more equity to investors to diversify their risks, and it is less costly, as fewer profits are lost. In contrast, it is very expensive for more profitable companies, so they will have less incentive to send out this signal. As entrepreneurs have superior knowledge and information about their own business to funders, retaining more equity can be observed as a positive signal of the development of companies and attract more investors, enhancing the probability of being succeed via equity crowdfunding. Thus, it seems plausible that less retained equity implies a higher level of uncertainty and is perceived negatively by investors (Ahlers et al., 2015; Li et al., 2018; Ralcheva & Roosenboom, 2016). Likewise, more equity retained lowers the probability of success, less percentage raised and fewer investors (Du et al., 2022). However, there is also empirical evidence that entrepreneurs who offer less equity to investors are more likely to achieve success in equity crowdfunding by attracting more potential backers (Vismara, 2016; Battaglia et al., 2021).

   As empirical evidence is contradictory, the signal of retained equity may be perceived differently, too: offering only minority holdings in the company may signal to investors that the company may not intend to go public, thus implying that investors may permanently hold unlisted stock. Minority holdings of unlisted companies can only be sold at a large discount and the selling process may be lengthy and expensive. Therefore, retained equity can work as a two-way signal.

5. Intellectual property rights: The protection of intellectual property right has a positive impact on the equity crowdfunding as it safeguards entrepreneurs from piracy and shows entrepreneurs' determination and confidence in establishing a prosperous business (Ralcheva & Roosenboom, 2016). In particular, patents send several signals to investors as the number of patents is considered a measure of the company's innovation ability and productivity (Griliches et al., 1986; Griliches, 1990; Lanjouw, 1998; Long, 2002). Therefore, a company with more patents than the industry average seems likely to be highly competitive. Eventually, this is an observable signal of innovation and can provide more information about the company's value to reduce information asymmetry in initial public offerings (Heeley et al., 2007). However, this only holds if there is a clear link between patents and the returns earned by patents. Thus, while companies with filed patents are more likely to attract financing resources to grow their business a certified third party enhances their reputation (Hsu & Ziedonis, 2013), this may not always apply (Ahlers, 2015; Rossi et al., 2020; Du et al., 2022).

Besides patents, also R&D and teams' education levels have a significant positive impact on fundraising success as they are perceived as a quality signal by external investors (Battaglia et al., 2021).

6. Maturity of the company: Age and thus the maturity of the companies may also be considered as a positive signal and thus has a positive impact on the success of the pitch independently of alternative success criteria (Du et al., 2022). A more mature company is more likely to have a proven business model and a track record of media coverage. Therefore, a higher age of a company seeking crowdfunding sends positive signals to potential investors.

9.4 Discussion and Conclusion

The success factors discussed above are categorized in the following Table 9.1 regarding their credibility, difficulty in obtaining information, and direction of impact.

Table 9.1 Summary and Relevance of Signals

Signal	Difficulty in signal creation	Impact	Source
Former external financing	Low level of difficulty → depending on management's network	Positive	Lukkarinen et al. (2016); Ralcheva/ Roosenboom (2020); Kleinert et al. (2020)

Table 9.1 (Continued)

Signal	Difficulty in signal creation	Impact	Source
Business angels / accelerator	Medium level of difficulty → depending on reputation of management/ founders: professionals (business angels) invest own money / → depending on expertise in the start-up community: Accelerators scan ideas for feasibility	Positive	Ralcheva/ Roosenboom (2016); Du et al. (2022)
Grants	High level of difficulty → independent juries/ experts need to be convinced, high competition	Positive	Ralcheva/ Roosenboom (2016); Lerner (2000)
Retained equity	Low level of difficulty → founders' own decision; yet careful consideration is needed due to ambiguous perception	Mixed	Negative: Ahlers et al. (2015); Li et al. (2018); Ralcheva/ Roosenboom (2020); Ralcheva/ Roosenboom (2016); Du et al. (2022) Positive: Vismara (2016); Battaglia et al. (2021)
Intellectual property rights	High level of difficulty → legal and technical requirements of patents have to be fulfilled → high costs of application and maintenance → credible communication of earning impact	Positive / conditionally positive (clear link to earning potential) / no impact	Positive: Ralcheva & Roosenboom (2016); Long (2002); Griliches et al. (1986); Griliches (1990); Lanjouw (1998); Hsu & Ziedonis (2013) Conditionally positive: Heeley et al. (2007) No impact: Ahlers (2015); Rossi et al. (2020); Ralcheva & Roosenboom (2020)

Table 9.1 (Continued)

Signal	Difficulty in signal creation	Impact	Source
Maturity of the company	No active signal → financing is needed in the near future and aging is not an option	Positive	Positive: Du et al. (2022)

Source: Authors' own elaboration.

So, companies seeking to attract equity crowdfunding investors should make sure to actively send signals that make success more likely.

It therefore makes sense to communicate former external financing in a way that the information is easily found, for example., on the company website and on social media. Business angel backing sends similar signals suggesting that professional investors and industry experts believe in the business model, approve the way the company is set up, and show this by investing their own money. Similarly, stock prices of publicly traded companies are regarded as a valid valuation, representing the consensus of market participants' actions.

Accelerator participation and winning grants signal that the founders have managed to establish a network of experts that scrutinized the business ideas, helped to improve it and, by awarding a grant, suggests approval of the viability of the business.

Consequently, start-ups should actively seek opportunities to participate in accelerators, expand their network to gain support and funding from early-stage investors such as business angels, and last but not least, apply for grants. This does not only directly impact finances, but also increases the chances of equity crowdfunding success if communicated properly.

Retained equity, however, is a double-edged sword, as existing research is inconclusive. On the one hand, one may argue that founders who retain a significant stake of their holdings are committed to the company, believe that it will succeed and plan to continue working on the company success, thus sending a signal to potential crowdinvestors that agency costs are low. On the other hand, retained equity may also signal that existing owners do not believe in the crowdfunding campaign's success and feel compelled to retain a larger proportion of their holdings. Therefore, careful consideration and communication is advisable to companies considering equity crowdfunding.

Although sending a completely different message, intellectual property rights or patents may or may not send signals to potential investors. Existing research's findings that intellectual property rights increase that chance of equity crowdfunding success may be due to the fact that potential investors see patents as intangible assets that are of immediate value. On the other hand, patent valuation is highly complex and not feasible for small investors, so it may be highly rational to ignore intellectual property rights in equity crowdfunding. Therefore, the link between patent and earning potential should be actively signaled if a start-up company seeks investors.

Maturity, namely, the age of a company is perceived as a positive signal by potential investors. Early-stage venture capital is regarded as riskier than later stage private equity, because older companies typically have business up and running and may need additional money to scale up operations. Therefore, it may be reasonably assumed that maturity can rather be viewed as a proxy for an established business. Consequently, companies should signal that they have a promising or, even better, proven business model.

In conclusion, companies should carefully analyse their situation before launching an equity crowdfunding campaign. Some success factors may already be in place and should be communicated accordingly. Tailoring other factors may involve time and effort. Therefore, timing and the particulars of a potential crowdfunding campaign should be consciously considered.

References

Ahlers, G. K. C., Cumming, D., Günther, Ch., & Schweizer, D. (2015): Signaling in Equity Crowdfunding, *Entrepreneurship Theory and Practice*, 1–45.

Battaglia, F. & Busato, F., & Manganiello, M. (2021): A cross-platform analysis of the equity crowdfunding Italian context: the role of intellectual capital, *Electronic Commerce Research* 22, 1–41.

Block, J. H., Colombo, M. G., Cumming, D. J., & Vismara, S. (2018): New players in entrepreneurial finance and why they are there, *Small Business Economics* 50, 239–250.

Bruton, G., Khavul, S., Siegel, D., & Wright, M. (2015): New financial alternatives in seeding entrepreneurship: Microfinance, crowdfunding, and peer-to-peer innovations, *Entrepreneurship Theory & Practice* 39(1), 9–26.

Courtney, C., Dutta, S., & Li, Y. (2017): Resolving information asymmetry: Signaling, endorsement, and crowdfunding success, *Entrepreneurship Theory and Practice* 41(2), 265–290.

Cumming, D., & Dai, N., (2010): Local bias in venture capital investments, *Journal of Empirical Finance* 17(3), 362–380.

Cumming, D., Meoli, M., & Vismara, S. (2021): Does equity crowdfunding democratize entrepreneurial finance?, *Small Business Economics* 56(2), 533–552.

Du, L., Bartholomae, F., & Stumpfegger, E. (2022): Success factors in equity crowdfunding–evidence from crowdcube, *Entrepreneurship Research Journal*. Advance online publication. https://doi.org/10.1515/erj-2021-0519.

Elitzur, R., & Gavious A. (2003): Contracting, signaling, and moral hazard: a model of entrepreneurs, 'angels,' and venture capitalists, *Journal of Business Venturing* 18(6), 709–725.

Griliches, Z. (1990): Patent statistics as economic indicators: A survey, *Journal of Economic Literature* 28(4), 1661–1707.

Griliches, Z., Pakes, A., & Hall, B. (1986): The Value of Patents as Indicators of Inventive Activity, NBER Working Paper No. w2083.

Heeley, M. B., Matusik, S. F., & Jain, N. (2007): Innovation, appropriability, and the underpricing of initial public offerings, *Academy of Management Journal* 50(1), 209–225.

Hossain, M., & Oparaocha, G. O. (2017): Crowdfunding: Motives, definitions, typology and ethical challenges, *Entrepreneurship Research Journal* 7(2), 20150045.

Hsu, D. H., & Ziedonis, R. H. (2013): Resources as dual sources of advantage: Implications for valuing entrepreneurial-firm patents, *Strategic Management Journal* 34(7), 761–781.

Huang, S., Pickernell, D., Battisti, M., & Nguyen, T. (2022): Signalling entrepreneurs' credibility and project quality for crowdfunding success: Cases from the kickstarter and indiegogo environments, *Small Business Economics* 58, 1801–1821.

Iurchenko, D. (2019): *Three Essays on Equity Crowdfunding and the Digitalization of Entrepreneurial Finance*, Doctoral Thesis, University of Lausanne.

Kleinert, S., Volkmann, C., & Grünhagen, M. (2020): Third-party signals in equity crowdfunding: the role of prior financing, *Small Business Economics* 54, pp. 341–365.

Lanjouw, J. O. (1998): Patent protection in the shadow of infringement: Simulation estimations of patent value, *Review of Economic Studies*, 65(4), 671–710.

Lerner, J. (2000): The Government as venture capitalist: The long-run impact of the SBIR program, *Journal of Private Equity* 3(2), 55–78.

Li, Y., Cao, H., & Zhao, T. (2018): Factors affecting successful equity crowdfunding, *Journal of Mathematical Finance* 8, 446–456.

Long, C. (2002): Patent signals, *The University of Chicago Law Review* 69(2), 625–679.

Lukkarinen, A., Teich, J. E., Wallenius, H., & Wallenius, J. (2016): Success drivers of online equity crowdfunding campaigns, *Decision Support Systems* 87, 26–38.

Mazzocchini, F. J., & Lucarelli, C. (2023), Success or failure in equity crowdfunding? A systematic literature review and research perspectives, *Management Research Review*, 46(6), 790–831.

Meyskens, M., & Bird, L. (2015): Crowdfunding and value creation, *Entrepreneurship Research Journal* 5(2), 155–166.

Miglo, A. (2021): Crowdfunding under market feedback, asymmetric information and overconfident entrepreneur, *Entrepreneurship Research Journal* 11(4), 20190018.

Mollick, E. (2014): The dynamics of crowdfunding: An exploratory study, *Journal of Business Venturing* 29(1), 1–16.

Ralcheva, A., & Roosenboom, P. (2016): On the road to success in equity crowdfunding, SSRN.

Ralcheva, A., & Roosenboom, P. (2020): Forecasting success in equity crowdfunding, *Small Business Economics* 55, 39–56.

Rossi, A., Vanacker, T. R., & Vismara, S. (2020): Equity Crowdfunding: New Evidence From US and UK Markets, SSRN.

Short, J. C., Ketchen, D. J., McKenny, A. F., Allison, T. H., & Ireland, R. D. (2017): Research on crowdfunding: Reviewing the (very recent) past and celebrating the present, *Entrepreneurship Theory and Practice* 41(2), 149–160.

Signori, A., & Vismara, S. (2018): Does success bring success? The post-offering lives of equity-crowdfunded firms, *Journal of Corporate Finance* 50, 575–591

Spence, M. (1973): Job Market Signaling, *Quarterly Journal of Economics* 87(3), 355–374.

Spence, M. (2002): Signaling in retrospect and the informational structure of markets, *American Economic Review* 92(3), 434–459.

Statista Research Department. (2020). Global crowdfunding volume by model category 2020. Statista. www.statista.com/statistics/946668/global-crowdfunding-volume-worldwide-by-type/.

Vismara, S. (2016): Equity retention and social network theory in equity crowdfunding, *Small Business Economics* 46(4), 579–590.

Vismara, S. (2018a): Signaling to Overcome Inefficiencies in Crowdfunding Markets, in: Cumming D. & Hornuf, L. (eds.): The Economics of Crowdfunding, Palgrave Macmillan, Cham, pp. 29–56.

Vismara, S. (2018b): Information cascades among investors in equity crowdfunding, *Entrepreneurship Theory and Practice* 42(3), 467–497.

Vismara, S. (2021): Expanding corporate finance perspectives to equity crowdfunding, *Journal of Technology Transfer* 1–11.

Yasar, B., Martin, T., & Kiessling, T. (2020): An empirical test of signalling theory, *Management Research Review* 43(11), 1309–1335.

Chapter 10

Making Finance Invisible: What Defines Embedded Finance and its Effects on User Experience?

Jibran Ahmed Bugvi and Tobias Endress

Chapter Overview

Embedded Finance is a rapidly emerging concept that has sparked considerable online attention. It is a multibillion-dollar market, and plenty of industry research and white papers have been released. The growth of Embedded Finance has been symbiotic with the rise of digital channels and platforms where the common currency is better user experience and seamlessly providing services at the point of context for customers. Despite its potential to disrupt traditional distribution models of financial services, Embedded Finance does not have a consistent and widely agreed definition that can form a foundation for further academic and professional research. This chapter discusses the existing definitions of Embedded Finance, divides them into schools of thought, and proposes a more robust and consistent definition that can fill the gap in the literature on Embedded Finance. It also explores drivers of adopting Embedded Finance under the framework of the unified theory of acceptance and use of technology.

DOI: 10.1201/9781003395560-10

10.1   Introduction

Embedded Finance is a fairly new term and some people consider it as an evolution from Open Banking (Schneider, 2023). Many people make regular use of payment services on an e-commerce platform or a ride-hailing app without using cash, purchase something using a Buy-Now-Pay-Later offering or use a price-freeze option on an online travel or airline platform–if you are one of them you have used Embedded Finance (EF). It is a growing phenomenon, with annual revenue of $22 billion expected to grow to $51 billion by 2026 (Harris et al., 2022) and with surging online-search interest (Ozili, 2022).

Improved User Experience (UX) is seen as one of the key reasons for its adoption and proliferation, creating opportunities for financial institutions, FinTech companies and digital platforms ecosystems. Despite its importance we still have only a limited body of knowledge on Embedded Finance and it appears that there is no agreement on a consistent definition.

In this chapter we will discuss the lack of a consistent Embedded Finance definition in academic literature and review the existing (limited) body of academic publications. We will discuss the drivers of adoption of this particular technology and how FinTech can be understood by using theoretical frameworks such as the Technology Acceptance Model and the Unified Theory of Acceptance & Use of Technology leading to practical implications and recommendations for best practices.

10.2   Background and Context

Open Banking has been a topic discussed for quite a while and was expected to open up the 'walled gardens' of the banking industry (Aytaş et al., 2021). It can also be considered a special form of Open Innovation (Chesbrough, 2012; Endress, 2023) focusing on banking and financial use cases. While the discussion about Open Banking concentrates largely on the technical aspects, like an API-driven ecosystem and system communication (Schneider, 2023), user acceptance and experience appear to become a topic in this context of increasing interest from academic and business practitioners. It seems that more and more companies understand that pure technical feasibility is not enough for a successful business case, but it needs to be part of a well-designed user journey. Embedded Finance lending companies like YouLend advertise that they approve a new loan every three minutes using just a few clicks, while BNPL players like Klarna and Affirm swear by the ideal one-click shopping experience once KYC is done, showing the importance of the user experience at the center of these propositions That's why we explore EF from a user experience point of view. This might include the consideration of the following constructs.

10.2.1 How to Measure the Usability of Embedded Financial Products

A reasonably simple measure to get an idea about usability is the number of clicks. It defines the effort the end-user takes when clicking or tapping their input devices, such as a mouse or touching pad (Harrati et al., 2016). A single type of click is considered as the unit of measurement, referring to both right and left, while a double click is counted as two consecutive clicks. Building on ideas from the human-computer interaction literature de Santana & Baranauskas (2015) argue that the usage data that can be determined from client-side user logs for usability evaluation are reliable and efficient metrics for usability insights. Still, clicks are not the only measure of good usability. Sometimes, more clicks are considered more convenient depending on the design and other factors like visual appeal or navigation times (see also Jones, 2012; Stojmenovic et al., 2019). This typically applies in financial transactions like loans, particularly from non-standard providers such as Atome BNPL in Asia, Akulaku in Indonesia where first-time users may not be comfortable with a few clicks loading them up with sizable financial exposure. Hence, *task duration* is another measure that should be considered in the usability context. The total time taken to achieve a particular task by a user or usability expert is used to measure the efficiency rate (Harrati et al., 2016). It is generally measured (approximated) in seconds as a difference between time stamps for a task's start and last data logs. Finally, the *Completion Rate* means the success rate of completion of tasks, one of the fundamental usability metrics for users to achieve a goal successfully. This is a highly relevant number in business use cases as it might have the most direct impact on the sales numbers. Cart abandonment is a big phenomenon in e-commerce and one of the aspects highlighted in particular by embedded payment service providers like Stripe, Adyen and Braintree is the ability to reduce cart abandonment by making the last mile payment experience seamless. Overall the usability of a software product is the extent to which the product is convenient and practical to use (Boehm et al., 1978). It requires the consideration of completion rate, clicks, task duration and more. It is well established that usability is influenced by learnability, efficiency, memorability, few errors and user satisfaction (Nielsen, 1993). However, when we use this regarding financial transactions, there might be more to consider than only the traditional measures for usability. Based on existing literature, particularly the unified theory of acceptance and use of technology (UTAUT) and its extension UTAUT2 (Venkatesh et al., 2012), we suggest including the following elements in the design consideration.

> *Performance Expectancy*: This is the degree to which using Embedded Finance will benefit consumers in online retailer transactions (modified from Venkatesh et al., (2012)). You could ask clients if they agree or disagree with whether they consider using the helpful product, increasing their effectiveness and/ or helping them pay more quickly. In practical terms, these questions could

be included in a net-promoter-score survey that many companies already use to measure client satisfaction (Fisher & Korbupleski, 2019; Hamilton et al., 2014). For example, with a Likert scale with a range of 1 to 7; with 1 as strongly disagree and 7 as strongly agree.

Effort Expectancy (EE): This is the degree of ease associated with consumers' use of technology (Venkatesh et al., 2012). It basically asks if learning to use this product is easy for the user, if it would be easy for the user to become skillful at using it, and if the user would find this product easy to use. EE can influence consumer adoption of technology products as consumers evaluate technology based on its perceived ease of use, which is assumed to improve lives.

Facilitating Conditions (FC): Consumers perceive the resources and support available to perform a behaviour (Venkatesh et al., 2012). FC might influence consumer adoption of technology products as FC enhance the perception that technology products are effortless and easy to operate. Mobile technology is increasingly used for EF transactions which makes this point important in terms of the technology used, whether it's web-view or application, Google's Android or Apple's IOS.

Innovativeness: Not only on the product side but also on the users' propensity to try new products (Manning, Bearden & Madden, 1995). Behavioral science suggests that personality traits like personal innovativeness may be significant determinants of adoption (Kováříková, Grosova, & Bara, 2017).

Table 10.1 Definitions of Embedded Finance

Type	Definition	School
Academic Literature	"Mobile finance functions offered by non-bank third-party financial service providers"… which "are organizations that have no direct relationship with government and banks" (Sam et al., 2020). Alipay & WeChat Pay are good examples.	1
Grey Literature	"Embedded Finance is non-financial companies offering financial products and services. It could be an e-commerce merchant providing insurance, a coffee shop app that offers 1-click payments, or a department store's branded credit card" (Sullivan, 2022). Examples include price free options on Hopper and Starbucks app wallets.	1
Academic	"The Shadow Banking system" (Wullweber, 2020).	1
Grey Literature	"Embedded finance is the use of financial tools or services — such as lending or payment processing — by a non-financial provider" (Dolgorukov, 2021), like BNPL.	1

(Continued)

Table 10.1 (Continued)

Type	Definition	School
Grey Literature	"Embedded finance is the placing of a financial product in a nonfinancial customer experience, journey, or platform" (Dresner et al., 2022), like Amazon lending.	2
Grey Literature	Bank and non-bank lenders offering Loans to customers buying both online and at physical points of sale"… including "business loans and working capital lines" (Lee, 2022). Several players like YouLend, Funding Societies, Funding Circle offer this.	2
Grey Literature	"Distribution of financial service product through someone else's customer experience" (Honig, 2021). Examples are embedded payment methods offered at checkout stage on Lazada, Shopee or other e-commerce platforms in Asia.	2
Grey Literature	"When a software platform uses a BaaS provider, this is typically called "embedded finance" because the platform adds the financial services as part of its core software" (Stripe, 2023). Stripe is a provider of such BaaS technology layer for platforms.	2
Grey Literature	"Embedded Finance is the integration of financial services directly into a business's products and services, via API. This enables both financial and non-financial businesses to offer services like payments, banking, lending and insurance without becoming regulated as financial entities or building any financial infrastructure themselves" (Open Payd, 2023).	2
Grey Literature	"Embedded Finance enables any brand, business, or merchant to rapidly, and at low cost, integrate innovative financial services into new propositions and customer experiences" (Mambu, 2022). Mambu is a provider of such propositions.	2
Professional Journal	"Embedded finance takes traditional financial services capabilities and places them inside consumer apps, making it quick and easy for everyday consumers to access them" (Fava, 2023). A good example is Apple Pay, allowing payments in app.	3
Academic Literature	"Financial service on the terms of the customer, from anywhere, anytime. There is no longer a need to visit banks that have access to their money. In some cases embedded Finance eliminates traditional banks" (Meng et al., 2021), like AliPay.	3

Table 10.1 (Continued)

Type	Definition	School
Grey Literature	"Embedded finance is the integration of financial services like lending, payment processing or insurance into nonfinancial businesses' infrastructures without the need to redirect to traditional financial institutions" (Jacobson, 2022). A good example is open banking provider Trustly that allows non-redirect options.	3
Professional Journal	Banks addressing "consumers rights at their 'point of need'–on ecommerce platforms, in apps from mobility service providers or on comparison portals"… "by embedding financial services into the products of non-bank companies, thus offering seamless processes and an increased level of convenience to their clients. Open Banking is what provides the foundation for this concept of 'embedded finance'" (Hensen & Kotting, 2022).	4
Grey Literature	Products "embedded in other things and places they go, with banks unseen in the background" (Crosman, 2021). A good example is Standard Chartered's "Nexus" service which powers EF for platforms but without being visible in many cases.	4
Grey Literature	"Embedded finance refers to the shift from time-consuming bank transfers to the use of financial services or tools by a non-financial provider" … " and "should create more simplicity and convenience by embedding the financial journey into a customer's normal non-financial journey" (Haselwood, 2022). One-click instalment and checkout solutions from BNPL fall under this category.	4
Grey Literature	"Embedded Finance is the integration of financial services or tools–traditionally obtained via a bank–within the products or services of a non-financial organization. Think of an online store offering short-term loans in the form of BNPL, or the digital wallet on your phone enabling instant contactless payments" (Carbonnier, 2022).	4

(Continued)

Table 10.1 (Continued)

Type	Definition	School
Grey Literature	"A nonfinancial software platform providing an adjacent financial service, for which it takes some degree of economic ownership. This allows the platform's customers to take advantage of a value-added offering within the native customer journey." (Harris et al., 2022). Uber allowing cards saved on file for automatic payment once cab door is closed is an example of this.	4
Book	"Embedded Finance" is embedded in another context–a checkout line, a mobile app and the like. From consumer perspective, it could be summarized as "invisible payments" or "invisible finance" because a key message is that the financial transaction becomes naturally integrated into what you are doing to the point it feels invisible." (Sieber and Guibaud, 2022). Examples in Asia include Foodpanda one-click payment.	4
Grey Literature	"Embedded Finance is not really designed to be finance at all. When you create a user journey that addresses common pain points, whatever that may be, and you happen to incorporate a financial element, that is embedded Finance. The end user shouldn't really notice the finance if it's properly embedded; it just becomes part of the product" (Jones, 2020).	4
Grey Literature	" Embedded Finance allows companies to create innovative financial offerings that are integrated into the act of purchasing a non-financial product or service" (Compton, 2021). Online Travel Agencies like Booking.com, Expedia and Agoda have perfected this, offering single checkout solutions, typically after the first transaction.	4

Perceived Security: For finance products, the customers' perception of the process of system and product design to securely protect consumer data is a crucial factor (Mohamad et al., 2021). In extension to UTAUT2, perceptions about the technology security system might be essential to gain consumer trust against unauthorized access and to minimize risk (Lee et al., 2013) and an important driver of the *Behavioral Intention to Use*, which defines the overall consumer intention to adopt new technology (Venkatesh et al., 2012).

10.2.2 Current Discussion on Embedded Finance

Scholarly research and a host of practitioner, industry sources, and grey literature defines Embedded Finance in various, sometimes conflicting ways. We aim to present an overview and group these into four distinct schools of thought.

From the aforementioned summary, it appears that business practitioners primarily drive the discussion, and there is still very little academic literature on Embedded Finance. The various definitions can be clustered in four different categories or "Schools of Thought" (see Figure 10.1).

School 1 definition is viewed as too broad. In practice, financial offerings by third parties can be provided outside of mobile technology and in partnership with traditional financial institutions under a Banking as a Service (BaaS) infrastructure. It also does not cover that most offerings benefit from being offered at the point of context, on platforms where users organically congregate.

School 2 does not cover the improvement in user experience. Just providing financial services on third party platforms does not explain why user adoption is so strong. Traditional financial institutions have been distributing services at the point of context in the offline world for decades, via auto-financing at car dealerships or educational loans offered in collaboration with universities without the same growth.

School 3 is not viewed as going far enough. Technology has the potential to revolutionize user experience and financial services, rather than introducing incremental improvements. As digital applications, the Internet of Things (IoT) get more ubiquitous, user experience should move towards seamless.

School 4 offers the most all-encompassing definition of Embedded Finance but it suffers from pitfalls, as a practical evolution to this ideal can be across a spectrum. A non-financial platform may be able to offer one-click checkout, Uber may be able to offer instant payment once the cab door is closed but these are ideals achieved on the second transaction, after a user provides a card or bank account credentials manually typed at checkout on the first transaction to be stored on file or tokenized. Therefore, there is a need to keep the definition open and account for the spectrum of EF offerings.

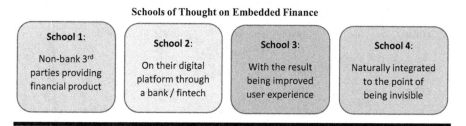

Figure 10.1   Schools of thought on embedded finance (own illustration).

10.2.3 A New Definition of Embedded Finance

Going forward, and for better common understanding, we will propose a new and amended and more differentiated definition of Embedded Finance that combines the appropriate elements of the four schools (Bugvi & Endress, 2023) while accounting for the shortcomings outlined. It considers the evolutionary development in different scenarios. Embedded Finance is defined as (a) financial products and services, (b) offered by non-financial companies or in partnership with traditional financial institutions and FinTech companies (taken from School 1 and 2, (c) at the point of context on digital platforms and applications where users organically congregate (taken from School 2), (d) with improved user experience at the core of the proposition (taken from School 3), (e) ideally naturally integrated into a non-financial product or service to the point of feeling invisible and seamless (taken from School 4). This new definition means Embedded Finance offerings can be viewed across a spectrum, illustrated as follows:

Distribution of financial services has historically followed a model where an intermediary provider like a bank would serve a utility function, providing financial products towards pursuance of an end goal, like purchasing goods and services. As technology evolved, the need to physically go to a financial service provider started to reduce, with cheques, credit, and debit cards and eventually ATMs allowing financial services to be accessed without needing to constantly visit a bank branch. With internet and mobile penetration increasing, new digital channels emerged which allowed financial services to be accessed anytime and from anywhere, making physical presence less relevant. At the same time, two sided digital platforms and eco-systems driven by e-commerce and consumer apps became popular points of congregation for millions of customers looking to fulfil an end need.

	Redirect	Clicks – 1st trx	Clicks – 2nd trx	Task completion time	UX control by 1 or more	
EF 1.0	Yes	Many	Many	Higher	Multiple	
EF 2.0	No	Few	Few	Lower	1	
EF 3.0	No	Few	1	Lower	1	Better UX

Figure 10.2   Spectrum of embedded finance per proposed new definition (own illustration).

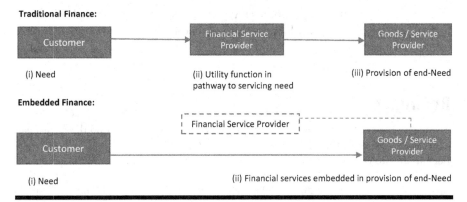

Figure 10.3 **Process comparison of traditional and embedded finance (own illustration).**

The rise of FinTech, proliferation of modular API based eco-systems enabling Banking as a Service (BaaS) (PPS, 2021), regulatory and commercial drive towards Open Banking lifting banks' monopoly over customer data (Hensen & Kötting, 2022) and growing acceptance of the superior customer experience offered by digital applications (Dresner et al., 2022) is changing the nature of financial services. The utility function of banks and intermediary financial services providers is therefore less relevant (Wullweber, 2020). Customers are now able to access financial services at the point of end-need, embedded in e-commerce and digital platforms which can own the customer experience, rather than having to go through a utility financial service provider.

10.3 Summary and Discussion

This chapter provides an overview of the current discussion on Embedded Finance. It can be noted that academic literature seems to have a hard time keeping up with a fast-growing area, and there is only a little academic research available at the moment. As a starting point for further discussion we proposed a more consistent definition of the term Embedded Finance and outlined the potential relationship between technical EF, perceived EF and behavioural intention to adopt EF, thereby empirically testing a key assumption of EF adoption, that it is driven by UX improvement based on existing literature. Given EF's position as one of the top FinTech trends with rising online interest (Ozili, 2022), rapidly growing volume already more than $2.6 trillion, yielding $22 billion in revenue and expected to double to $51 billion by 2026 (Harris et al., 2022), the contributions here are key as this provides a stronger foundation for academics and practitioners to study Embedded Finance while focusing on drivers of adoption, in particular User Experience, which is seen as spearheading it's phenomenal growth. It also provides value for industry practitioners on how to win EF business, as the battle for user attention on crowded technology platforms heats up.

References

Aytaş, B., Öztaner, S. M., & Şener, E. (2021). Open banking: Opening up the 'walled gardens.' *Journal of Payments Strategy & Systems*, 15(4), 419–431.

Boehm, B., Brown, H., & Lipow, M. (1978). Quantitative Evaluation of Software Quality. TRW Systems and Energy Group.

Bugvi, J. A., & Endress, T. (2023). Making Finance Invisible: Embedded Finance Adoption and User Experience. *Proceedings of the AIT SOM Doctoral Colloquium 2023*, 42–53.

Carbonnier, L. (2022, April 13). *Why embedded finance is the next big thing*. Fintech Futures.

Chesbrough, H. (2012). Open Innovation: Where We've Been and Where We're Going. *Research Technology Management*, 55(4), 20–27.

Compton, P. (2021). *Embedded Finance: Creating a seamless future for financial services* (Rise FinTech Insights, pp. 4–5). Barclays Bank. https://rise.barclays/content/dam/thinkrise-com/documents/Rise-FinTech-Insights-Embedded-Finance-DIGITAL.pdf.

Crosman, P. (2021). U.S. banks give embedded finance a whirl. Will it catch on? *American Banker*, 186(168), 5–6.

de Santana, V. F., & Baranauskas, M. C. C. (2015). WELFIT: A remote evaluation tool for identifying Web usage patterns through client-side logging. *International Journal of Human-Computer Studies*, 76, 40–49.

Dolgorukov, D. (2021, August 27). *Embedded Finance: What It Is And How To Get It Right*. Forbes.

Dresner, A., Murati, A., Pike, B., & Zell, J. (2022). *McKinsey–Embedded Finance Global Banking & Securities*.

Endress, T. (2023). Open Innovation Ecosystem in Asia. In T. Endress & Y. F. Badir (Eds.), *Business and Management in Asia: Digital Innovation and Sustainability* (pp. 35–48). Springer Nature Singapore.

Fava, D. (2023). Where Behavioral Finance and Embedded Finance Intersect Clients encounter myriad opportunities for impulse spending. How does that affect financial planning and goal setting? In *54 Journal of Financial Planning*. www.envestnet.

Fisher, N. I., & Kordupleski, R. E. (2019). Good and bad market research: A critical review of Net Promoter Score. *Applied Stochastic Models in Business and Industry*, 35(1), 138–151. https://doi.org/10.1002/asmb.2417.

Hamilton, D. F., Lane, J. V., Gaston, P., Patton, J. T., MacDonald, D. J., Simpson, A. H. R. W., & Howie, C. R. (2014). Assessing treatment outcomes using a single question: The Net Promoter Score. *The Bone & Joint Journal*, 96-B(5), 622–628.

Harrati, N., Bouchrika, I., Tari, A., & Ladjailia, A. (2016). Exploring user satisfaction for e-learning systems via usage-based metrics and system usability scale analysis. *Computers in Human Behavior*, 61, 463–471.

Harris, M., Davis, A., Adams, B., & Tijssen, J. (2022, September 12). *Embedded Finance: What It Takes to Prosper in the New Value Chain*. Bain & Company.

Haselwood, S. (2022, December 20). *Embedded finance: a game-changing opportunity for banks*. The Global Treasurer.

Hensen, J., & Kötting, B. (2022). From open banking to embedded Finance: The essential factors for a successful digital transformation. In *Journal of Digital Banking* (Vol. 6). Henry Stewart Publications.

Honig, C. (2021). The (Opt) Ins and Outs of Embedded Finance. *Best's Review, 122*(6), 32–34.

Jacobson, A. (2022, September 20). *What Is Embedded Finance?* Builtin.

Jones, A. A. (2012). *The Impact of Website Navigational Usability Characteristics On User Frustration and Performance Metrics* [Ohio University]. https://etd.ohiolink.edu/apexprod/rws_etd/send_file/send?accession=ohiou1339618564.

Jones, F. (2020, November 23). *What is embedded Finance?* 11FS.

Kováříková, L., Grosová, S., & Baran, D. (2017). Critical factors impacting the adoption of foresight by companies. Foresight, 19(6), 541–558.

Lee, L. Y.-S. (2013). Hospitality industry web-based self-service technology adoption model. Journal of Hospitality & Tourism Research, 40(2), 162–197.

Lee, P. (2022). Banks Missing Out on Embedded Finance. *Euromoney, 53*(630), 28–31.

Mambu. (2022). *Embedded Finance: Who will win the battle for the next digital revolution?*

Manning, K. C., Bearden, W. O., & Madden, T. J. (1995). Consumer innovativeness and the adoption process. Journal of Consumer Psychology, 4(4), 329–345.

Meng, S., He, X., & Tian, X. (2021). Research on Fintech development issues based on embedded cloud computing and big data analysis. *Microprocessors and Microsystems, 83*.

Meng Sam, K., & Han Chan, W. (2020). Factors affecting the adoption of embedded mobile finance functions. *Journal of Information Technology Management, XXXI*(2).

Mohamad, M. A., Radzi, S. M., & Hanafiah, M. H. (2021). Understanding Tourist Mobile Hotel Booking Behaviour: Incorporating perceived enjoyment and perceived price value in the modified technology acceptance model. Tourism & Management Studies, 17(1), 19–30.

Nielsen, J. (1993). *Usability engineering*. Academic Press.

OpenPayd. (2023, February 14). *What is embedded finance and how is it changing businesses?* Open Payd Blog.

Ozili, P. K. (2022). Assessing global interest in decentralized Finance, embedded Finance, open Finance, ocean finance and sustainable Finance. *Asian Journal of Economics and Banking, 7*(2), 197–216.

PPS. (2021). *Exploring Embedded Finance: The Future of Integrated Financial Services*.

Schneider, M. (2023). Open Banking and Digital Ecosystems. In T. Endress, *Digital Project Practice for New Work and Industry 4.0* (1st ed., pp. 169–179). Auerbach Publications.

Seiber, S., & Guibaud, S. (2022). *Embedded Finance: When Payments Become An Experience* (1st ed.). Wiley.

Stojmenovic, M., Biddle, R., Grundy, J., & Farrell, V. (2019). The influence of textual and verbal word-of-mouth on website usability and visual appeal. *Journal of Supercomputing, 75*(4), 1783–1830.

Stripe. (2023). *Introduction to banking-as-a-service (BaaS) for software platforms*. Stripe.

Sullivan, T. (2022, October 3). *What is embedded finance? 4 ways it will change fintech*. Plaid.

Venkatesh, V., Thong, J. Y., & Xu, X. (2012). Consumer acceptance and use of information technology: extending the unified theory of acceptance and use of technology. *MIS Quarterly*, 157–178.

Wullweber, J. (2020). Embedded Finance: the shadow banking system, sovereign power, and a new state–market hybridity. *Journal of Cultural Economy, 13*(5), 592–609.

Chapter 11

The Buy-Now-Pay-Later Ecosystem: New (Algo) Rhythms of Spending and Reframed Relationships

Ruffin Relja, Philippa Ward, and Anita Lifen Zhao

Chapter Overview

Buy-now-pay-later (BNPL) is changing young consumers' spending and relationships to credit through an integrated digital ecosystem predicated on algorithmic marketing. Whilst BNPL has the capacity to liberate young consumers by fostering a more entrepreneurial disposition to credit, this view is founded on the supposition that consumers have the necessary knowledge and capability to make informed financial decisions. However, the use of algorithms means that young consumers are, perhaps, more accurately framed as being constrained and any inherent patterns of damaging behavior maintained. Therefore, while the provision of BNPL appears to offer opportunities such as greater accessibility and flexibility, it inevitably evidences numerous disadvantages, such as impulsive borrowing and financial vulnerability, which are intensified by a lack of regulation. These complexities create a challenging operational space for consumers, service providers, retailers, and regulators alike–arguably changing the relationships between them and necessitating continued consideration of the evolving nature of digital consumer credit solutions.

DOI: 10.1201/9781003395560-11

11.1 Introduction

This chapter discusses the interlock of buy-now-pay-later (BNPL) consumption and social media platforms to consider the development of an integrated ecosystem that currently circumscribes credit usage for many young consumers, reshaping their approach to spending, and to the relationships with the other actors present in the system. The chapter also delves into how the application of algorithms across both domains is creating a space fraught with differential outcomes, leading to the possible amplification of inequalities.

11.2 The Promotion of New Digital Consumer Credit Solutions

Marketing has long helped normalize consumer credit through ubiquitous advertising and the extensive provision of new credit solutions (Husz, 2021). Through this, several possible problems emerge that relate to the pervasive promotion of new digital consumer credit products: push marketing fosters impulsive borrowing that lacks prior intention or clarity of purpose; there is poor product disclosure; digital delivery can change repayment dynamics, and digital credit raises consumer protection concerns–particularly in relation to data usage and sharing (Mazer & McKnee, 2018). These complexities create a challenging operational space for consumers, service providers, retailers, and regulators alike. Additionally, such concerns generate a novel climate where interactions and exchange are reframed and combined to create the specter of manipulation and possible exploitation.

However, such drawbacks do not belie the opportunities that are also present in this emerging market. The possibly progressive outcomes of digital consumer credit have been extolled in much research (see for example: Hasan et al., 2021 Li et al., 2020; Zhong, & Jiang, 2021). Such benefits have particular salience for consumers previously excluded by traditional financial services (Bourreau & Valletti, 2015). This is because such digital forms of credit, ostensibly, make financial access 'easier', making it more convenient and swifter, which simultaneously generates new consumption opportunities.

Therefore, these financial products concomitantly intensify household borrowing and increase the risk of over-indebtedness (Yue et al., 2022). Risk here is predicated on excluded consumers often experiencing more restricted financial well-being in terms of their current money management stresses and expected future financial security (Netemeyer et al., 2018) and their having lower financial literacy, both in relation to objective and subjective knowledge (Sun et al., 2022). Lower financial literacy is particularly significant in relation to digital consumer credit, as many such products, and their management, are more complex than those to which excluded consumers will previously have been exposed or used. This discrepancy can substantially diffuse the benefits wrought by reduced information asymmetry between lenders and borrowers in digital consumer credit services. This is because a lack of knowledge means that, whilst information may be found more easily, the borrower is not able to utilize it effectively to make an informed choice. So, potentially financially vulnerable consumers can engage with digital consumer credit services with relative ease, without apprehending the possible unintended consequences that may transpire.

Therefore, the overall picture is one where the extensive development of digital consumer credit products, the relatively low consumer adoption barriers and the intricate interplay between benefits and risks creates a complex context where consumers' approach to spending is being reshaped (Koskelainen et al., 2023). As are consumers' relationships with the other actors present in the system, be they the digital credit provider, the retailer, or others who generate content that promotes, or cautions against, the use of such financial services. Hence, consumers are now surrounded by a digital ecosystem, powered by digital credit, that serves up a myriad of opportunities to purchase.

11.3 Buy-now-pay-later–a Distinctive Digital Consumer Credit Product

BNPL products can be defined as third-party short-term credit agreements, that consumers access through dedicated provider apps or as one of the payment options at retailers' checkouts. The agreements usually enable deferred payment of the purchase price or split it into instalments spread across a few months, consumer preference differs between countries as to which BNPL form predominates. Most BNPL providers do not charge interest or fees unless a repayment is missed, or borrowers elect a longer settlement period (Relja et al., 2023a). In many countries, there is no requirement for extended credit checks and BPNL regulation is negligible, as lawmakers are yet to address this new digital format. Conversely, many BNPL providers use significant technological capabilities to embed this digital credit product within an enhanced service proposition, seeking to make it ubiquitous.

Therefore, BNPL with its adept application of FinTech and sophisticated digital marketing utilization, has become a quintessential contemporary form of unregulated short-term digital consumer credit (Johnson et al., 2021). BNPL largely adheres to the precepts that consumers now "… demand intelligent, however easy-to-use financial services independent of location and time, and at continually decreasing costs" (Gomber et al., 2017, p. 537). But rather than simply becoming another new digital credit solution, BNPL has morphed, in many instances, into a consumption platform, where the customary relationships between customer, retailer and payment provider are renegotiated (Relja et al., 2023b) and are increasingly intertwined with social media content and influencers, specifically 'Finfluencers' (de Regt, 2023).

The growth and potential of BNPL as a form of consumer credit is evident in recent figures from GlobalData (2023), which suggest that, by the end of 2023, the digital credit product will account for nearly 60 percent of the transaction values across five primary categories (food and drink, health and beauty, media and entertainment, electrical goods and home appliances, clothing and footwear). Currently, GlobalData (2023) suggests that the global BNPL "… market size will be valued at 309.2 billion [US Dollars] in 2023 and [that it] is expected to grow at a compound annual growth rate (CAGR) of 25.5% over the forecast period [to 2026]." Given this scale and anticipated trajectory, there is little doubt that BNPL is a substantial consumer credit mechanism, although it is still significantly smaller than the global credit card payment market, which reached 521.8 billion US Dollars in 2022 (Imarc Group, 2022).

BNPL services are now operated by numerous companies. These include Afterpay Ltd., Klarna Bank AB, Sezzle Inc., Splitit Payment Ltd., BNPL pioneers and now synonymous with this form of short-term credit; PayPal Holdings Inc. and Openpay Group Ltd., digital payment specialists; alongside Amazon Payments Inc. and Apple Pay Ltd., and other providers rooted in various forms of technological innovation and solutions. However, BNPL services are increasingly being offered by traditional credit providers too, including American Express Co., Barclays Plc., Citigroup Inc., and Monzo Bank Ltd. The entry of providers with established reputations potentially increases consumer trust and reduces perceived risk in this form of online payment, especially when the retailer is unfamiliar (Cardoso & Martinez, 2019). The diversification of market players demonstrates that BNPL has become an established digital consumer credit product and one that is likely to form a major part of the contemporary consumption landscape for the foreseeable future.

This is particularly the case as BNPL use is widespread among younger cohorts (Statista, 2022), such as Millennials (born 1980–1994) and Generation Z (born 1995–2009). These younger consumers have a receptive attitude to BNPL, and many prefer to engage with new digital consumer credit solutions rather than utilize alternate traditional financial products. Additionally, these younger consumers frequently have a limited credit history, making traditional credit products difficult to access. Many also experience more restricted financial well-being as they are in the early stages of their careers and are simultaneously seeking to establish an independent life with its intendent financial requirements. Equally, given their limited experience and the lack of formal education in the domain (Lusardi, 2015), many have low financial literacy. This can make these young consumers particularly financially vulnerable.

This vulnerability is potentially heightened as many young consumers additionally prefer the immediate and frictionless procedures and simple account management capacity that BNPL affords, making access to credit almost effortless. This creates a volatile admixture of credit opportunity and consumer naivety that fuels BNPL market growth. This mix also fosters the *illusion* of financial well-being, as it generates a position where the young consumer may feel they have "… control over day-to-day finances; have the capacity to absorb financial shock; have ability to meet [their] financial goals; and [specifically] have the financial freedom to make the choices that allow one to enjoy life (Collins & Urban, 2020; Netemeyer et al., 2018)" (Koskelainen et al., 2023, p. 508).

BNPL, therefore, offers potential financial freedoms, but is less tangible than other traditional, or even, digital payment forms. But perhaps most importantly, the attendant BNPL apps that wrap around the core consumer credit product, proliferate consumption choices triggered by algorithms (for example, promotion of preferred retailers, discount notification). What is, therefore, created is an integrated ecosystem, which contains both the BNPL app and associated social media, and that frames both choice and the means to pay for it, offering young consumers a single portal to (over)spending.

Consequently, such BNPL offers are more a digital consumption platform than they are simply a new consumer credit solution. In that respect, these BNPL digital consumption ecosystems bound young consumers' financial capability. namely their ability and the opportunity to act (Scott et al., 2018; Serido et al., 2013). The pervasiveness, and power, of such digital ecosystems has often been noted, as users are immersed in the technology, hence they do not perceive it, and its use, as being a separate exercise from their everyday activities (Baskerville et al., 2020). Therefore, these digital ecosystems become embedded and persistent, and are a persuasive force, which seek to prime attitudes and nudge choice behavior (Dennis et al., 2020).

11.4 The Nature and Power of Algorithmic Marketing

This reframing of BNPL is principally predicated on the application of algorithmic marketing, which seeks to curate tailored retail offers alongside customized financial discounts and deals. Here the BNPL consumption platform acts as a digital infrastructure that draws together consumers and retailers and enables exchange between the actor groups through the digital consumer credit product that lies at its core. The emergence of such a 'platform assemblage' (Kozinets, 2022) has the capacity to alter customers' spending, both in relation to what is bought and when. This is grounded on the abundance of data generated and available through the embedding of such digital ecosystems in consumers' everyday activities and the appearance of varied digital-sensing tools used in the financial landscape (Gomber et al., 2017). Such tools enable BNPL providers to combine various data sources (browsing history, retailer transactions, repayment data, social network data) to both identify young consumers' consumption patterns and to build highly targeted recommendations (Gomber et al., 2017). As such, BNPL consumption platforms are not 'neutral' (Gillespie, 2010), as the explicit intent is to extract such data to affect the choices and the spending of the young consumers who are its chief users.

To enable the effective generation of data, these BNPL consumption platforms need to create an 'enclosed space' in which consumers can be observed, tracked and predictions made that serve to enhance consumer desire. This requires consumers' activities to be constrained by the platform (Zuboff, 2019) and yet be simultaneously empowered by them (Kozinets, 2022). For example, on a BNPL consumption platform, only retailers who 'subscribe' are displayed. This delimits the consumption choices that the young consumer can make but may also expose them to brands and products that they would otherwise not come across. Additionally, those retailers who pay the BNPL platform more to enjoy preferential advertising displays are foregrounded and those retailers who do not engage in such promotional spending are demoted to secondary positions, hence consumers are required to expend more effort to effectively 'hunt out' these retailers' offers. Such practices thereby establish "outright manipulation and constrained self-determination" (Breidbach & Maglio, 2020, p. 180). This market-based form of constraint is both enabling but through the application of predictive analytics to consumer activities it equally seeks to nudge young consumers within these BNPL consumption platforms.

Such predictive analytics are built on algorithms that, in the contemporary context, are best understood as being "enacted by practices which do not heed a strong distinction between technical and non-technical concerns, but rather blend them together. In this view, algorithms are not singular technical objects that enter into many different cultural interactions, but are rather unstable objects, culturally enacted by the practices people use to engage with them" (Seaver, 2017, p. 5). This perspective enables consideration of the devices on which the software runs, the software programming, and the producing and consuming of content, as well as the valuing and using of data (Kozinets, 2022). Therefore, this conceptualization highlights that algorithms are embedded manifestations of contemporary consumer culture, that both have socially generative and responsive qualities, and are not 'merely' a benign technical instrument. This position led Kozinets et al. (2017, p. 667) to coin the term 'networks of desire' to describe the interconnected web of actors (chiefly consumers, companies, platforms, and influencers/content creators), that are part of a wider social system, and for whom, through the application of algorithmic technologies, consumption interests are created and intensified.

Other, more challenging, terminology refers to such algorithmic marketing approaches as 'surveillance capitalism' (Zuboff, 2019) and highlights the potential biases that the inferences shaped by such systems engender, even going so far as to suggest that the outcomes "… are used to manipulate, assess, predict, and nudge individuals, often without their awareness and nearly always without any oversight or accountability" (Gawer, 2021, p. 12). This raises significant concerns and suggests that there are likely to be ethical consequences that affect individual consumers and society more generally, particularly as the availability of anonymized, big data sets and analytic practices become ever more sophisticated (Wirtz et al., 2023). Similar customer privacy and vulnerability worries (Koskelainen et al., 2023) can be extended to BNPL, particularly given the potential centrality of this form of platform assemblage to young consumers' consumption practices, as well as to their financial capability. Here, algorithmic marketing, underpinned by behavioral economics, seeks to influence young consumers to make certain decisions in relation to the financial services that they use (Cai, 2020) to facilitate access to curated lifestyles, neatly packaged within the BNPL consumption platform.

11.5 Consumer Credit Marketing Algorithms

Recent work has gone even further, suggesting that technologically supported credit marketing practices, and the application of algorithms specifically, shape class distinction (Pellandini-Simányi, 2023). Here, customers are seen as passive objects of algorithms, segmented, and 'fed specific marketing messages'; they are also viewed as subjects of algorithms, where the digitalization of choice is facilitated, with both preferential and detrimental consequences. BNPL consumption platforms have certainly been a stage for the proliferation of targeted marketing messages and demonstrated the potential to generate varied outcomes for young consumers, offering possible liberation from traditional credit forms to which they may not have access, alongside the promotion of unsustainable consumption and over-indebtedness.

Many young consumers, given their limited financial literacy, also hold a range of misnomers about the relationship between BNPL and wider credit systems. For instance, in the UK, a significant number assume that on-time repayment of BNPL debit immediately increases their credit scores (Relja et al., 2023a), whilst not appreciating that each BNPL transaction and 'defaulted' repayments (90 days or more) are noted on credit reports, and in the case of the latter stay there for six years (Experian, 2023). Such specific inaccuracies, and more generally uninformed positions on digital financial services, are entwined with young consumers' extensive reliance on social media. BNPL providers make extensive use of social media, and there is copious consumer-created BNPL content, alongside the pervasiveness of 'FinTok' as a means for young consumers to 'educate' themselves. In the United States of America, Generation Z and Millennials in particular (56 percent in total) report using social media to garner financial advice: both groups rely on Instagram, but Generation Z also use TikTok, whilst Millennials additionally employ Facebook (Credit Karma, 2021).

In a recent study of BNPL FinTok, Aggarwal et al. (2022, pp. 351–352) identified four common types of content: "Memes (highly spreadable and replicable videos, often depicting humorous or sardonic content); Lifestyle (videos in which creators discussed, criticized, or celebrated purchases made using BNPL); Promotional (videos in which creators advertised products that could be purchased using BNPL services or advertised the BNPL products themselves); and Advisory (videos in which creators provided information or cautioned viewers about using BNPL products)." Whilst these different types of content are evident, the nature of the algorithms that drive TikTok mean that young consumers who view one form of content, for example, lifestyle videos celebrating purchases made using BNPL, see more of the same material and simultaneously have messages that provide counterpoint excluded. This again amplifies the tone of the original material viewed, and simultaneously perpetuates constrained self-determination. Additionally, BNPL providers can comment on, or even promote, such content through the web of connectivity that is the BNPL ecosystem, potentially lending further opportunities to manipulate consumers' attitudes and choice behaviors. Given this, it is unsurprising that there are significant anxieties concerning how social media accelerates BNPL use, normalizes debt, and even seeks to make approaches to defaulting on repayments humorous.

In relation the use of social media in wider [digital] marketing ecosystems, Redmond (2023) suggests consideration of who is the consumer and who is the customer, and if their interests coincide, of what constitutes data and what information, alongside if social media provisions sovereignty, which "involves the self-interested, objective and analytical evaluation of market offerings by the consumer" (p. 2). Firstly, when social media is considered, the viewers of the content are purely consumers, as they pay nothing for access, and the customers are the advertisers and those paying for the data generated, namely the BNPL consumption platform providers in this context. The interests of the two groups do not necessarily align and content creators are keenly aware that the money they generate comes directly from the 'customer' rather than the consumer. Secondly, social media provides its *customers* with considerable data on its *consumers*. This data is the saleable commodity at the heart of social media platforms. This notion underpins the third point that social media consumers may well be subjects of the system rather than served by it, and that it is the customers of social media who have sovereignty. Consumers, and their data, are however, the currency that is traded via social media and keeping them engaged and returning to consume more is critical.

Many social media consumers spend considerable time each day using such platforms and are influenced by their interactions on these sites. For instance, over one-third of Generation Z spend more than two hours daily on social media, Millennials are, however, the most active users with 32 percent posting either daily or multiple times a day (Coe et al., 2023), many stating this affects their choices. For young consumers social media has become habituated and the 'influencers' [irrespective of the veracity of what they present] are often more trusted than traditional sources of financial advice. When such social media engagement by young consumers is allied with the use of the BNPL consumption platforms, what results are refashioned approaches to purchasing, ones where young consumers can spend now and not worry, even later when repayment is due, with some content creators even posting about the size of their accumulated BNPL debt in humorous memes. In this sense, the issue becomes if what is fostered is choice or, rather, 'choicelessness'.

11.6   An Evolving Set of Relationships

Choice is also reframed in terms of the traditional relationships that exist between consumer and retailer in the BNPL ecosystem. The BNPL consumption platforms, and the associated social media content, promote the digital consumer credit provider to a position of primacy. Retailers are a necessary constituent of the BNPL ecosystem but are no longer primary. It is access to this form of digital consumer credit that is paramount for young consumers, as it enables them to manage their finances in what are increasingly turbulent and uncertain economic conditions (Relja et al., 2023b).

Consumers can use BNPL to 'feel' as if they are able to make use of what they see as *their* borrowed future money. They are, in essence, first focusing on the means of access to consumption that BNPL affords and then using this platform to delimit the menu of consumption choices available to them. Here, the retailers' chief connection comes to the BNPL provider as it is the consumption platform, and the retailers' (paid for) relationships with it, that are critical. These associations enable the BNPL provider to offer targeted savings and discounts, as well as curate the development of a lifestyle proposition. This effectively mediates the consumption experiences of these young consumers, and potentially engenders dependence, both in terms of access to credit, but also by circumscribing the set of retailers and brands with whom consumers develop a relationship.

This presents retailers and brand owners with considerable challenges and may lead them to make decisions about which BNPL consumption platform providers they deal with, or if they elect to use the BNPL services of companies that currently operate more as a traditional credit product, offered only at point of purchase. If such patterns develop, they will further serve to delineate consumption choices for young consumers, as the extent to which consumers are then willing to engage with different BNPL providers becomes a salient feature and the future battleground for BNPL provision.

11.7   BPNL and the New (Algo)rhythms of Spending

When taken in the round, whilst BNPL may liberate young consumers from the tyranny of 'credit scores' (Kear, 2017), it might be said to simultaneously increase the responsibilization of individuals (Burton, 2008). Here, the issue of governance is transferred to the individual consumer through an 'appeal of freedom', and they are responsible for self-steering and self-care. BNPL consumption platforms are certainly offering young consumers a new means of access to goods and services, but there is also an implicit assumption that these consumers can make decisions that are advantageous to them, and thereby exercise self-governance. Therefore, it might be expected that BNPL furthers the entrepreneurial disposition of consumers to credit (Langley, 2008) but, given the issues raised above, concerns of inequality and susceptibility are also heightened, specifically given the allying of FinTech and digital marketing capabilities.

The application of algorithmic marketing that lies at the core of BNPL consumption platforms, and within the associated social media sites that these young consumers use to gain information, actively delimits, and potentially curtails consumers' capacities to act freely. The algorithms applied offer constrained self-determination by firstly categorizing these young BNPL users and then secondly by providing tailored retail offers. Hence, what a young consumer can access is, therefore, defined through the platform and reinforced via social media. This has considerable potential to lead to attitudinal and behavioral nudging, the outcomes of which can be unfavorable for the young consumer, for instance the buildup of debt, unnecessary accumulation of goods and spending on services, and reinforcement of unsustainable financial habits.

What is perhaps even more concerning is that the defaults that these young consumers may well develop in terms of BNPL will, in turn, be made manifest in future credit prospects. In essence, the data surrounding young consumers' BNPL activities will be the meat of further algorithms that will decide on their access, or more likely the curtailment of their access, to future financial opportunity. As such, the algorithms used by BNPL providers, and indeed the wider financial services industry, shape young consumers' rhythms of current spending and define their future financial well-being. Without effective regulation, consumer education, and more consideration of the issues that result from the application of algorithms in relation to new digital forms of consumer credit, the future for young consumers is fraught with differential outcomes and substantial inequalities. This was recently highlighted as one BNPL consumption platform provider in the UK elected to make opting out of its credit services easier by managing this from within the platform settings. Up to this point, consumers could only 'leave' if they spoke to the provider's customer service team. The aim of such a tactic simply seems to be making it too 'inconvenient' to leave. Hence, once the young consumer is a BNPL user they were caught, constrained, and remained the object and subject of the BNPL provider's algorithmic marketing. Whether the move to ease young consumers' ability to leave was enacted to start returning control or a more cynical response to mounting external pressure is unclear. What is apparent though is that BNPL consumption platforms, and probably other new forms of digital credit services, will continue to reshape consumer spending and raise numerous questions and concerns.

11.8 Conclusion

Figure 11.1 summarizes the interplay between the primary actors in the BNPL ecosystem. It depicts the way these relationships define the space for consumer action and their longer-term prospects.

Young consumers inhabit the intersection created by the algorithmic marketing practices deployed by BNPL platform providers and social media. The BNPL platform

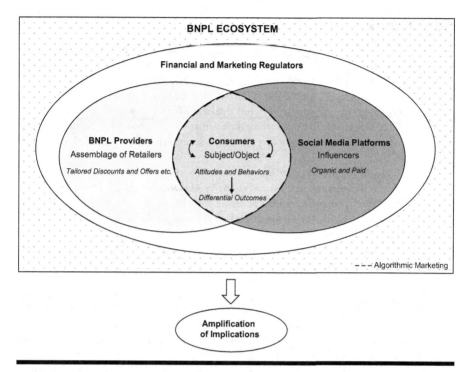

Figure 11.1 The BNPL ecosystem.

providers seek to offer an assemblage of retailers. The aim is to curate a lifestyle via access to specific goods and services. Through this, the short-term credit product that lies at the core of BNPL platform provision is enclosed within a structure that provides consumers with personalized discounts and offers. These benefits are then entwined with the messages fashioned by social media influencers, irrespective of whether those communications are paid for by the BNPL provider or are organic content. Therefore, consumers are both simultaneously the subject and object of algorithmic marketing that shapes their attitudes and behaviors. Consequently, differential outcomes are made manifest and potential inequalities are forged within the BNPL ecosystem.

That system is currently one with limited intervention from either financial or marketing regulators across much of the globe. However, the role of this actor is pivotal for the future. At present, regulators are playing catch-up as the speed and capability for novelty demonstrated by the BNPL providers incapacitates their ability to act preemptively. This results in an ecosystem that is driven by the FinTech provider. Such motivations are invariably bound to seeking profitability at the expense of the consumer. The potential amplification of inequalities that results is supported by young BNPL users' low levels of financial literacy and capability. The consequences of this confluence of factors could well create ripples that are sustained into the future financial well-being of young consumers for generations to come.

References

Aggarwal, N., Kaye, D., & Odinet, C. K. (2022). #Fintok and Financial Regulation. *54 Arizona State Law Journal 333*, U Iowa Legal Studies Research Paper No. 2022–26, UCLA School of Law, Law-Econ Research Paper No. 23-01.

Baskerville, R. L., Myers, M. D., & Yoo, Y. (2020). Digital first: the ontological reversal and new challenges for information systems research. *MIS Quarterly, 44(2)*, 509–523.

Bourreau, M., & Valletti, T. (2015). Enabling digital financial inclusion through improvements in competition and interoperability: What works and what doesn't. CGD Policy Paper, 65, 1–30.

Breidbach, C. F., & Maglio, P. (2020). Accountable algorithms? The ethical implications of data driven business models. *Journal of Service Management, 31(2), 163–185.*

Burton, D. (2008). *Credit and Consumer Society*. Routledge.

Cai, C. W. (2020). Nudging the financial market? A review of the nudge theory. *Accounting and Finance, 60*, 3341–3365.

Cardoso, S., & Martinez, L. F. (2019). Online payments strategy: How third-party internet seals of approval and payment provider reputation influence the Millennials' online transactions. *Electronic Commerce Research, 19(1)*, 189–209.

Coe, E., Doy, A. Enomoto, K., & Healy, C. (2023, April 28). Gen Z mental health: The impact of tech and social media. *McKinsey Health Institute*. www.mckinsey.com/mhi/our-insights/gen-z-mental-health-the-impact-of-tech-and-social-media.

Collins, M. J., & Urban, C. (2020). Measuring financial well-being over the lifecourse. *European Journal of Finance, 26(4–5)*, 341–359.

Credit Karma (2021, July 13). Gen Z turns to TikTok and Instagram for financial advice and actually takes it, study finds. [Press Release]. www.creditkarma.com/about/commentary/gen-z-turns-to-tiktok-and-instagram-for-financial-advice-and-actually-takes-it-study-finds.

Dennis, A. R., Yuan, L., Feng, X., Webb, E., & Hsieh, C. J. (2020). Digital nudging: numeric and semantic priming in e-commerce. *Journal of Management Information Systems, 37(1)*, 39–65.

de Regt, A., Cheng, Z., & Fawaz, R. (2023). Young People Under 'Finfluencer': The Rise of Financial Influencers on Instagram: An Abstract. In: Jochims, B., Allen, J. (eds) *Optimistic Marketing in Challenging Times: Serving Ever-Shifting Customer Needs*. AMSAC 2022. Developments in Marketing Science: Proceedings of the Academy of Marketing Science. Springer, Cham.

Experian (2023). Does short-term buy now pay later credit affect your credit score? www.experian.co.uk/consumer/help-discover/discover/guides/short-term-buy-now-pay-later.html.

Gawer, A. (2021). Digital Platforms and Ecosystems: Remarks on the Dominant Organizational Forms of the Digital Age. *Innovation: Organization & Management, 24*, 1–15.

Gillespie, T. (2010). The politics of 'platforms'. *New Media & Society, 12(3)*, 347–364.

GlobalData (2023). Buy Now Pay Later (BNPL) Market Size, Share, Trends and Analysis by Spend Category (Clothing and Footwear, Furniture, Travel and Accommodation, Sports and Entertainment), Region and Segment Forecast to 2026. Report Code: GRCBBR00004FS (May, 2023), 1–89.

Gomber, P., Koch, J. A., & Siering, M. (2017). Digital Finance and FinTech: current research and future research directions. *Journal of Business Economics, 87*, 537–850.

Hasan, M., Le, T., & Hoque, A. (2021). How does financial literacy impact on inclusive finance? *Financial Innovation, 7(1)*, 1–23.

Husz, O. (2021). Money cards and identity cards: de-vicing consumer credit in post-war Sweden. *Journal of Cultural Economy. 14(2)*, 139–158.

Imarc Group (2022). Credit Card Payment Market Size: Global Industry Trends, Share, Size, Growth, Opportunity and Forecast 2023–2028. Report ID: SR112023A4922, 1–143.

Johnson, D., Rodwell, J., & Hendry, T. (2021). Analyzing the impacts of financial services regulation to make the case that buy-now-pay-later regulation is failing. *Sustainability, 13(4)*, 1992.

Kear, M. (2017). Playing the credit score game: Algorithms, 'positive' data and the personification of financial objects. *Economy and Society, 46(3–4)*, 346–368.

Koskelainen, T., Kalmi, P., Scornavacca, E., & Vartiainen, T. (2023). Financial literacy in the digital age–A research agenda. *Journal of Consumer Affairs, 57(1)*, 507–528.

Kozinets, R. V. (2022). Algorithmic branding through platform assemblages: Core conceptions and research directions for a new era of marketing and service management, *Journal of Service Management, 33(3)*, 437–452.

Kozinets, R., Patterson, A., & Ashman, R. (2017). Networks of desire: How technology increases our passion to consume. *Journal of Consumer Research, 43(5)*, 659–682.

Langley, P. (2008). Financialization and the consumer credit boom. *Competition & Change, 12(2)*, 133–147.

Li, J., Wu, Y., & Xiao, J. J. (2020). The impact of digital finance on household consumption: Evidence from China. *Economic Modelling, 86*, 317–326.

Lusardi, A. (2015) Financial Literacy Skills for the 21st Century: Evidence from PISA. *Journal of Consumer Affairs, 49(3)*, 639–659.

Mazer, R., & McKee, K. (2018). *Digital Consumer Credit: Four Ways Providers can Improve Customer Experience*. Consultative Group to Assist the Poor. CGAP Policy Paper, 1–41.

Netemeyer, R. G., Warmath, D., Fernandes, D., & Lynch Jr, J. G. (2018). How am I doing? Perceived financial well-being, its potential antecedents, and its relation to overall well-being. *Journal of Consumer Research, 45(1)*, 68–89.

Pellandini-Simányi, L. (2023). Algorithmic classifications in credit marketing: How marketing shapes inequalities. *Marketing Theory*, Advance online publication.

Redmond, W. (2023). A Note on Marketing Systems and Social Media. *Journal of Macromarketing*, Advance online publication.

Relja, R., Ward, P., & Zhao, A. L. (2023a). Understanding the psychological determinants of buy-now-pay-later (BNPL) in the UK: a user perspective. *International Journal of Bank Marketing*, Advance online publication.

Relja R., Zhao, A. L., & Ward, P. (2023b). Friend or foe? How buy-now-pay-later is seeking to change traditional consumer-retailer relationships in the UK. In K. Bäckström, C. Egan-Wyer, and E. Samsioe (Eds.). *The Future of Consumption–How Technology, Sustainability and AI will Revolutionize Retail*. Palgrave Macmillan.

Scott, J. K., Vu, N. N., Cheng, Y., & Gibson, P. (2018). Financial capability: literacy, behavior, and distress. *Financial Services Review, 27*, 391–411.

Seaver, N. (2017). Algorithms as culture: some tactics for the ethnography of algorithmic systems. *Big Data and Society, 4(2)*, 1–12.

Serido, J., Shim, S., & Tang, C. (2013). A developmental model of financial capability: a framework for promoting a successful transition to adulthood. *International Journal of Behavioral Development, 37(4)*, 287–297.

Sun, S., Chen, Y. C., Ansong, D., Huang, J., & Sherraden, M. S. (2022). Household financial capability and economic hardship: An empirical examination of the financial capability framework. *Journal of Family and Economic Issues, 43(4)*, 716–729.

Statista. (2022). *Buy Now, Pay Later (BNPL)*. [Digital & Trends Dossier].

Wirtz, J., Kunz, W. H., Hartley, N., & Tarbit, J. (2023). Corporate digital responsibility in service firms and their ecosystems. *Journal of Service Research, 26(2)*, 173–190.

Yue, P., Korkmaz, A. G., Yin, Z., & Zhou, H. (2022). The rise of digital finance: Financial inclusion or debt trap? *Finance Research Letters, 47*, 102604.

Zhong, W., & Jiang, T. (2021). Can internet finance alleviate the exclusiveness of traditional finance? Evidence from Chinese P2P lending markets. *Finance Research Letters, 40*, 101731.

Zuboff, S. (2019). *The age of surveillance capitalism: The fight for a human future at the new frontier of power*. Profile Books.

Chapter 12

Zero Trust in Banking and FinTech

Tobias Endress

Chapter Overview

This chapter discusses the concept of Zero Trust Architecture (ZTA) and its application in the banking and financial services industry. It highlights the increasing need for collaboration in API-based ecosystems and the potential risks associated with data protection and transaction security. It emphasizes the importance of secure information management and the challenges faced by organizations in the financial services industry regarding IT security. It introduces the history and key elements of Zero Trust, including user and location authentication, device management, application/service access control, real-time risk intelligence, and trust algorithms. The practical implementation of Zero Trust in a bank or financial services organization is also discussed. The chapter concludes by emphasizing the need for management attention and proper design and preparation when implementing Zero Trust ecosystems, including identifying protected resources and applying the least privilege access principle.

12.1   Introduction

Banks and FinTech companies are operating complex IT ecosystems, often with globally distributed operations, including remote workforces and third-party connectivity, which are contributing to an increasingly challenging risk landscape (Rafla

DOI: 10.1201/9781003395560-12

et al., 2022). The increasing need for collaboration in API-based ecosystems based on Open Banking (Schneider, 2023) and Embedded Finance (Bugvi & Endress, 2023) while this kind of collaboration enables new use cases and business models but these approaches also raise questions about data protection and transaction security. This is becoming increasingly demanding also from a management perspective. Depending on the specific business model, sharing information with Third-Party Providers (TPP) or other ecosystem partners might be needed. The adequate and secure management of shared digital information with all parties involved in the ecosystem is a central prerequisite for successfully implementing such strategies (Müller et al., 2020). Whenever humans or machines work together, information exchange must respect compliance and trust (Ryan & Falvey, 2012). Every partner must have access to the necessary information to process the clients' requests. At the same time, it needs to be ensured that unauthorized access is not possible and the data is protected from misuse. Still, security breaches happening in the financial services industry are not an uncommon phenomenon. The IT security company Sophos surveyed 5600 IT professionals, of whom 444 worked in the financial services industry. It revealed that the financial services industry is attacked less frequently than most other industries, but still, about 55% of organizations were attacked by ransomware, and the number is increasing year-on-year (Sophos, 2022). In another survey with more than 3600 participants (IT and security professionals) around the globe, it was reported that about 51% had sustained a data breach in the last 12 months (IBM, 2021). Hence, organizations and data owners might need to invest in their information management and enhance their knowledge about data governance for streamlined processes without unnecessary risk exposure. Many people fear the accessibility of data in the cloud and the loss of control. So far, we must remember that we must take care of all components, gateways, devices, and programs in our own infrastructure but also consider the ecosystem partners (TPP). It can be argued that, in particular, small and mid-size companies might have fewer resources to implement and maintain security mechanisms than specialized providers, but it also depends on the appropriate system architecture. The concept of zero-trust (ZT) is a widely discussed topic, and many companies make this concept part of their defence and security strategies. Researchers at the US National Institute of Standards and Technology (NIST) defined zero-trust as an evolving set of cybersecurity and privacy paradigms that move defences and security mechanisms from static, network-based perimeters to focus on users, assets, and resources (Rose et al., 2020). This means it includes various elements to verify valid access attempts in the verification process. Accordingly, it requires a different design and architecture of the application or service. The fundamental principles of zero-trust authentication build on various elements, including user/ location, device, and application/service authentication. Zero Trust Architecture (ZTA) generally builds on Zero Trust principles to plan industrial and enterprise infrastructure and workflows (Rose et al., 2020). Some consider it the next generation of cybersecurity and describe a paradigm shift from perimeter to Zero Trust designs (DelBene et al., 2019). The demand for products that support Zero Trust designs. is on the rise. Research firm

Markets and Markets projects that the global Zero Trust security market will grow from $19.6 billion in 2020 to $51.6 billion by 2026. In this chapter, we will introduce the various elements of zero-trust and will discuss the practical implementation in a bank or financial services organization.

12.2 History of Zero Trust

The term Zero Trust is fairly new. However, the underlying concept was already in place before the term was coined. The enterprise strategy called "black core" developed by the Defense Information Systems Agency (DISA) and the Department of Defense (DoD) can be seen as predecessor paving the way. Black core involved a paradigm shift from a perimeter-based security approach to a model that emphasises the security of individual transactions (Department of Defense CIO, 2007). The concept of deperimeterisation was developed and improved into the broader concept of Zero Trust, which was later coined by John Kindervag (2010; Cunningham, 2018). Zero Trust then became the term for various cybersecurity solutions where security no longer relies on implicit trust based on network location, but focuses on assessing trust on a transactional basis for every request.

While Zero Trust was initially championed by government agencies and there is still a strong push, especially in the US administration towards ZTA (Biden, 2021). Still, meanwhile many private companies also start to adopt Zero Trust strategies in their products. Solutions such as Centrify, iWelcome, Microsoft (Office 365), Okta, and Ping Identity just to name a few examples of those technology enablers have solutions that could be considered as Zero Trust architectures (Cunningham, 2018). The adoption of Zero Trust gained momentum in 2019. Only 16% of organizations surveyed by Okta stated four years prior that they either had a Zero Trust initiative in place or would have one in place in the coming 12–18 months. In 2022 that number was already 97% (Okta, 2022).

12.3 Key Elements of Zero Trust

The zero-trust concept builds on various elements that are considered to verify valid access attempts. Unlike walled-garden systems that classify all requests from a specific origin as authorized, the zero-trust concept is based on the idea that every request must be verified.

According to He et al (2022) ZTA is built on the following five basic assumptions:

1. The network is in a dangerous environment all the time.
2. There are external or internal threats in the network from beginning to end.
3. The location of the network is not enough to determine the credibility of the network.

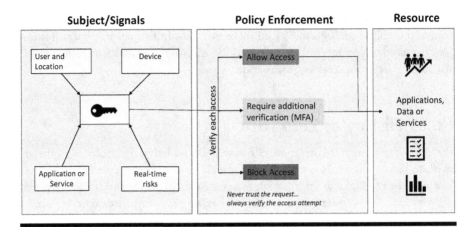

Figure 12.1 Schematic overview of Zero Trust Architecture.

4. All devices, users, and network traffic should be authenticated and authorized.
5. Security policies must be dynamic and calculated based on as many data sources as possible (p. 2).

Banks and FinTech companies have very high requirements regarding security. In fact, they "sit on a goldmine of sensitive data: corporate financial data, customer data, credit card data, and more. Digital innovations, complex IT processes, accelerated cloud adoption, remote workforces, and a growing reliance on third-party vendors contribute to a challenging risk landscape in banking and financial services" (Mahendru, 2023). This has implications for the system design and architecture of the application or service. ZTA requires and supports strong authentication methods and includes multi-factor authentication (MFA). An access control engine or policy decision point is responsible for policy enforcement (PE). It allows access, might require additional verification or can block access to the requested resource (application, data or service). All communications are encrypted.

12.3.1 User and Location

User authentication can be an important pillar of ZTA. A comprehensive user database with specific access rights would be a prerequisite. The authentication can include multiple factors and different types of users may need different handling (for example, business users, clients and partners, IT users, or technical accounts). There are, for example, many proposals for biometric authentication that can be used to verify the authenticity of users due to their distinctiveness and the use of human physiological characteristics for identity authentication. It is already a common practice to use sensors and apps in smartphones to collect fingerprint data or face recognition for identity authentication, but this method only applies to some series of mobile phones and is not very comprehensive. The security of one-factor authentication is weak. Henderson (2019) proposed multi-factor authentication that combines factors such as a fingerprint sensor and an LED pulse oximeter, aiming to optimise the shortcomings of a single fingerprint scan. Abuhamad et al. (2020) in their research utilised sensors in smartphones to capture user behaviours such as jogging and exercising while holding a smartphone, and combined this with contextual information such as text messages, voice and video chats for authentication. The method does not require sensitive software or hardware permissions that could compromise the user's privacy. It requires a good understanding of the business case and the ecosystem (social and technological) to design appropriate policies. Additional, geolocation might be considered to ensure that the access is needed and legal. In general, it should be the aim to restrict user access to only the resources that are necessary for a given role or task (least privilege access principle).

12.3.2   Device

"Authenticating and authorizing the device is just as important as doing so for the user/application. This is a feature rarely seen in services and resources protected by perimeter networks" (Gilman & Barth, 2017, p. 39). ZTA is involved heavily in managing access control to corporate resources. Hence, an important element is to identify what resources and assets the company owns, including corporate-owned and possibly BYOD devices. Creating a device inventory can help the organization to keep track of this information. The organization needs to implement mechanisms to identify devices requesting resources (Teerakanok et al., 2021).

12.3.3   Application or Service

Zero Trust Architecture (ZTA) can significantly reduce vulnerabilities and risks in networks when the organization creates application or service specific discrete, granular access rules. It can be argued that some of severe cases of security breaches could have been prevented using basic zero trust principles on the application level (DelBene et al., 2019). The access to the application or service depends on context and role of the request (for example, is the requesting application or service on a list of approved applications for this specific resource?), form of the request (for example, any unusual parameter?) and patch level (Rose et al., 2020). Depending on these factors, the policy enforcement might grant access to the resource or block it. Machine learning algorithms may be of help in optimizing the implementation of ZT policies across a complex environment (Hosney et al., 2022).

12.3.4   Real-time Risk Intelligence

Additional to signals originating from the context of the request there is also information concerning real-time risks and threat intelligence to be taken into consideration. This is specifically addressed by Security Orchestration Automated Response (SOAR) and Security Information and Event Management (SIEM) services. SIEM tools collect and log organisational cybersecurity information from your entire internal network. When something suspicious, abnormal or suspicious is detected, the SIEM service raises an alert. SOAR tools use a combination of human intelligence, artificial intelligence (AI) and machine learning (ML) to identify the most pressing risks and analyse enormous amounts of data into actionable and meaningful insights. Unlike SIEM services, SOAR services are able to respond to issues and resolve them. However, while SOAR solutions can be very advanced they are not perfect and can't entirely solve security issues (Zawalnyski, 2023). It is important to understand limitations, add additional security measures and supervise the service. Microsoft Sentinel, IBM Security SOAR, and Splunk are prominent examples of such SOAR and SIEM services (Zawalnyski, 2023; Shoard & Davies, 2022). Sometimes those provider services are used in combination, for example, with bi-directional synchronisation, for increased security and wider application (IBM SOAR, 2023).

12.3.5 Trust Algorithm

In order to access the requested resource each access needs to be verified. The trust algorithm for this verification in a ZTA is not necessarily very complex and might simply follow a few consecutive steps including identity authentication, access control, and trust assessment. A typical trust algorithm might include the following steps (Rose et al., 2020):

- *Access request:* The request for access to a resource includes information about the requester, which might include location of origin, and other information such as their operating system version, software used, and patch level.
- *Subject database:* This database contains information about the individuals or processes requesting access to resources. It includes their attributes and privileges, which form the basis for resource access policies. User identities may consist of account IDs and authentication results. Privileges should be assigned to individuals based on their specific needs, rather than fitting into a predefined role. This information is stored in an identity management system and policy database.
- *Asset database (and observable status):* This database contains information about the status of enterprise-owned assets, both physical and virtual. It includes details such as the operating system version, software present, integrity, location, and patch level. Access to assets may be restricted or denied based on a comparison of the asset's status with the information in this database.
- *Resource requirements:* These policies complement the user ID and attributes database and define the minimum requirements for accessing a resource. Requirements may include authentication assurance levels, network location restrictions, data sensitivity, and asset configuration requests. These requirements are developed by both data custodians and those responsible for the relevant business processes.

▪ *Risk intelligence:* This refers to information about general threats and active malware found on the internet. It can include specific details about suspicious communication from devices, such as queries for potential malware command and control nodes. Threat intelligence can come from external services or internal scans and discoveries, providing attack signatures and mitigation strategies.

The importance of each data source can be determined by a proprietary algorithm or configured by the enterprise. These weight values reflect the significance of the data source to the enterprise. Depending on these factors and the security posture of the asset, access may be restricted or denied. The signals and their weighting in the trust algorithm needs to be monitored and regularly adjusted if needed. The various signals are not equally important; some information, such as user credentials, might be more important and weighted higher, comparing to other factors such as network traffic, in determining the trust level of a subject. At the moment, "there is no optimal solution, guideline, or reliable approach in weighting such factors; the enterprise implementing ZTA needs to continuously observe and adjust these parameters over time to ensure it functions accurately as intended" (Teerakanok et al., 2021, p. 7).

The final determination is then passed to the Policy Administration (PA) for execution. The PA's role is to configure the necessary Policy Enforcement Points (PEPs) to enable authorized communication. Depending on the Zero Trust Architecture (ZTA) deployment, this may involve sending authentication results and connection configuration information to gateways, agents, or resource portals. The PA can also temporarily pause a communication session for reauthentication and reauthorization according to policy requirements. Additionally, the PA is responsible for issuing commands to terminate connections based on policy, such as after a time-out, completion of a workflow, or due to a security alert.

It is a best practice that develop a ZTA trust algorithm contextually, but this may not always be possible with the infrastructure components available in the ecosystem. A contextual TA can help to mitigate threats where an unauthorized access simulates requests close to a "normal" set of access requests for a specific element or insider attacks. Still, it is important to balance security, usability, and cost-effectiveness when designing and implementing trust algorithms. Continually prompting an element for reauthentication against behaviour that is consistent with historical trends and norms for their regular function and role within the system might cause usability issues (Rose et al., 2020).

12.3.6 How to Design Zero Trust Ecosystems

The design of Zero Trust ecosystems requires some preparation. It is necessary to identify all the protected resources and needed access rights based on the least privilege access principle. It might be helpful to map the transaction flows (Campbell,

2020). Building the zero trust architecture is the core of the implementation task. Most companies leverage the experience of established players in the Zero Trust industry to build their own ZTA on a specific industry solution (for example, Forrester's NGFW/ZTX, Google BeyondCorp, Palo Alto Networks Prisma Access, Deloitte Zero Trust Access, VMware's NSX, or Zscaler Private Access) and use the features provided as a starting point for the integration. In any case the organization needs to create a zero trust policy. Once the ZTA is established it is important to monitor it closely and adjust the policy with the latest information and experience from the environment. An article published by Deloitte recommended five actions to increase cyber resilience and enhance cybersecurity in financial services (Rafla et al., 2022).

1. Implement network segmentation to reduce the spread of potential attacks (for example, production versus nonproduction and micro segmentation, application ringfencing).
2. Limit privileges to the needed minimum and enforce dynamic access control.
3. Establish all needed security controls as foundational elements in cloud environments before migrating operations to the environment.
4. Business expansion or consolidation can introduce complexity during the integration or divestiture process. Advanced technology including software-defined perimeter management or secure access service edge can be leveraged to enable secure ZTA for the ecosystem while maintaining consistent and broad cybersecurity controls.
5. Improve data inventory, classification and governance structures. It is essential to understand where data is located, its relevance, and which individual and service should have access to. This supports not only compliance with data sovereignty but is also relevant for adherence to privacy laws and management of the overall data risk position.

While all of these actions seem not very complicated it can be quite challenging to implement and follow them stringently in a fairly complex and distributed production environment such as an Open Banking ecosystem. The existence of legacy systems, unclear and concurrent data streams might cause significant challenges in the design and maintenance of such ecosystems. Developing a ZTA can be demanding and might require significant changes to the security architecture. However, there are different guidelines available that can be helpful in this context. The NIST National Cybersecurity Center of Excellence and its collaborators, for example, the developed Cybersecurity Practice Guide will help users develop a plan for migrating to ZTA. It demonstrates a standards-based reference design for implementing a ZTA and describes approaches to how to incorporate available technology to build interoperable, open, standards-based zero trust architecture and implementations that follow the concepts and principles (Kerman et al., 2022). It is important to remove implicit trust from all requests and related subjects. All devices located no matter whether they are inside or outside the corporate network are treated the same as devices connected from an external network (Teerakanok et al., 2021).

The design and implementation of ZTA is a demanding task and not without challenges. A fragmented approach to zero-trust can create security gaps. Which can be a big issue as it might be difficult to migrate all systems and processes at the same time. It should also be noted that all-in-one zero-trust products don't exist and it is important to develop an ecosystem that suits business needs. Especially, legacy systems in the financial industry may not adapt to zero trust. Zero trust requires ongoing administration, and maintenance. Zero Trust also might cause productivity issues, in particular, during the setup and initial phases of the environment. And lastly, zero trust isn't without security risks (Shea & Turpitka, 2022). Hence, the project team requires beside technical expertise, risk experts, legal advice, business analysis and attention from senior management.

12.4 What's Next? Looking Beyond Zero Trust

Zero Trust can be an important step towards increased security in complex technological ecosystems such as those typically in place in Open Banking and Embedded Finance business cases. Still, it can't solve all security issues and the development progresses fast, both on the side of the attackers and in the quest for appropriate security solutions.

Some companies enhance Zero Trust solutions with proprietary enhancements. Google, for example, also included in its BeyondCorp architecture a reverse proxy to hide the service details from the subject (Google, 2020). When a subject makes a service request, the reverse proxy encrypts the traffic before it checks device and user context. Only when all checks are passed does it route the proxy request to the application or service, thus leaving the subject blind to any characteristics of the system internals. Unlike a traditional network tunnel, BeyondCorp's reverse proxy solution does not require the requestor to install or configure anything, making it very easy to migrate or onboard with this solution (Campbell, 2020).

Another example for the evolution of Zero Trust is the Zero Trust eXtended (ZTX) framework. Forrester launched ZTX in 2018. While essentially keeping its original Zero Trust roots, ZTX introduces a new control-mapping framework that extends Zero Trust to an ecosystem with seven main pillars: data, networks, people, workloads, devices, visibility and analytics, and automation and orchestration (Turner & Cunningham, 2021; Campbell, 2020). This extended framework now gives organizations alternative ways in which they can achieve Zero Trust based on their business case and risk-mitigation agendas. Access management can be redefined and it can enable new business models. The extension of Forrester's Zero Trust strategy aims to be more prescriptive and more open to technologies that help to drive strategic goals. It is the idea that nothing in this new framework should be without a direct correlation with a successful Zero Trust process. Every organization could leverage this evolution and use quantifiable measures of its own criteria for any strategic plans or vendor integrations in the plan to improve its business ecosystems (Cunningham, 2018).

It seems very likely that the rapid development of API-based ecosystems in the financial services industry would benefit from further development of industry-specific solutions with predefined interactions with the most important vendors and ecosystem partners.

12.5   Summary and Conclusion

Zero Trust is an interesting concept that can help banks and FinTech companies to enhance cybersecurity in Banks and FinTech organizations. The credo 'Trust No One. Verify Everything' does not only apply to cryptocurrencies but can also be followed in system design and ecosystem development. Still, it is clear that it is not a panacea to prevent all kinds of cyber fraud and security breaches. However, if designed and implemented correctly, it can be an essential pillar in the security concept of an organization and empower secure real-time interaction within an API-based ecosystem for financial information and transactions. SOAR and SIEM providers provide external risk information to be included in the security policies. The design and setup of a ZTA environment requires diverse teams and support from management. It might be a piece of good advice to start small, scale slowly and keep people and Zero Trust in mind (Shea & Turpitka, 2022). Improving a data inventory and establishing appropriate organizational structures to follow up on policy changes is crucial for the long-term success of a strategy built on Zero Trust. Security in an ecosystem is a job that requires knowledge and ongoing improvement. Interaction with partners (TPPs, clients, vendors) is also very important, not only during the setup but also after the launch during the ongoing operations (run the bank).

While Zero Trust is a technical concept, its implications go far beyond network teams or the IT department. It has profound implications for the design of digital ecosystems from a business perspective. It appears that the banking industry is only beginning to understand the benefits of this technology for use in cases of API-based ecosystems such as Open Banking and Embedded Finance. The paradigm shift needs to be embraced and the transition carefully orchestrated. Roles, access rights and data inventories need to be redesigned. This can be a fairly demanding management task.

Overall Zero Trust can play a valuable part in a security strategy in digital ecosystems. However, it needs to be managed carefully and embedded in a more comprehensive strategy. It is not possible to reduce risks to "zero". Managing complex digital infrastructure requires knowledge about the underlying mechanisms and policies. ZTA needs to be monitored and regularly adjusted if needed to achieve the best value and risk reduction for the business.

References

Abuhamad, M., Abuhmed, T., Mohaisen, D., & Nyang, D. (2020). AUTo Sen: Deep-Learning-Based Implicit Continuous Authentication Using Smartphone Sensors. *IEEE Internet of Things Journal, 7*(6), 5008–5020.

Biden, J. R. (2021, May 12). *Executive Order on Improving the Nation's Cybersecurity.* The White House. www.whitehouse.gov/briefing-room/presidential-actions/2021/05/12/executive-order-on-improving-the-nations-cybersecurity/

Bugvi, J. A., & Endress, T. (2023). Making Finance Invisible: Embedded Finance Adoption and User Experience. *Proceedings of the AIT SOM Doctoral Colloquium 2023*, 42–53.

Campbell, M. (2020). Beyond Zero Trust: Trust Is a Vulnerability. *Computer, 53*(10), 110–113.

Cunningham, C. (2018, March 27). Next-Generation Access and Zero Trust. *Forrester.* www.forrester.com/blogs/next-generation-access-and-zero-trust/.

DelBene, K., Medin, M., & Murray, R. (2019). *The Road to Zero Trust (Security)* [White Paper].

Department of Defense CIO. (2007). *Department of Defense Global Information Grid Architectural Vision Vision for a Net-Centric, Service-Oriented DoD Enterprise.* www.acqnotes.com/Attachments/DoD%20GIG%20Architectural%20Vision,%20June%2007.pdf.

Gilman, E., & Barth, D. (2017). *Zero Trust Networks: Building Secure Systems in Untrusted Networks.* O'Reilly.

Google. (2020, September 15). *BeyondCorp Zero Trust Enterprise Security.* Google Cloud. https://cloud.google.com/beyondcorp.

He, Y., Huang, D., Chen, L., Ni, Y., & Ma, X. (2022). A Survey on Zero Trust Architecture: Challenges and Future Trends. *Wireless Communications and Mobile Computing, 2022*, 1–13.

Henderson, L. (2019). *Multi-Factor Authentication Fingerprinting Device Using Biometrics* [Villanova University]. http://fog.misty.com/perry/FP/LH_ECE_5991_report.pdf.

Hosney, E. S., Halim, I. T. A., & Yousef, A. H. (2022). An Artificial Intelligence Approach for Deploying Zero Trust Architecture (ZTA). *2022 5th International Conference on Computing and Informatics (ICCI)*, 343–350.

IBM. (2021, November 16). *Cyber Resilient Organization Study 2021.* IBM. www.ibm.com/resources/guides/cyber-resilient-organization-study/.

IBM SOAR. (2023, May 1). *IBM Security App Exchange—Microsoft Azure Sentinel for IBM SOAR.* https://exchange.xforce.ibmcloud.com/hub/extension/exchange.xforce.ibmcloud.com/hub/extension/9b0cf8a90909e8f79e35de1b2062f839.

Kerman, A., Souppaya, M., Scarfone, K., Symington, S., & Barker, W. (2022). *Implementing a Zero Trust Architecture, Volume E: Risk and Compliance Management* (Special Publication 1800-35E). NIST National Cybersecurity Center of Excellence. www.nccoe.nist.gov/projects/implementing-zero-trust-architecture.

Kindervag, J. (2010). *Build Security Into Your Network's DNA: The Zero Trust Network Architecture.* Forrester Research. www.virtualstarmedia.com/downloads/Forrester_zero_trust_DNA.pdf.

Mahendru, P. (2023, January 3). Zero trust network access in banking and financial services. *Sophos News*. https://news.sophos.com/en-us/2023/01/03/zero-trust-network-access-in-banking-and-financial-services/.

Müller, J. M., Veile, J. W., & Voigt, K.-I. (2020). Prerequisites and incentives for digital information sharing in Industry 4.0–An international comparison across data types. *Computers & Industrial Engineering, 148*, 106733.

Okta. (2022). *The State of Zero Trust Security 2022: Assessing identity and access management maturity in global organizations* [Whitepaper]. www.okta.com/sites/default/files/2022-09/OKta_WhitePaper_ZeroTrust_H2_Campaign_.pdf..

Rafla, A., Norton, K., & Nicholson, M. (2022). *Zero Trust for Financial Services*. Deloitte United States. www2.deloitte.com/us/en/pages/advisory/articles/zero-trust-for-financial-services.html.

Rose, S., Borchert, O., Mitchell, S., & Connelly, S. (2020). *Zero Trust Architecture*. National Institute of Standards and Technology.

Ryan, P., & Falvey, S. (2012). Trust in the clouds. *Computer Law & Security Review, 28*(5), 513–521.

Schneider, M. (2023). Open Banking and Digital Ecosystems. In T. Endress, *Digital Project Practice for New Work and Industry 4.0* (1st ed., pp. 169–179). Auerbach Publications.

Shea, S., & Turpitka, D. (2022, October). *Top 6 challenges of a zero-trust security model | TechTarget*. TechTarget Security. www.techtarget.com/searchsecurity/tip/Top-risks-of-deploying-zero-trust-cybersecurity-model.

Shoard, P., & Davies, A. (2022). *Magic Quadrant for Security Information and Event Management* [Gartner Reprint]. www.gartner.com/doc/reprints?id=1-2BDGWSVV&ct=221011&st=sb.

Sophos. (2022). *The State of Ransomware in Financial Services 2022* [White Paper]. www.sophos.com/en-us/whitepaper/state-of-ransomware-in-financial-services.

Teerakanok, S., Uehara, T., & Inomata, A. (2021). Migrating to Zero Trust Architecture: Reviews and Challenges. *Security and Communication Networks, 2021*, 1–10.

Turner, S., & Cunningham, C. (2021). *Zero Trust eXtended (ZTX) Ecosystem* [Best Practice Report]. www.forrester.com/report/The-Zero-Trust-eXtended-ZTX-Ecosystem/RES137210.

Zawalnyski, A. (2023, May 24). The Top 10 SOAR Solutions. *Expert Insights*. https://expertinsights.com/insights/the-top-soar-solutions/.

Chapter 13

Sustainable Development Goals as Unintended Consequences of Digital Transformation Strategies: Case of Siam Commercial Bank

Sundar Venkatesh and Nguyen Quynh Phuong

Chapter Overview

This chapter explores the implications of digital transformation in the banking sector, focusing on its impact on business strategies, cost reduction, revenue generation, and the unintended yet significant contribution to Sustainable Development Goals (SDGs). Using the case study of Siam Commercial Bank (SCB) in Thailand, we highlight how digital transformation, driven by clear business objectives, leads to reduced costs, increased revenues, and the emergence of new business models. The successful implementation of digitalization demonstrates that what benefits business can also benefit society, showcasing the potential for digital transformation to serve both commercial interests and the achievement of SDGs.

DOI: 10.1201/9781003395560-13

13.1   Introduction

Digital Transformation is being pursued by large incumbent commercial banks. Ambitious transformational goals backed by large-sized investments have seen many banks redefine their business models. Branch and deposit/lending-driven strategies give way to mobile and customer acquisition strategies. There has been a decline in the number of bank branches in countries such as Thailand, even as the number of individuals with bank accounts has sharply increased. We share a case study of SCB, one of Thailand's leading banks, to demonstrate that provision of financial services through digitally transformed banks has positive externalities through easier operations and increased access for account holders. Digital transformation has the potential to enable banks to address opportunities at the "bottom of the pyramid" while creating a "level playing field" by making access to financial services more ubiquitous and thereby catalyzing the achievement of related SDGs.

13.2   SCB

Established in 1906 as Thailand's first indigenous bank, SCB's major shareholders at the end of 2020 were His Majesty King Maha Vajiralongkorn Phra Vajiraklaochaoyuhua (23.35%) and Vayupak Fund 1, established by the country's Ministry of Finance, (23.10%). With assets of over 3200 billion Thai Baht (1 USD = 30 Thai Baht, approximately), SCB was one of the top four banks in the country.

The bank's net profits declined from 2016 to 2019. Part of the reason for the decline was the increase in operating expenses. At the analyst meeting, the bank's management had explained that investments in digital transformation, many of which were classified as operating expenses for financial reporting purposes, were largely responsible for the increase in operating expenses. Growth in Net Interest Income and Non-Interest income were modest.

SCB's revenues came from three business segments: Corporate, SME and Retail and Wealth. The Retail and Wealth segment was a dominant contributor to the bank's revenues and was expected to remain so. As the bank's management reported to its shareholders:

> *Given the Bank's strategic direction to grow fee income from bancassurance and wealth products, the contribution from the Retail & Wealth Segment is expected to rise over time.*
>
> (Siam Commercial Bank, 2020, p.39)

Retail services included home loans, personal loans, car hire purchases, credit cards, debit cards, currency exchange facilities and overseas remittances, and investment and bancassurance products. Key subsidiaries aligned with serving the customers in the Retail and Wealth Management segment included SCB Assets, SCB Securities, SCB Julius Baer and SCB Protect. SCB Julius Baer was SCB's partnership with Switzerland's premier private bank to provide world-class wealth management services to high-net-worth customers. SCB Protect operated as an insurance brokerage, both life and non-life, to capture Thailand's underpenetrated mass insurance market. The formation of wealth management and insurance subsidiaries was part of a range of new initiatives launched by the bank to exploit benefits resulting from its large-scale digital transformation.

13.3   Launching the Digital Transformation at SCB

SCB formally launched its Digital Transformation (DT) journey in 2016. In their message to shareholders, the bank's board of directors noted

> *In the financial services industry, fundamental shifts in customer behaviour and the regulatory landscape, driven by digital technologies, are redefining the operating environment and business paradigm.*
>
> (Siam Commercial Bank, 2016, p.19)

To meet this challenge, SCB launched a multi-year transformation program to, among other things, enable a new customer experience by embracing digital technologies. The transformation journey was expected to enable the bank's progress towards its vision of being "The Most Admired Bank" for all its shareholders.

SCB identified transformation of four key foundations on which the digital transformation would be built:

1. People: This involved putting greater emphasis on capability-building and workforce management.
2. Process: The goal was to redesign and digitize the existing processes to be more *customer-centric and operationally efficient* by leveraging digital technologies such as AI and Big Data Analytics.
3. Product: The intent was to build advanced product capabilities with an agile development process and open architecture to shorten time to market, *differentiate from competitors and maximize value creation* for customers.
4. Technology: The bank aimed to develop best-in-class digital technology infrastructure as a key enabler for new capabilities, for example, a new mobile banking platform and a new payment engine (Siam Commercial Bank, 2016).

The company's management highlighted the impetus for these investments by informing investors that

> *Given the importance of this ambitious program, the Bank will be committed to allocating a significant portion of its investment plan in the next two or three years to uplift these key foundations.*
>
> (Siam Commercial Bank, 2016, p.43)

Changes in the industry that followed, such as the waiver of digital transaction fees in 2018, bore testimony to the SCB's management's prognosis about fundamental shifts in the industry. In March 2018, leading banks in Thailand waived digital transaction fees. Fees for digital transactions with other banks, money transfers across banking zones, bill payments and cash withdrawals were all dropped. Analysts estimated this move would cause a 5% decline in the banks' profits. Why did the banks drop the fees and lose a lucrative source of revenue?

News agency Reuters reported that banks were feeling the pressure from non-banking competitors. Customers were switching to alternative methods of money transfer such as government-backed money transfer service, PromptPay, startup Omise and digital wallets offered by telecom companies such as TrueMoney (Reuteurs, 2018). The fee waiver was seen as a strategy by the banks to retain customers by sacrificing a substantial transaction fee income. Clearly, the industry shifts, and consequent challenges, noted by SCB's board in 2016 were making quick forays into the financial performance of banks. These changes also highlighted the difficult tradeoffs that banks were having to make. Often, the tradeoffs involved the sacrifice of current profitability to secure long-term competitiveness.

For analysts, it was clear that, with its Digital Transformation, SCB was embarking on a major investment plan. Unlike in the case of traditional investments, such as in physical plant and machinery, the size of the investment outlay remained unclear, even though the bank's management had indicated in several public communications that it would be about 40 billion baht (Banchongduang & Paweewun, 2018).

13.4 The Strategy Underlying the Digital Transformation

Broadly, SCB planned its DT as a three-phase process. In the first phase, the bank labelled *fixing and building the foundation*; the bank would build new foundations and capabilities. In this phase, the bank would develop a digital platform, enhance the use of technologies, and build analytics capabilities. The second phase was to *transform the business model and organization*. In this phase, the bank would embark on a "bank as a platform strategy" while promoting new growth areas such as wealth management, digital lending and developing capabilities for capturing and processing big data. The final phase was to *realize value from the transformation program* through distinctive customer value propositions. Revenue enhancement and cost reduction would follow, leading to enhanced Return on Assets (ROA).

To reap long-term value from its investments in DT, SCB identified two key steps to kick-start the journey. One was to acquire new customers through or migrate existing customers to the new digital channel. The second was to stimulate digital customers to execute transactions online and keep them engaged. The bank launched several initiatives to acquire/migrate and transact/engage customers.

One of the initiatives was the development of a digital product named *I-onboarding*. By late 2018, this product had gained traction. More than 90% of individual account openings and 85% of juristic onboarding[1] were done digitally. According to the bank's estimates, individuals save more than 50% of their time by onboarding digitally compared to physical onboarding. Juristic entities saved more than 90% of their time. The longer-term plan was to use I-Onboarding as a platform for cross-selling and upselling based on insights from customer analytics. Other banks offered similar products that substantially eased customer onboarding. To a large extent, the launch of I-onboarding and similar products was aided by regulatory changes that supported e-KYC. Reduced time and increased convenience of opening accounts digitally would lead to increased account openings. Knowledge of the customer through the accounts opened could lead to targeted sales through digital channels. Ease of account opening also highlighted the need for enhancing customer satisfaction. Dissatisfied customers could easily switch without even closing their existing accounts.

Another initiative was launching the bank's *SCB Easy* app, designed as the entry point for digital retail customers. In just over four years, the app was downloaded 13.1 million times (Countrymeters, 2023). An increase in financial transactions through SCB Easy was expected to increase customers' embrace of a "do-it-yourself" approach to executing financial transactions. If customers were to buy mutual funds on the digital platform, it could cut the costs of commission that the bank had traditionally paid for such sales to the staff at the branches.

SCB Mae Manee was designed to help sellers accept payments through a QR code from any mobile banking app. Within 12 months between 2017 and 2018, the bank had more than a million merchants on its Mae Manee app.

The bank launched its *SCB Business Anywhere*, a digital banking platform for its corporate customers. The forum included features that supported data visualization, cash management, and transfers and payments (Siam Commercial Bank, 2022b). Between its launch in late 2018 and the end of 2020, the platform had acquired 92 000 corporate users.

With these initiatives, the share of digital transactions in total transactions showed impressive growth. For example, by the end of 2020, SCB reported 3.05 billion (2017: 91 million) transactions annually, with 77% (2017:32%) being digital.

Alongside the digital migration, SCB has continuously reduced its branch network. Some of the frequent transactions through branches, such as payments of bills, were not only made accessible and possible through the digital platform but were also no longer possible at the branches. The number of branches had reduced from

1170 in 2016 to 854 by the end of 2020. In its presentation to analysts in January 2021, the bank declared

> *Along with digital migration, we have continuously reduced branch network.*
> (Siam Commercial Bank, 2021, p.36)

Success was no longer measured by the number of footfalls at branches. SCB's Chief executive and president, Arthid Nanthawithaya, noted that mobile banking services had 40–50% lower operating costs than branch services (Banchongduang & Paweewun, 2018).[2] An increase in digital transactions and a reduction in the number of branches were expected to reduce the cost-to-income ratio and enhance the bank's ROA.

Impressive as the customer acquisition and engagement data were, analysts knew that these were sufficient conditions for a profitable Digital Transformation strategy. For example, an increase in the number of monthly transactions and an increase in the share of digital transactions could conceivably result from lower transaction costs. But did a rise in digital transactions lead to increased revenues and improved bottom lines? The bank's analysis indicated that digital users generated higher revenues, held products over more extended periods, and had higher average credit card spending. Though these associations were evident, it was unclear whether there was a causal relationship between a customer being active on the digital channel and positive financial outcomes for the bank. It could well be that the causality moved in the opposite direction, namely, those who spent more on credit cards were also more likely to go digital with their banking.

13.5 Digital Platform

Addressing analysts at SCB's analyst conference on October 25, 2018, Thien-Ngern, the bank's Chief Digital Transformation officer, drew parallels between banks and telecom companies. "Everyone uses mobile phones, but the margins have moved from the service provider to the application provider", he noted (SCBx, 2018). With companies like Google, Grab, Alibaba, and Gojek launching their lending business, margins were likely to shift from banks to these companies. These companies will use banks, of course, but as a dumping ground(?). The only way out for banks from becoming a low-margin, commodity type of company servicing the types of Google would be to position themselves as a platform. "Our differentiation will be our positioning of Bank as a Platform", Thien-Ngern, concluded.

Elaborating on the Bank as a Platform idea, Dr. Arak Sutivong, the bank's Chief Strategy office and Chief Financial officer in 2019, said at the analyst conference in January of that year that SCB saw itself as an ecosystem (SCBx, 2019).

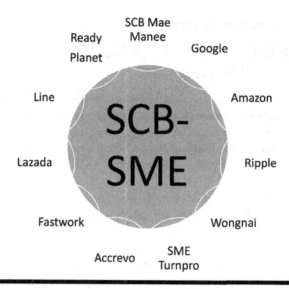

Figure 13.1   The SCB-SME ecosystem adapted from SME Customers in Siam Commercial Bank (2019a).

SCB's SME Ecosystem illustrated what management meant by a bank as a platform. Figure 13.1 provides a pictorial of the SME ecosystem. SCB intended to be part of its SME customers' activities whether they are transacting as business owners or consumers.

"Because banks are payment platforms and lending platforms, we are welcome across all verticals", noted Sutivong (SCBx, 2019). One example of how SCB, as a lender, could embed itself in a vertical was its partnership with Lazada.

Lazada is a leading e-commerce company in Southeast Asia. It is majority owned by China's Alibaba (Business Wire, 2016). It is one of the partners featured in SCB's SME ecosystem. SCB partnered with Lazada to create an SME digital lending platform to serve Lazada's sellers. This project leverages Artificial Intelligence (AI) technology powered by SCB Abacus, a subsidiary of SCB, to enable instant credit approval (Siam Commercial Bank, 2018). Clearly, this partnership had the potential to open new markets for SCB at a meager cost of customer acquisition. Customers were likely to be attracted by the convenience and speed of service. Processing times were expected to be reduced to 15 minutes from 3 to 7 days that it currently took for SME loans.

Attractive as the partnership was for creating new revenue streams for SCB, it was unclear whether Lazada would partner exclusively with SCB or open its platform to other banks, including direct competitors to SCB. It was also likely that Lazada would enter the SME lending market on its own, given its Alibaba parentage and consequent association with Ant Financials.

13.6 Sustainable Finance

13.6.1 SDGs Achieved Through Improved Access to Financial Services

A widely accepted definition of sustainable finance is "the process of taking **environmental, social and governance (ESG) considerations** into account when making investment decisions in the financial sector, leading to more long-term investments in sustainable economic activities and projects"(European Commission, n.d.). Target 10 of Sustainable Development Goal 8 aims to

> *Strengthen the capacity of domestic financial institutions to encourage and expand access to banking, insurance and financial services for all.*
> (United Nations, n.d.)

Though SCB's strategy for digital transformation did not specifically address issues of sustainable finance and sustainable development goals, we find that the sustainability element resulted, perhaps as an unintended consequence, of the bank's digital transformation strategy. We identify three areas where we find this sustainability outcome because of the bank's digital transformation strategy.

One was the change from branch-based banking to mobile banking. From a peak of 1210 branches in 2015, the number of branches reduced to 854 in 2020 as it drove its digital transformation strategy on the back of mobile banking. Branches had high-cost operations. They were replicating much of the work that could be done through mobile banking. Footfalls at the branches were seeing a decline. More of the transactions were being done digitally. Between 2018 and 2021, as the bank's digital transformation strategy gathered momentum, transactions increased from 1.5 billion to 4.6 billion per year. The share of digital increased over the same period from 47% to 85% (Siam Commercial Bank, 2022a). There was also a branch rationalization at work. Alongside the reduction in number of branches, branch sizes shrunk. Full-service branches gave way to, what was called box branches or express branches. At these branches, machines were provided that handled typical transactions. The number of staff at these branches was reduced to a minimum.

The staff work was limited to guiding customers on how to use the machines. But the digital transformation strategy also saw how SCB improved the ease of opening bank accounts and transacting on mobiles. Their award-winning apps, SCB Easy and Biz Anywhere, ensured that people could open an account without coming to a branch. Account opening could be done quickly and efficiently, sometimes in less than 15 minutes. The penetration of mobile phones in Thailand, at nearly 80% in 2022, ensured that most people could easily open a bank account (Statista, 2023). Of course, this was not seen only in the case of SCB; other banks in Thailand also followed the same route to customer acquisition. At the core of the digital transformation strategy of all commercial banks was the race to acquire more customers. In the process, financial inclusion was improved because it became a positive externality. As the banks aimed to onboard more customers as part of the digital transformation strategy, the number of accounts opened also increased substantially. Banks were acquiring more customers to monetize them in future by selling financial and other services. This drive also achieved the social purpose of providing access to financial services to many, notwithstanding the fact the articulated strategy of the bank's digital transformation did not explicitly include such a goal.

A second interesting feature related to the above discussion of SCB's digital transformation strategy was to tap into business at the "bottom of the pyramid" (Prahalad et al., 2012). Typically, commercial banks have not effectively addressed the lower end of the market. In a typical commercial bank, the task of acquiring customers at the bottom of the pyramid is high. Those with the means to make small deposits or with small borrowing needs were not seen as economically viable. The task of officers going out into the field and acquiring these customers far exceeded the potential benefits to the bank. Digital transformation made the acquisition of such customers less costly to the bank. Lending to such customers was riskier without reliable financial data, a characteristic customer in this segment. Evaluating the credit risks of lending to customers at the bottom of the pyramid became more accessible with the data acquisition and analytic capabilities developed through the Digital Transformation strategy. Using the social media posts of its potential customers in this segment or their selling habits through online platforms such as Lazada, the bank was able to analyze its customer profile and understand the credit risk better. In its presentation to analysts, the bank bullet points this opportunity:

- *AI-based lending with instant approval and gamification features*
- *Expansion into new, underserved segments*
- *Incorporation of big data into underwriting, risk* (Siam Commercial Bank, 2022a).

Yield on these loans was typically higher because customers were considered high-risk and, therefore, were willing to pay a higher rate. SCB's reorientation towards the bottom of the pyramid meant that its new businesses, like food delivery brand Robin Hood, were promoted to support this aspect of its Digital Transformation strategy. SCB claims,

> There are fees for using the platform or GP. But for Robinhood, there is no GP fee. Helping to increase sales opportunities. Solve the problem that cannot be sold on online platforms due to the high cost. In addition, merchants receive payments within an hour, resulting in a cash flow to expand the business.
>
> (Siam Commercial Bank, n.d.)

Sellers on Robinhood became account holders of SCB. SCB could see the sales and cash flow data of these SMEs. As a result, a new kind of customer base was generated for the bank. At the same time, the purpose of financial inclusion was also served very well. Many of these small businesses have typically been starved for access to organized financing. The literature shows these small businesses depend on informal finance from lenders who charge usurious rates; and often find themselves in financial ruin after borrowing at exorbitant rates (Gill & Singh, 2006). Access to commercial lending from large bank meant that these businesses now had a chance to grow their business profitably. Financial inclusion became a reality since these small businesses could now access finance at rates proportional to the risks they posed and not at phenomenally high rates and backbreaking. Digital transformation, on the one hand, opened an interesting market for SCB. On the other, it also served the purpose of widening financial inclusion by making affordable loan products and deposits available to small and medium enterprises and other customers at "the bottom of the pyramid".

A third element that we noted was using strategic Digital Partnerships as part of SCB's DT strategy. SCB used Digital partnerships to extend the reach of its financial services, entering partnerships such as those with convenience stores 7–11. Even as the number of branches was reduced in SCB, and customer onboarding was increasingly being done digitally, many customers, especially in the rural markets, transacted for business and personal needs in cash. They needed to have a service through which they could deposit some money, withdraw cash in a bank, and do it safely and reliably. The digital partnership with 7–11 provides a classic example of an initiative through a digital transformation that expands financial services' reach to remote areas at a very low cost. 7–11 had nearly 10 000 plus branches spread all over the country, and this was a far larger network of outlets than SCB had ever operated. In one stroke, SCB provided access to its essential financial services through the vast network of 7–11 outlets, increasing its customer base. On the other hand, it helped contribute to the sustainable development goal of making finance available to all.

> *SCB's strategy places importance on digital technology development allowing the bank to develop platform banking along with strong banking partnerships to create a multi-dimensional digital ecosystem. Teaming up with strong and leading platforms, partners, and key players in each sector is the key to developing new capabilities to prepare for growth in the current business world, enabling us to achieve our goal of delivering the best things to our customers and to grow steadily together with them, the then SCB Chief Executive Officer Arthid Nanthawithaya.*
>
> (Siam Commercial Bank, 2019b)

13.7 Conclusion

In conclusion, we would like to highlight in this chapter that digital transformation is often undertaken with clear business strategies in mind, and these business strategies revolve around two objectives reducing costs and increasing revenues through new business models and opening additional revenue streams. But in some ways, these digital transformation strategies contribute to SDGs, possibly as an unintended consequence. We say unintended because there was no articulation of these social consequences when SCB presented its digital transformation strategy to its investors. It turns out that when done well, digital transformation serves the bank's business interests and contributes to achieving SDGs, mainly target 10 of goal #8. The SCB case clearly shows that what is good for business can be good for society, even if it is not by design. It is expected that as banks, not only in Thailand but elsewhere in the world of emerging markets, invest heavily in digital transformation, they are going to see opportunities at "the bottom of the pyramid", and this, in turn, will lead to allowing economically weaker customers access to financial services at commercially viable rates. Exploitation is avoided, as might be the case when customers obtain these services at the bottom of the pyramid through the informal sector. Digital transformation can potentially connect large-scale traditional commercial banks and financial services companies to customers at the bottom of the pyramid, benefiting both sides. On the one hand, is access to fair price finance for the customers and on the other is access to new blue ocean markets for the commercial banks.

Notes

1 Juristic account opening refers to account opening by legal entities such as companies and partnerships.
2 Bangkok Post, "SCB's Digital Transformation take shape", 31 August, 2018.

References

Banchongduang, S., & Paweewun, O. (2018, August 31). *SCB's digital transformation takes shape Bangkok Post Learning*. Bangkok Post. www.bangkokpost.com/learning/easy/1531582/scbs-digital-transformation-takes-shape.
Business Wire. (2016, April 12). *Alibaba Acquires Controlling Stake in eCommerce Platform Lazada*. www.businesswire.com/news/home/20160411006370/en/Alibaba-Acquires-Controlling-Stake-in-eCommerce-Platform-Lazada%20on%20February%209.
Countrymeters. (2023). *Thailand population*. Countrymeters. https://countrymeters.info/en/Thailand.
European Commission. (n.d.). *Overview of sustainable finance*. Retrieved June 18, 2023, from https://finance.ec.europa.eu/sustainable-finance/overview-sustainable-finance_en#what.
Gill, A., & Singh, L. (2006). Farmers' Suicides and Response of Public Policy: Evidence, Diagnosis and Alternatives from Punjab. *Economic and Political Weekly*, 2762–2768. https://mpra.ub.uni-muenchen.de/146/.

Prahalad, C. K., Di Benedetto, A., & Nakata, C. (2012). Bottom of the pyramid as a source of breakthrough innovations. *Journal of Product Innovation Management, 29*(1), 6–12. https://doi.org/10.1111/j.1540-5885.2011.00874.x.

Reuteurs. (2018). *Thailand's top banks to waive off digital transaction fees*. Reuteurs. www.reuters.com/article/thailand-banks/thailands-top-banks-to-waive-off-digital-transaction-fees-idUSL3N1RB2VI.

SCBx. (2018). *Webcast: 9M18/3Q18 Financial Results: Analyst Meeting Presentation*. SCB X Public Company Limited. http://scb.listedcompany.com/wp.html/t/vdo/e/am3q2018.

SCBx. (2019). *Webcast: 2018 Financial Results, SCB X Public Company Limited*. SCBx. http://scb.listedcompany.com/wp.html/t/vdo/e/am4q2018.

Siam Commercial Bank. (n.d.). *5 advantages when ordering food from the Robinhood app*. Retrieved June 18, 2023, from www.scb.co.th/en/personal-banking/stories/order-food-delivery-robinhood.html.

Siam Commercial Bank. (2016). *Annual Report 2016*. www.scb.co.th/content/dam/scb/investor-relations/documents/financial-information/en/2016/annual-report/annual-report-2016.pdf.

Siam Commercial Bank. (2018, June). *Online Loans to SMEs through AI-powered platform*. www.scb.co.th/en/about-us/news/jun-2018/nws-lazada.html.

Siam Commercial Bank. (2019a). *2018 Financial Results: Analyst Meeting Presentation*. Siam Commercial Bank. www.scb.co.th/content/dam/scb/investor-relations/documents/presentation/en/Analyst presentation 4Q18_Final.pdf.

Siam Commercial Bank. (2019b). *SCB and CP ALL announce key digital financial partnership*. www.scb.co.th/en/about-us/news/mar-2019/nws-digital-financial-partnership-7-11.html.

Siam Commercial Bank. (2020). *Digital Banking Digital Culture Annual Report 2020 Form 56-1 One Report*. www.scb.co.th/content/dam/scb/investor-relations/documents/financial-information/en/2020/annual-report/2020annualreport-eng.pdf.

Siam Commercial Bank. (2021). *2020 Financial Results: Analyst Meeting Presentation*. Siam Commercial Bank. www.scb.co.th/content/dam/scb/investor-relations/documents/presentation/en/2020analyst-meeting-presentation.pdf.

Siam Commercial Bank. (2022a). *2021 Financial Results: Investor Presentation*. www.scb.co.th/content/dam/scb/investor-relations/documents/presentation/en/4q21-analyst-presentation.pdf.

Siam Commercial Bank. (2022b). *SCB Business Anywhere*. www.scb.co.th/en/corporate-banking/digital-banking-services/business-anywhere.html.

Statista. (2023). *Thailand: smartphone penetration rate 2019–2028*. Statista. www.statista.com/statistics/625455/smartphone-user-penetration-in-thailand/.

United Nations. (n.d.). *Goal 8 Promote sustained, inclusive and sustainable economic growth, full and productive employment and decent work for al*. Retrieved June 18, 2023, from https://sdgs.un.org/goals/goal8.

Chapter 14

Working With, Not Against: An Asian Cooperative Approach in Developing FinTech

Chris Lobello and Jayant B. Ramanand

Chapter Overview

FinTech, particularly as it concerns digital assets and crypto currencies, is often seen as being at odds with traditional finance, a not unsurprising view given that many of the initial promoters of cryptocurrencies saw their new tools as a means to bypass government regulations and the existing financial industry. In Asia though many FinTech and DeFi entrepreneurs are working closely with the existing structures and the regulators to leapfrog technology gaps and bring Asian finance to the fore of global digital innovation. This chapter examines the way in which the history and culture of Asian business has, in a generalized sense, led to a greater tendency for Asia-based FinTech startups to embrace local regulators and work with them as cooperative partners, an approach at odds with the aforementioned view. Firms looking to establish FinTech operations in this region, or competing with Asia-based challengers, will be well served to take note of this approach and prepare their strategy accordingly.

DOI: 10.1201/9781003395560-14

14.1 Whither Digital Innovation in Asian Finance?

At the time of this writing (the summer of 2023) the U.S. Securities and Exchange Commission (SEC) is leading a major crackdown against the cryptocurrency industry through lawsuits targeting two major FinTech firms – cryptocurrency platform Coinbase, and Binance, the world's largest cryptocurrency exchange (CoinGecko, n.d.). This effort has been very direct in its condemnation of the firms, for example, stating that Binance CEO Zhao Changpeng is leading a "web of deception" (U.S. Securities and Exchange Commission, 2023).

This recent turmoil comes after last year's cryptocurrency challenges where purportedly stable coin LUNA lost more than 99% of its value before delisting. Asian markets are well-versed in some of the challenges in pegging currencies: remembering the 1997 Asian Crisis, Korean firm Terraform Labs, the creator of LUNA, should not have been unaware that pegging to one currency while holding assets in another is a substantial risk. In the late '90s the Korean Won lost more than half of its value during an Asian crisis that was largely driven by similar asset-liability mismatches (Kim, 2006).

But the world of digital assets is much broader and will ultimately be much larger than that of cryptocurrencies alone, and the digital transformation embedded within FinTech and decentralized finance (DeFi) is continuing to grow. Asia Pacific in particular has seen strong investment growth in FinTech with record raises of US$50.5bn in 2022 and with greater funding opportunities in Asia than in North America or Europe (KPMG, 2023). Further, governments are aggressively pursuing opportunities in FinTech, both to better service their citizens and to pursue financial market strength. "Hong Kong as one example HKMA has collaborated with the Central Bank of the United Arab Emirates (CBUAE) to enhance collaboration between the financial services sectors of the two jurisdictions. Agreeing to strengthen cooperation in three major areas including financial infrastructure, financial market connectivity between the two jurisdictions and virtual asset regulations and developments" (Hong Kong Monetary Authority, 2023).

Yet the path to this dominance follows what might seem to be an unlikely route due to cultural and regulatory issues unique to Asia. To understand the growth of DeFi in Asia one must consider the benefit of technology leapfrogging, generalized aspects of Asian cultures, and importantly, how most Asian nations view the role of their regulators.

14.1.1 The Birth of Decentralized Finance

While there are a number of factors driving the growth of decentralized finance there is no doubt that one of the most critical is the development of blockchain, an electronic system of storing data in such a way that makes it extremely difficult (but not quite impossible) to change or hack. For thousands of years the financial system has existed to provide trust: trust that our silver coins are full weight and purity; trust

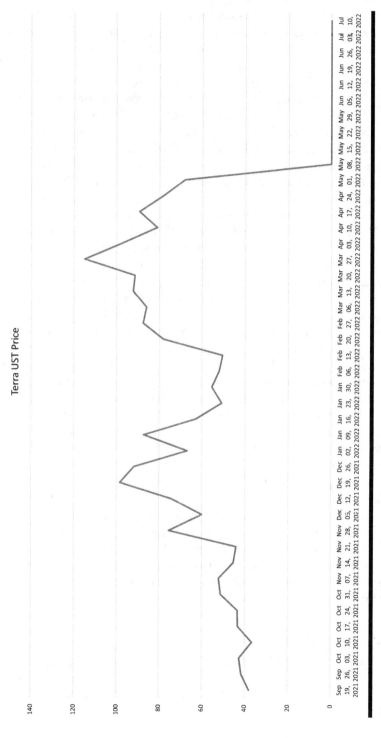

Figure 14.1 LUNA collapses after UST loses its peg to the US Dollar.

that money stored with a bank would be returned when requested; and trust that when we send money to someone far away the funds will actually be delivered. This trust is a necessary component for business to flourish and economies to grow.

But this trust comes at a not insubstantial cost as middlemen bankers have historically taken significant fees out of the funds travelling through their systems. Transaction fees that often rose to several percent of a move in assets had a significant and much greater impact on a business's margin or an individual's earning power, particularly when layered over multiple transactions. As such when the mysterious and probably apocryphal Satoshi Nakamoto developed blockchain in 2008 it was instantly seen as a disruptive agent (Ducree, 2022). Now, instead of having to pay others a substantial fee to provide and enforce trust between parties involved in a financial transaction, those self-same parties could themselves employ a blockchain solution to provide that trust and keep the fees for themselves. Sending a payment overseas? Whereas before one would pay the bank (or more likely several banks along the way) to send the funds and convert the currencies then report back to you that the payment had been made, now the two originating parties can make a peer-to-peer transaction that would be much quicker and provide complete confidence along with a perpetual, immutable record that the payment had been made and received.

Early proponents of blockchain noted that this could be taken all the way to the core of the financial system - currencies. Who needs a government to tell people that a currency holds value when people themselves can provide the strength and trust behind the money? This idea is of particular attraction to those people who are concerned about personal privacy and perceived overly-demanding government control. They see blockchain as providing a pathway to freedom. It is against this background that Bitcoin was first developed and many of the cryptocurrency's initial proponents were of this crypto-anarchist bent. The digital changes envisioned by early promoters of cryptocurrencies were not just disruptive, they were expected to be literally revolutionary.

Whether cryptocurrencies do in reality provide the anonymity (pseudonymity?) their promoters search for - the nearly, immutable and permanent nature of a blockchain record could in fact assist an inquisitive and persistent government in their enquiries - the roots of cryptocurrency adoption, and of DeFi in general, are embedded in beliefs of individual freedom and escape from government control. How is this rather North American perspective received in the Asian context, and how does that impact the opportunity for the digital transformation of Asia's financial systems?

14.1.2 *Note the Regulator*

Before examining that question, it is perhaps best to first examine one of the key constraints facing any attempt at innovation in finance - the regulator. Trust in our financial system is so critical to economic success and social stability that all governments recognize the importance of stability and faith in financial market practitioners. The days of bank runs and market panics are not completely behind us but they are at least greatly reduced and the impacts muted (Hoffner, 2022). This has been accomplished through something antithetical to the crypto-anarchists, namely a good deal of government regulation.

While proper and sensible regulation does seem to have largely stabilized the financial system in recent decades it does come at the cost of strict rules and expensive compliance procedures that combine to squash innovation. Established banks view this as jointly limiting their ability to innovate and protecting their interests by keeping newcomers away from their established business. Following the many rules of different regulators is both expensive and demanding of talent and knowledge. Over the years most financial institutions have been happy to focus on the protective benefits of regulation as contributing the most to their profitability (Claessens, 2009). After all, if innovation was more difficult overall, they did not have to worry about losing ground to others, and could instead focus on maintaining their hefty margins in the absence of strong competition. In more than two decades of working for traditional financial firms it was clear that the regulator was viewed as a barrier to competitive entry that offered specific value to the existing players. The UK's Financial Conduct Authority (FCA) looked at this issue for asset managers as one example where they found a distinct lack of competition, in particular price competition, across the industry (KB Associates, n.d.).

Remember as well that most financial institutions face a number of regulators spread across multiple countries depending on the exact nature of their services. Starting a bank or broker from scratch is already an expensive challenge. Doing so with a new and untested product that needs to be approved by multiple regulators that are naturally risk averse is an order of magnitude more difficult. This kept traditional financial firms focused on the status quo and averse to innovation and disruption. Why should any firm want to interfere with the status quo?

14.1.3   The Internet Interferes with the Status Quo

The first home banking service is generally acknowledged as being that offered by the United American Bank, a small bank headquartered in Tennessee (Sudman, 2017). Customers could ring in using a secure modem to transact basic banking services, all done via the telephone. The large banks soon followed and a remote digital banking slowly began to take shape. It took another leap ahead in 1995 when Wells Fargo replaced its former dial-in service with the first true internet banking offering (Wells Fargo, n.d.). Still, adoption was slow as at that time few people felt great comfort with internet-driven technology and the traditional system worked fine for most customers. Even now electronic banking in the United States has trailed behind much of the rest of the world. It is expected that US digital banking users will only just pass 200 million, or just over ¾ of the potential market size, this year. That is after a pandemic-related boost to adoption that saw many over-60 customers taking up internet banking for the first time as a matter of necessity amidst closed physical locations and concerns over meeting face-to-face (Insider Intelligence, 2021).

Meanwhile in Asia growth accelerated much more quickly. Indian banks for one initiated their own internet banking services just a year after the US in 1996 with ICICI the first to launch, followed soon after by HDFC Bank and Indusind Bank (Suhas & Ramesh, n.d.). China Merchants Bank launched that country's first internet payment system in 1997 with other banks soon spreading the technology across the country (Yuan, Lee, & Kim, 2011). In both of these countries as in many other Asian nations the growth was fueled by technological leapfrogging. With many consumers in Asia being underbanked or even completely outside of the banking system they were able to best meet their needs by completely leapfrogging over traditional banking services to use online banking, just as many emerging economies skipped over landline penetration and moved straight to mobile phones.

Yet until this point the service provided was only really different in the delivery mechanism. The providers were still the established, licensed banks and the product offering was an online version of what was already being done in the brick-and-mortar locations. True innovation was hampered by the regulatory limitations that kept small, innovative firms locked out of client contact while keeping the larger firms from ever wanting to change the product offering.

To better understand exactly how reticent regulators had been in accepting change it is perhaps best to look at an example from as late as 2005, when one of these writers was newly posted as the country head of CLSA, which is a financial services firm that provides equity broking, research institute, across Asia. CLSA was, at the time, the top-ranked Asian equity broker as measured by client feedback to the Greenwich polls and was regularly voted number one in Asiamoney's annual ranking of the region's brokers. CLSA was one of five international brokers awarded a full dealing license as, for the first-time foreign brokers were to be allowed to execute their own trades on Bursa Malaysia. These five foreign brokers were understandably in a rush to begin trading.

CLSA's efforts hit a bump however when it was noted that existing Malaysian regulations noted that all trade data, electronic or not, had to be entirely stored within Malaysia. This of course made sense when all the brokers were Malaysian and both paper records and electronic data were stored in local systems that needed to be available to the regulator, but was impossible for any firm trading regionally or globally as data would necessarily be stored with the centralized trading systems located in regional head offices. The bump turned into a wall when, on the first approach, the regulator said that they would not change this rule, nor amend it to a practical solution meeting everyone's needs. In meeting after meeting the officers noted the issue and recognized that shifting all global systems to Malaysia was not a serious option, but no one was willing to consider any change. Eventually it was not until this writer, CLSA's head of operations, and the group's global head of legal met with the number two person at the commission that he said, 'Well that doesn't make sense, does it?' and changes could be made. In exchange for various promises about access to any required data the regulator amended the rule.

The point here is that even when it was obvious that the old rules were untenable and inappropriate for the intended goal of introducing trading by foreign brokers the overwhelming response from several levels of leadership at the regulator was to say 'no.' This is certainly not unique to Malaysia. Regulators around the world are, understandably, known for their conservatism. Technological innovation was set to disrupt the world of finance and offer superior service and better pricing, but was being kept from the market as the need for regulatory approval made it impossible for smaller startups to introduce their products to clients and subsequently meant that the existing financial institutions saw no need to improve.

What was unique and positive for Malaysia was the fact that their regulatory system is lean enough and flexible to allow for rapid change when needed. This is, in this writer's opinion, an example of a simpler regulatory approach in that things can be done quickly, albeit in ways that might not seem obvious to those unfamiliar with the local approach. While some might describe Asia's regulatory environment as being more complex because of a lack of complete and clear rules this is really simply an issue of being more difficult for outsiders to navigate. The systems themselves are certainly leaner and more streamlined, and with an understanding as to the workings they also offer an easier environment to bring about change. Had the hard drive question been an issue in certain other markets it would have required a lengthy and challenging effort to change the rule. In Malaysia, once the correct and authorized person was approached the waiver was given to the firm by the end of the day.

14.1.4 Come Play in the Sandbox

The innately conservative approach from regulators shifted in 2016 when the UK's Financial Conduct Authority (FCA) opened the first FinTech sandbox. This was done with the stated goal of removing "unnecessary barriers to innovation" for firms delivering financial services in the UK (Financial Conduct Authority, n.d.-a). The idea was to recognize that. in any system of disruptive innovation. ideas and technologies need to be tested, yet that establishing a fully-licensed firm to engage in that testing was typically financially impossible given existing rules about capital requirements and limitations on service innovation. Therefore, startups were to be allowed to test their new offerings in a clearly defined and limited sandbox (Financial Conduct Authority, n.d.-b) with set limits and protections for clients, particularly individual consumers. This testing would take place under close monitoring by the FCA[TE17] [CL18] and with the understanding that they could stop the test at any time if they felt that either the existing systems or individual consumers were facing any risk.

For the first time the regulator had established an environment that allowed for innovation and the testing of potentially disruptive systems and technologies. Asian markets soon followed. The Monetary Authority of Singapore (MAS) released a consultation paper on its own sandbox just weeks after the FCA's effort opened, and would go on to add Sandbox Express in 2019 with a focus on even quicker acceptance and turnaround. Hong Kong opened its sandbox in the fall of 2016, India in 2019, and the aforementioned Malaysia in 2017. Across Asia many regulators were quick to adjust (Rosha, 2022) and establish sandbox environments that promoted FinTech innovation and disruption while ensuring the stability of their financial systems and the economic safety of their retail investors and banking customers.

Meanwhile in the United States the sandbox concept has lagged behind and has still not produced a single, centralized federal sandbox, primarily because the US regulatory system is much more complex with different regulators observing different aspects of the finance industry, and with regulation at both the federal and, depending on the exact business of the firm, state level–the latter meaning of course 50 different states (U.S. Government Accountability Office, 2016). No single US agency had the authority to create a broad, inclusive, state and federal level sandbox, and that includes the Federal Reserve and the Securities and Exchange Commission.

Asian governments are thus aided in their sandbox efforts by much simpler regulatory frameworks that can allow for easier sandbox development. Asian countries generally have far fewer organizations to deal with as can be expected when considering the table below showing a partial representation of the US regulatory system. Still these fewer entities in most Asian countries can sometimes be more confusing for overseas groups as there is less specificity in the rules, with a general tendency towards a more teleological approach as opposed to the deontological structure more prevalent in the West. The Asian environment gains even more benefit through another key factor–the Asian perspective on governments in general and regulators specifically.

14.1.5 The Asian Perspective

Remember that the core technological innovation at the heart of DeFi is blockchain, and that this was primarily advanced by people who do not trust the government and want less government involvement in their business. Furthermore, they tend to see any government action as interference with market forces and Adam Smith's invisible hand.

While it is a significant generalization, most Asian cultures have a more accepting and benign view of government participation in their markets. This is at least partially due to the fact that Asian business people often see their government as an important partner in making money. The history of this perspective is explored thoroughly in Joe Studwell's excellent book *Asian Godfathers* (Studwell, 2007).

Studwell looked at some of the richest families across Southeast Asia, many purporting to have built themselves up from humble beginnings through hard work and innovation. He found that in almost all cases these individuals and families owe their success to close cooperation with the government. This is especially true for the ethnic Chinese minority that plays such an important role in many Asian nations. Studwell postulates that ethnic Chinese business people were often in the unique role of being able to help the new nations (the ones in Studwell's focus had

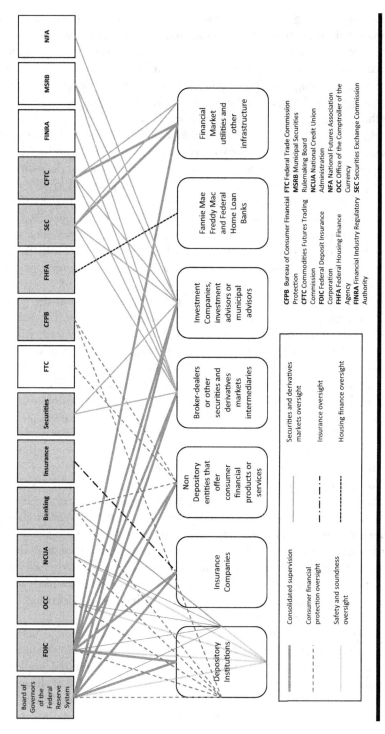

Figure 14.2 Regulatory Jurisdiction by agency and type of regulation.

left or were soon leaving colonial control) yet were not, due to their status as an ethnic minority, in any way a political threat. In this way many of these famous and wealthy people built their financial success on the back of serving as managers for cashflows they monitored for both governments and local politicians. These tycoons became experts at managing cashflow, and used this cashflow to keep their political supporters happy. In this process they typified cooperative approaches to wealth-building that saw government cooperation as beneficial.

As such, and with full recognition that this is a significant generalization across a complex and diverse region, governments in Asia are often seen by business people and entrepreneurs in a more benign light, or at least not with active antipathy, and with the expectation that they might actually be able to help citizens in their efforts to get rich. There are certainly roots for this in Confucian teaching. As Charles Goodhart explained in his comparison of Asian and Anglo-Saxon models Asia holds a proportionately greater share of its financial system under public/government control (Goodhart, 2009). The end result is, as Andrew Sheng of the China Banking Regulatory Commission (Sheng, 2010) puts it, a regulatory and governance style that is 'more consensual and pragmatic.'

An example of this can be seen in Singapore where many hold the government in high regard and where the government has been quite direct in fostering digital innovation in finance. The well-regarded 'Men in White,' the early rulers of modern and independent Singapore, were known for their dedication to the people of Singapore and for their trustworthiness. In more modern times government linked funds have been serious investors in both FinTech and DeFi. The Monetary Authority of Sinapore's (MAS) Managing Director Ravi Menon was quite specific about this when he said "Singapore's FinTech journey is about innovation, inclusion and inspiration. Everything we do in FinTech must always have a larger purpose–to improve the lives of individuals, to build a more dynamic economy, to promote a more inclusive society" (Monetary Authority of Singapore, n.d.).

This focus on participating in digital innovation to drive Singapore's growth has very direct and immediate consequences. When recently working at a FinTech startup that was applying for a place in Singapore's sandbox the firm's senior management team certainly felt that it was very important to get the firm's Singapore office up and running quickly, both to help the regulators feel more comfortable with the sincerity of our application and to send the signal that we wanted to succeed jointly with Singapore. As a result of this cooperative mindset, one is far less likely to find crypto anarchists in Singapore and far more likely to find entrepreneurs looking to work closely with the government.

So Asia generally sees two great advantages over the US when it comes to digital innovation. First, a simpler and more streamlined regulatory system makes it easier for innovative startups to work with rule makers to test and implement their improvements. Second, a greater tendency towards acceptance of the government as a benign player that can aid in one's success causes innovators to want to work with the government to whatever reasonable level makes the most sense.

As one example the CEO of MANTRA Finance, a vertically integrated DeFi eco-system, is very specific in stating that he understands the importance of working with regulators. "With our origins in Hong Kong, it only makes sense to work with regulators within the region that have taken a pro-innovation stance. Building trust is a critical element to inflow of capital, institutional money looks to licenses as a means to signal a good actor in the financial world." This DeFi platform recently established an operation under Dubai regulation, working with the global family of regulation to best pursue its goals.

Similarly Hex Trust, a digital asset custody firm at which both of these authors previously worked, sees an embrace of regulation as a competitive advantage as it steers serious players and traditional financial firms to work with those who have taken the time to pass the barrier to entry of gaining appropriate licensing. "Our aim is to be one step ahead of the regulators so that once licenses and policies get rolled out, we're the first company to be able to obtain them" said Hex Trust CEO Allessio Quaglini (Quaglini, n.d.). The challenge of licensing has long helped keep new competition away from traditional financial firms and banks, and key FinTech startups recognize the value of this barrier.

In January 2023, the HKMA sought industry insight (Hong Kong Monetary Authority, 2023) to regulate virtual assets in Hong Kong. Respondents generally supported the proposed regulatory requirements for licensed VA trading platforms. Many of the comments sought clarification of the technical and implementation details. Key comments related to retail access to licensed VA trading platforms, the criteria for token admission, compensation arrangements for the risks associated with custody of client assets, trading in virtual asset derivatives, implementation details and the transitional arrangements.

Key comments where the approach differs from western regulators is an openness to allow retail users to access a new asset class. They have set conditions forward to ensure that access is provided with regulatory guidance. They believe that licensed VA trading platforms should comply with a range of robust investor protection measures covering onboarding, governance, disclosure and token due diligence and admission, before providing trading services to retail investors.

This new regime to trade crypto assets was opened to the public on 1 June 2023.

Of course, other markets are also looking to adopt this progressive approach, and not all of Asia is managing the development as well as Singapore's example. India is one country that, despite its very early start with bank digitalization in the late '90s (or perhaps to an extent because of that early progress) is seemingly failing to follow up with further digital disruption. In recent months the web3 brain drain from India has its citizens heading to Singapore or to the neighboring Middle East, where Dubai has embraced FinTech and DeFi developments (BeInCrypto, 2021). To an extent these shifts are driven by a much friendlier tax environment, but the regu-latory regime is also key. Whereas regulators in most of Asia are keen to work with FinTech innovators, India's representatives seem to have not yet realized that the dis-intermediation of Trust is here to stay and that finance is fundamentally changing.

Other Asian markets are responding to Dubai's efforts by honing their own competitiveness. After several Web3 service providers made the shift to the Emirati city earlier in 2022 Singapore for one appears to have taken this as a sign to be more progressive and swifter in regulatory approval for this space. Operators are keen to work with Singapore, and other governments, to further their advance in this space.

14.1.6 Sustainable Digital Innovation in Asian Finance

These three key differences: frequent positioning that benefits from technological leapfrogging, a simpler regulatory framework that allows for easier approval of testing and eventual change, and a cultural approach that very often sees the government as a potential partner in driving digital transformation and not an enemy, all combine to leave Asia at the center of FinTech creativity and acceptance.

This is especially important in China. The transformation of China's retail financial services over the past three decades is nothing short of astounding. Just before the pandemic the Asian branch of the Chicago Quantitative Alliance (CQA) hosted its annual meeting in Shenzhen and was joined by several board members from the parent CQA organization. These were very senior, C-Suite and board level experts in the financial services industry. At dinner the first night one of the visiting Americans sat next to a young Chinese fund manager who started to explain the versatility and benefits of Alipay and Wechat Pay. The fund manager discussed how the financial end of the app fit with reviews, advertisements, special offers, scheduling, and other tools to provide a seamless problem solver for getting through one's day. The visitor was amazed at how much the systems could do. He was then shocked after dinner when we were walking down the street and he stopped to purchase some sliced pineapple from a street vendor. He took some carefully prepared renminbi out of his pocket to pay, only to be told that cash was not accepted. His new friend the fund manager had to pay for him using Alipay.

The next day the visitor came to the local fund manager before the first session and asked a question that had been troubling him the entire night: was the fund manager not concerned that they were giving all of that data and insight to the government, and that it might somehow be used against them? The Alipay user replied that he was not overly concerned. He pointed out that various marketing services were also tracking all sorts of activities of the American when he was engaged in online shopping, and that the businesses were then using that information to their advantage against him. While he did not trust the private businesses to promote his interests, he felt that so long as he was living a good life the government would wish to look out for him, or at least to do him no harm.

This very different view of government trustworthiness is significant. A recent study by a public relations consultancy suggests that 91% of Chinese citizens trust their government, compared to only 39% of respondents in the same group's study of the US (Edelman, 2022). While such metrics should certainly be queried, these numbers fit with conversations and interactions with Chinese citizens who take pride in China's recent growth and accomplishments. Thirty-five years ago, the Chinese financial system barely functioned and now it provides the world's most advanced retail offerings.

This comfort and confidence provide key opportunities for the continued digital disruption of financial services in China and the rest of Asia. The idea of social credit scores, or of credit scores sourced through a data-driven review of individual behavior, would be an anathema to many in the west. Yet such comfort, whether justified or misplaced, does allow entrepreneurs to work with Asian governments to create powerful new digital solutions. Meanwhile in the US people continue to work with FICO scores, a system first developed in the 1950s that limits itself to a tiny subset of available data and does nothing to consider some of the most basic components of the question of loan repayment (assets for example are studiously ignored.)

For now, many Asian markets are working closely with digital entrepreneurs to develop the next generation of tools that will drive financial interactions. The latest DeFi buzzword for example is the 'DeFi mullet,' which is a Web 2.0 inter-face linking to a Web3 engine, allowing greater back-end functionality through what will appear to be the original product. As Asia continues to see above-average growth in its economies and its population, it will continue to look for oppor-tunities to leapfrog to more efficient and trustworthy financial markets, relying on a trust-based approach of cooperation with the regulators. It is of course dan-gerous to consider Asia as a single region, and its many governments, cultures, languages, and regulators provide their own challenge to entrepreneurial digital finance providers. Still, the current cooperative effort has greatly contributed to Asia's successes in the space to date, and look set to continue to provide a boost to sustainable digital innovation.

14.2   Conclusion

Various Asian countries are leading the world in both digital finance innovation and adoption (Infosys, n.d.). The roots of this can be seen in the opportunity for techno-logical leapfrogging, the region's economic growth, and a constructive approach to engagement with regulators. Many Asian countries recognize the challenges they face in their pursuit of ongoing development and hence are working to actively encourage cooperative ventures that will improve and rapidly progress their financial markets and systems. Going forward this cooperative effort, combined with the gen-erally streamlined regulatory oversight of Asia should continue to position the region well for sustainable digital innovation. Entrepreneurs looking to develop leading edge, transformative technology for finance should focus on the many opportun-ities offered by the Asian approach while being suitably mindful of the challenges presented by each unique Asian market. Most importantly follow the generalized Asian way of working with the regulator, not against.

References

BeInCrypto. (2021, November 19). Brain Drain: Indian Crypto and Web3 Companies Migrate to Dubai. Retrieved from https://beincrypto.com/brain-drain-indian-crypto-and-web3-companies-migrate-to-dubai/.

Claessens, S. (2009). Competition in the Financial Sector: Overview of Competition Policies. IMF Working Paper, WP/09/45.

CoinGecko. (n.d.). CoinGecko exchanges. Retrieved June 8, 2023, from www.coingecko.com/en/exchanges.

Ducree, J. (2022, June 21). Satoshi Nakamoto and the origins of Bitcoin. Cornell University.

Edelman. (2022). Trust China. Retrieved from www.edelman.com/trust/2022-trust-barometer/trust-china.

Financial Conduct Authority. (n.d.-a). Regulatory sandbox. Retrieved from www.fca.org.uk/firms/innovation/regulatory-sandbox.

Financial Conduct Authority. (n.d.-b). Regulatory sandbox. Retrieved from www.fca.org.uk/firms/innovation/regulatory-sandbox.

Goodhart, C. (2009). Banks and the public sector authorities. *Banks and Bank Systems*, 4(4).

Hoffner, B. (2022). Hong Kong: Private Emergency Loans, 1965. *Journal of Financial Crises*, 4(2), 877–896. Retrieved from https://elischolar.library.yale.edu/journal-of-financial-crises/vol4/iss2/40.

Hong Kong Monetary Authority. (2023, January). Conclusion of Discussion Paper on Crypto-assets and Stablecoins.

Hong Kong Monetary Authority. (2023, May 30). Hong Kong's external position remains strong. Retrieved from www.hkma.gov.hk/eng/news-and-media/press-releases/2023/05/20230530-5/.

Infosys. (n.d.). The Fintech Sun Rises in the East. Retrieved from www.infosys.com/milken/fintech-sun-rises.html.

Insider Intelligence. (2021, May 10). US digital banking users will surpass 200 million in 2022.

KB Associates. (n.d.). FCA Asset Management Market Study 2017: Final Report. Retrieved from https://kbassociates.ie/fca-asset-management-market-study-2017-final-report/.

Kim, K. (2006). The 1997–98 Korean Financial Crisis: Causes, Policy Responses, and Lessons. Paper presented at The High Level Seminar on Crisis Prevention in Emerging Markets, July 10–11.

KPMG. (2023). Q4'22 Venture Pulse Report. Retrieved from kpmg.com/xx/en/home/campaigns/2023/01/q4-venture-pulse-report-global.html.

Monetary Authority of Singapore. (n.d.). Fintech. Retrieved from www.mas.gov.sg/development/fintech.

Quaglini, A. (n.d.). The Big Crypto Questions: Alessio Quaglini, Hex Trust. *Elliptic*. Retrieved from https://hub.elliptic.co/analysis/the-big-crypto-questions-alessio-quaglini-hex-trust/.

Rosha, S. (2022, July 25). Emerging giants thrive in Asia Pacific's sandbox. *Nikkei Asia*. Retrieved from https://asia.nikkei.com/Opinion/Emerging-giants-thrive-in-Asia-Pacific-s-sandbox.

Sheng, A. (2010). The regulatory reform of global financial markets: An Asian regulator's perspective. *Global Policy*, 1(2), 203–214.

Studwell, J. (2007). Asian Godfathers. Profile Books.

Sudman, T. (2017, June 30). Nine young bankers who changed America. *ABA Banking Journal.* Retrieved from https://bankingjournal.aba.com/2017/06/nine-young-bankers-who-changed-america-thomas-sudman/.

Suhas, D., & Ramesh, H. N. (n.d.). E-banking and its growth in India – A synoptic view. *Journal of Management Research and Analysis,* 5(4), 376–383.

U.S. Government Accountability Office. (2016). Financial regulation: Complex and fragmented structure could be streamlined to improve effectiveness. Retrieved from www.gao.gov/products/gao-16-175.

U.S. Securities and Exchange Commission. (2023, June 6). SEC charges hedge fund adviser and Binance CEO for engaging in insider trading scheme. Retrieved from www.sec.gov/news/press-release/2023-101.

Wells Fargo. (n.d.). First in online banking. Wells Fargo History. Retrieved from www.wellsfargohistory.com/first-in-online-banking/.

Yuan, X., Lee, H. S., & Kim, S. Y. (2011). Present and future of internet banking in China. *Journal of Internet Banking and Commerce.*

Chapter 15

Blockchain and Financial Services: An Overview of Application Fields in Payment Transactions and for Securities Services

Marc Nathmann

Chapter Overview

Blockchain technology has attracted significant attention in the financial industry in recent years. Originally conceived as the basis for the cryptocurrency Bitcoin, Blockchain has evolved into a technology that has the potential to fundamentally change the way financial transactions are conducted. It is primarily a technology that can make transfers of money and/or assets significantly more efficient and could make various intermediaries, such as payment processing or securities trading service providers, redundant.

This chapter discusses the application areas of Blockchain in the financial industry and its impact on payments and securities.

15.1 The Blockchain Technology

The Blockchain is essentially a decentralized and transparent digital ledger that securely and immutably records information about transactions. Unlike traditional

    DOI: 10.1201/9781003395560-15

centralized databases, where a central authority is responsible for managing and validating transactions, the Blockchain enables peer-to-peer validation and verification of transactions. This means that transaction history can be reviewed and confirmed by all participants in the network, increasing trust in the integrity of the data.

15.1.1 Application Areas in the Financial Industry

One area where Blockchain has a major impact in the financial industry is in payment processing. Traditional international payments are often time-consuming and expensive, as they must be routed through multiple intermediaries and banks. With Blockchain technology, payments can be processed in real time and at a lower cost. By using Blockchain, financial institutions can make transactions directly without intermediaries, resulting in faster and more efficient payments.

Another application area for Blockchain is securities trading. Securities trading typically requires the involvement of intermediaries such as stockbrokers and settlement houses to facilitate and monitor transactions. By using Blockchain technology, assets can be digitized and traded on the Blockchain as so-called "tokens" (in the following, Blockchain-based payment units are referred to as "coins" and securities as "tokens"). This enables a direct peer-to-peer transaction between parties, reducing the need for intermediaries. In addition, Blockchain provides improved transparency and traceability of transactions, which can help combat fraud and manipulation.

Blockchain technology also offers solutions for identity management and know-your-customer (KYC) processes. Because Blockchain is a secure and immutable digital ledger, identity information can be securely stored and verified. This allows financial institutions to make the KYC process more efficient and secure. Customers can have their identity verified once on the Blockchain and then share this information with different service providers as needed, rather than having to perform separate identity checks with each new provider.

15.1.2 Obstacles

However, despite the promising applications of Blockchain in the financial industry, there are also challenges and barriers to its wider adoption. One of the biggest challenges is to integrate and interoperate existing systems and infrastructures. The shift to Blockchain requires close collaboration between different players and the creation of uniform standards.

Another obstacle is scalability. Current Blockchain networks such as Bitcoin and Ethereum have limited transaction capacities, which can lead to bottlenecks and high transaction costs. To widely deploy Blockchain technology in the financial industry, scaling solutions need to be developed to improve network performance.

Overall, Blockchain technology has the potential to transform the financial industry by improving efficiency, security and transparency. Applications range from payment processing to securities trading to identity management. Despite the challenges, many financial institutions are already realizing the benefits of Blockchain and are focusing on integrating it into their existing systems. It remains to be seen how Blockchain technology will evolve and what impact it will ultimately have on the financial industry.

15.2 Blockchain Based Payment Methods

15.2.1 Application Areas

Payment transactions are extremely complex, which makes Blockchain an obvious choice for increasing efficiency. Payment transactions (especially cross-border ones) are characterized by the fact that every single payment transaction between payer and payee passes through a broad network of intermediary actors for settlement and clearing: Bank service providers, central bank networks, central banks, credit card schemes, and the like, just to name a few. In addition, significant fluctuations in money markets and, last but not least, the negative interest rate policies of most central banks have led to a rather broad loss of confidence in "sovereign money."

Against this background, many initiatives by state and private actors have emerged with and in the wake of Bitcoin, either to develop private forms of money or to digitize state-issued, namely, central bank-issued, money. Essentially, "private money" based on the idea of Bitcoin and digital central bank money, as well as stable coins as an interim solution, have emerged to date.

15.2.1.1 Bitcoins in the Sense of "Private Money"

Since Bitcoin was supposed to be a means of payment independent of banks and especially state actors, namely central banks, Blockchain-based means of payment are often considered "private money". Exactly this scope should be considered a failure with regard to Bitcoin. It may be doubted that there is a scope for "private money" outside the black market. Ultimately, money essentially fulfills the function of a means of payment (among others). This requires low volatility because the value of money should remain stable for payment transactions. Furthermore, there must be a general trust in its acceptance and value stability. Currently, it is not readily apparent that non-state actors could guarantee acceptance and value stability for nationwide payment instruments. For this reason, most supervisory authorities do not regard "private money" such as Bitcoin as money or an alternative to money, but as a store of value or an investment vehicle (BaFin, n.d.)

15.2.1.2 Stable Coins

Stable coins can be assessed completely differently. The debate about stable coins flared up when Facebook announced that it was launching its own "currency", Libra, on the market. The basic idea of stable coins is to make digital coins capable of payment transactions by securing them.

Stable Coins follow the original idea of Bitcoins to establish virtual currencies as an alternative means of payment. If virtual currencies, as the example of Bitcoin shows, suffer from the problem of extremely high volatility, which at least makes it difficult to use them as a means of payment, stablecoins aim to establish value stability. Stable Coins are intended to ensure three functions, similar to money (Mertten, 2023):

1. Unit of account
2. Medium of exchange
3. Store of Value.

The idea is that it is a digital banknote. An instrument is issued that transaction parties recognize as the fulfillment of a monetary debt, legally speaking, in lieu of payment. To prevent the volatility dilemma of bitcoins, for example, the value is not in the coin itself, but the coin represents other assets and is thus stabilized.

For example, to guarantee the literal stability of the value, they are tied to a stable asset such as fiat currencies (for example, USD, EUR) or commodities (for example, gold). Thus, Stablecoins serve as a digital representation of the underlying asset and are designed to avoid price volatility often observed with traditional cryptocurrencies such as Bitcoin. Blockchain technology enables the efficient issuance, transfer, and custody of Stablecoins by providing transparency, security, and traceability of transactions. Stablecoins can be used to facilitate cross-border payments, financial transactions, and as an alternative to traditional fiat currencies.

There are already several platforms and projects that offer digital securities and Stablecoins on the Blockchain. For example, platforms such as Ethereum enable the creation and trading of tokens representing digital securities. At the same time, there are Stablecoin projects such as Tether (USDT) and USD Coin (USDC) that are based on the Blockchain and act as digital representations of fiat currencies.

The advantage with Stablecoins in practical terms is twofold:

1. Stablecoins allow payments to be processed securely and extremely efficiently. There is no longer any need for complex payment schemes or payment channels via central banks. A real peer-to-peer payment can be made at favorable conditions.
2. Unlike "private money," the value of the coins is stable. The currency basket or the underlying assets represent a genuine real value, so that on the one hand the trust is based on conventional fiat currencies or other assets. At the same time, the risk of a loss of value is significantly reduced.

Furthermore, Stablecoins can be used for payments within a product universe, and this was probably also a core idea of Facebook on which the Libra plans were based. Large corporations in particular can use Stablecoins to create an internal means of payment for their own products. The advantage is obvious. Customers, who are also users of the Stablecoin, can pay for products in an internal corporate currency.

Especially in cross-border payment transactions, transaction costs are likely to decrease with widespread use. The use of Stablecoins not only reduces transaction costs, but can also reduce price fluctuation risks, provided that the coin itself remains stable due to the currency basket. This is why Stablecoins are also referred to as "stable".

15.2.2   Central Bank Digital Currencies (CBDC)

Facebook's announcement of its intention to issue a Stablecoin caused near panic among central bankers around the world, who feared that the state monopoly on money could face significant private competition. As a result, more and more central banks are planning so-called CBDCs (Central Bank Digital Currencies), namely, cryptocurrencies issued by central banks (see, for example: Eurogroup, 2023).

The aim is to make the processing of international payments much more efficient, faster and cheaper. For example, international transfers of a digital Euro to another currency area could be made within seconds and with little to no transaction costs. In addition, there is competitiveness vis-à-vis other nations also working on introducing digital central bank money (European Central Bank, 2020).

Programmed payment processes would allow Euro payments and other financial services to be handled automatically. The error-proneness and bureaucracy of manual processes would be bypassed. Automation leads to an integration of performance and consideration. Particularly in international commercial transactions, performance and consideration have often diverged to date. The automated process would allow payments to reach the supplier within seconds of receipt of the goods. The programmable CBDC could also be used by devices such as cars, sensors and machines, which could be equipped with their own wallet and thus participate directly in the Blockchain network (Internet of Things). The digital Euro could drive the digitalization of industry and the machine economy and promote the competitiveness of European companies (Birne & Omlor, 2020).

15.2.3   Regulatory Issues–Bitcoins and "Private Money"

Within the European Union, particularly in Germany, Bitcoins are not considered a means of payment from a regulatory point of view (for example, BaFin, n.d.). Its classification regulates Bitcoin as a financial instrument, which means that within the EU similar framework conditions apply as for securities or securities-like instruments (Patz, 2021).

This assessment also applies (almost) worldwide, in so far as legislators or regulatory authorities have dealt with the classification of Bitcoins or similarly structured coins (Frank-Fahle et al., 2019).

It may also be considered legally doubtful that private actors are allowed to create and/or issue "money". The reason is understandably obvious. The creation of money is a core area of sovereign state action (for example, Möslein & Omlor, 2021).

15.2.3.1 Stable Coins–Basic Classification

The regulatory classification of stable coins is much more complex. Structurally, there is much to be said for assuming as a starting point that stable coins are initially a type of investment vehicle similar to an investment fund.

A mutual fund, as conventionally understood, is a financial instrument managed by a fund manager to collect capital from investors and invest it in a variety of securities such as stocks, bonds, money market instruments, or other financial instruments. A mutual fund is often referred to as an investment company or investment company with variable capital (ICAV). This is a legal structure specifically designed to manage mutual funds.

Stablecoins fall under this definition without any problems. The practical focus may be on payment processing, but structurally, capital is first received from the public, namely, the participants or buyers of the respective coin. This capital is then invested (according to terms similar to the investment terms) in assets, the basket of currencies. Ultimately, a Stablecoin would then be, to put it simply, a payment-capable ETF.

Of course, this classification seems a bit strange at first glance, since the stable coin is not only an instrument for processing payments in terms of its objective, but also a kind of digital banknote. In the case of investment funds, on the other hand, the increase in value or investment of value is typically at the ideal centre. From a legal point of view, however, this is not important. Legally, the only decisive factor is that a central body collects capital in order to then invest it collectively.

This is precisely how the regulatory responsible party can be determined. This is because the entity that receives the capital is responsible. This body determines and is responsible for the investment and is "master" of the capital.

15.2.3.2 Problems of Classification

Simply classifying Stablecoins as a payments ETF is, of course, completely unsatisfactory. It structurally misses the payments function in regulatory terms. Securities regulation is fundamentally different from payments regulation. Securities regulation aims to ensure investor protection, promote the integrity of capital markets, and ensure the orderly functioning of securities trading. Payments regulation, on the other hand, focuses on the safety, efficiency, and stability of payment systems and the protection of consumers in payment transactions.

The regulation of securities is also generally based on specific securities laws and regulations that govern trading in securities, regulate the issuance of securities, and establish requirements for issuers and market participants.

Payment regulation, on the other hand, is usually based on different legal foundations that deal with various aspects such as security, data protection, consumer protection, and interoperability.

As a consequence, the regulation of securities is often more complex and diverse than the regulation of payments. Because securities can encompass different asset classes, such as equities, bonds, mutual funds, and derivatives, regulators must establish specific rules and regulations for each of these asset classes. In contrast, payments regulation focuses on the transfer of funds and processing of payments, which typically involves fewer complex requirements.

In securities regulation, the focus is often on assessing and monitoring risks associated with investments, such as the risk of price losses, issuer insolvency, or market manipulation. Payments regulation, on the other hand, tends to focus on the security of transactions, preventing fraud, ensuring privacy, and protecting consumers from fraudulent payments.

15.2.3.3 Legislative Efforts

For this reason, there are, for example, efforts in the EU with MiCAR to create a regulatory level playing field for Stablecoins in order to be able to regulate specifically. After promulgation and entry into force at the beginning of 2023, the various regulatory complexes will become effective in two steps at the beginning and in the middle of 2024 (Council of the EU, 2022). MiCAR applies to natural and legal persons who engage in activities regarding the issuance, public offering or admission to trading of crypto securities or who offer crypto-specific services. Thus, it is not a complete regulation of Blockchain technology, but a fundamentally technology-neutral set of regulations around trading or investing in digital assets. Thus, MiCAR is genuine capital market law, although curiously not for financial instruments (Maume, 2022a). The central MiCAR regulatory idea is not to subject issuers of Stablecoins to the selective obligation to publish a prospectus or whitepaper only, as is the case when offering securities or other tokens (Maume, 2022b).

15.2.3.4 CBDCs

Unlike private money, CBDCs are "real" (central bank) money. There is state recognition and a sovereign act of creation. A CBDC therefore represents a currency in the monetary law sense. In contrast, privately issued "cryptocurrencies" are not intended to be centrally and state-controlled. However, the concrete design is still more than unclear in many cases.

15.2.4 Practical Issues in the Use of Blockchain-based Payment Methods

The following sections discuss practical issues of Blockchain-based payment methods in business contexts and outlines the use of smart contracts.

15.2.4.1 Advantages of Blockchain-based Payment Methods

In general, Blockchain-based payment methods can help improve financial inclusion, especially in regions with limited access to traditional banking services. Because Blockchain platforms are often based on open standards, they can be used by anyone with internet access, regardless of their geographic location or access to traditional bank accounts. This is a key advantage, particularly for transactions in countries with poorly developed banking infrastructure, and can better connect such countries to international payment flows and provide the basis for investment.

It is precisely through the use of stable coins that payments can be processed in real time. Unlike instant payments run via central banking systems, no or at least fewer intermediaries are required. This enables faster and more efficient transactions, as validation and settlement can take place directly between the parties involved.

As a result, significant cost savings appear possible. Costs for intermediaries or clearing houses are eliminated, as are the associated fees and costs. This can be particularly advantageous for cross-border payments, as traditional transfer fees and exchange rate charges can be eliminated.

Blockchain technology offers a high level of security and transparency. Transactions are verified and stored in a decentralized and distributed network, which reduces the risk of fraud and manipulation. The Blockchain also enables the tracking and verification of transactions, which increases users' trust in the payment system.

15.2.4.2 Combination with Smart Contracts

In combination with smart contracts, there are further significant advantages. The automation of payments, in that smart contracts define predefined rules and conditions can be mapped. Smart contracts are stored in the Blockchain, which means that all transactions and payments are public and transparent. By executing payments via smart contracts, transactions are secured by mathematical algorithms and cryptography. This minimizes the risk of errors, fraud, and unauthorized access. Smart contracts also provide the ability to encode terms and conditions and agreements in a secure and trusted environment.

15.2.4.3 Challenges of Blockchain-based Payment Methods

The biggest challenge is the still unclear legal situation. There is hardly any regulatory level playing field, so that even the regulatory classification causes difficulties.

Almost all conceivable areas of law are affected. Even within the EU, the obligations or even the licensing requirements for issuers are difficult to classify, and worldwide they are almost unmanageable. This is followed by various civil law issues.

On an unclear legal basis, the trust needed in payment systems is difficult to establish, which is a prerequisite for acceptance.

The solution to the core challenge therefore lies with the legislators. It is up to them to create the necessary legal framework.

Nevertheless, the following can be stated:

■ Bitcoins and "private money" are not and will not be suitable for payment transactions.
■ Stable Coins offer promising options to establish payment systems on this basis.
■ The same is true for CBDC's if state creators find market-driven implementation solutions.

15.3 Blockchain Based Securities: Application Areas

Digital securities are digitized versions of traditional financial instruments such as stocks, bonds, and mutual funds. By using the Blockchain, these securities can be created as so-called "tokens" and placed on the Blockchain. The advantages of digital securities include their increased liquidity, lower transaction costs, and the ability to enable real-time trading and settlement. The Blockchain also offers improved traceability and verifiability of ownership rights, which facilitates the process of transacting and managing securities.

Unlike in payments, the use of a Blockchain in securities enables two things:

■ The issuance of tokens, or digital securities, or digital securitization
■ The execution of securities transactions based on a Blockchain to eliminate the need for intermediaries and make trading or transferring securities more efficient.

There are also other areas of application that go beyond the scope of this article. In recent times in particular, works of art or other valuable objects have been made digitally investable via so-called NFTs (Non-Fungible Tokens). However, as far as can be seen today, these are not investment vehicles that can be used across the board in the narrower sense, but rather niche products.

15.3.1 Issuance of Digital Securities: "The ICO"

The issuance of digital securities takes place through a so-called ICO ("Initial Coin Offering"), similar to the IPO in the initial share offering. An ICO essentially means corporate financing without intermediaries such as banks and stock exchanges. Capital is raised through the issuance of tokens by a company and acquisition directly by the investor. An ICO can fulfill the financing function in that an investor receives a virtual equivalent in the form of a token for real money.

Although market capitalization has increased from zero to around USD 150 billion since 2013, in absolute terms ICO is a niche area of corporate financing both internationally and in Germany.

15.3.1.1 Procedure of the ICO

The process of an ICO has not yet been standardized, as it is a relatively new financing method. The company or project to be financed is regularly presented in a "white paper". The white paper is often placed on a "funding page" on the Internet. It contains the details of the financing.

In addition, there is often a term sheet that outlines the essential legal framework. This usually also contains the definition of the rights from the token.

However, every ICO presupposes a token as the means of securitization and the object of sale. Accordingly, the first step is the generation of the token, also called Token Generating Event. Thus, the tokens are generated and offered for sale for the first time. This represents the ICO in the narrower sense:

- In the case of a utility token, the cash flow is matched by a liability in the form of a subsequent obligation to supply goods or services. The financing thus consists of the granting of a loan.
- In the case of a security token, the cash flow is usually offset by participation rights in subsequent profit distributions or lending rights. For the most part, these are not equity interests.
- In the case of hybrid tokens, there is a hybrid between utility and security tokens.

There is also the possibility to combine an ICO with smart contracts and thus, in addition to the securitization of the right, trigger profit distributions when certain parameters occur. Recently, the option of mapping securities transactions on the Blockchain has also been discussed. The difference to an ICO is that a conventional security is issued and the transactions to acquire it are mapped in a Blockchain (Nathmann, 2019).

15.3.1.2 Legal Classification

The following section introduces the legal implications for banks and FinTech organization from securities law and civil law.

15.3.1.3 Securities Law

Lege lata: The specific legal classification of tokens regularly causes difficulties. The existing securities laws often cover tokens only partially and not always in a factually accurate manner.

For example, European definitions of securities do not allow for a clear qualification of security tokens. Although the EU legislator tends to qualify such rights as securities that are comparable to classical securities, such as shares or similar (see: Recital 8 of Directive 2014/65/EU (MiFID II)), the decisive factor for the European definition of securities is the exhaustive list in Art. 4 (1) No. 44 MiFID II. Furthermore, the tradability is also important (as in most global securities laws).

Therefore, MiFID II does not allow for a generalized statement either. This is noteworthy insofar as both ICO and tokens were already known during the creation of MiFID II. This certainly raises the question of whether the directive-maker deliberately omitted or simply overlooked the inclusion of tokens in MiFID. The current discussions at the EU level, however, rather speak for the latter (see: ESMA, Advice Initial Coin Offerings and Crypto Assets from 9.1.2019). Only those tokens that promise their holders to participate in future cash flows generated by the ongoing (or liquidated/sold) project generally need to be considered securities, while pure currency and utility tokens are exempt from securities regulation in the EU.

Internationally, the legal situation is highly inconsistent. Some countries consider ICOs and tokens to be subject to financial market regulation, while other countries, such as Singapore, have created so-called "sandboxes" and exempt the business models from essential obligations in whole or in part.

Even within the EU, the classification of tokens is not uniform. In the Netherlands, for example, ICOs are in principle permission-free according to the AFM. Further services around ICO and token trading can be provided in the "sandbox". In this context, financial service providers can conclude individual agreements with the supervisory authorities and thereby temporarily suspend regulatory requirements.

In the Czech Republic, on the other hand, financial regulators seem to assume that ICOs and their respective players are generally subject to national securities supervision laws.

In Malta, the Malta Digital Innovation Authority (MDIA) Act, the Innovative Technology Arrangements and Services (ITAS) Act and the Virtual Financial Asset (VFA) Act have been in place since July 2018. This basically regulates all players involved in ICO. With these regulations, Malta wanted to create a comprehensive regulatory framework for ICO.

Liechtenstein has also implemented similar plans with effect from January 2020. The law provides for a so-called token container model. The token serves as a container for rights of all kinds. This also aligns the token transfer with civil law so that a token transaction is fully defined (Nathmann, 2019).

Lege ferenda: Consequently, there is a need for action in terms of securities law. More and more legislators are recognizing this need. As a result, there are more and more attempts to define tokens as securities and thus, of course, to subject them to securities regulation.

A relatively early legislator was Germany. With the implementation of the amending directive to the Fourth EU Money Laundering Directive, a legal definition of the term "crypto tokens" was introduced by Section 1 (1a) sentence 3 KWG:

> (...) Crypto tokens within the meaning of this Act are digital representations of a value which has not been issued or guaranteed by any central bank or public body and does not have the legal status of currency or money, but which is accepted by natural or legal persons as a means of exchange or payment or serves investment purposes on the basis of an agreement or actual practice and which can be transmitted, stored and traded electronically (...).

Security tokens are thereby also qualified as crypto tokens. Thus, the previous view is regulated by law. What appears to be difficult about the definition is that it mixes virtual currency units and security tokens, although security tokens as a financing instrument pursue a completely different objective.

The MiCAR is also an attempt to establish a regulatory level playing field for tokens at the EU level. The central fact of the MiCAR is the crypto-asset. There, MiCAR also contains a definition of token. According to Art. 3 para. 2 no. 2 MiCAR, token is a similar to the solution in the German Banking Act "(...) *digital representation of value or rights that can be electronically transmitted and stored using distributed ledger technology or similar technology* (...)". Otherwise functionless tokens such as Bitcoin and other currency tokens fall under this very broad definition. In contrast to the German regulation, (pure) utility tokens are also explicitly covered as a subcase. In addition, MiCAR will be applicable to Stablecoins (e-money tokens and value-referenced tokens).

It is expected that other jurisdictions with similar definitions will gradually follow.

Consequently, tokens then represent regulated securities. Other special regulations, which are also contained in MiCAR, for example, relate to regulatory requirements for service providers, in particular issuers or exchanges. Here, requirements are set up based on the usual requirements in securities law, namely with regard to capital adequacy, prospectuses, etc.

15.3.1.4 Civil Law–Problems de Lege Lata

The token represents rights, but is itself (as far as can be seen) neither a thing nor a right in the vast majority of civil law systems. However, the rights from the token are not securitized by the token in the civil law sense. The securitization in the token is a legal nullum as a pure real act. Although tokens are technically comparable to a deed, the token nevertheless lacks the characteristic of a deed. A paper wallet is also not a deed, since only a private key, namely, a legitimation instrument, is present in paper form. There is also and in particular no protection under the substantive law, in that no acquisition in good faith is possible. The acquisition of a token from a non-entitled person is out of the question. In these cases, the transaction will be reversed (for example, Kaulartz & Matzke, 2019).

However, there are discussions in Europe about recognizing a property-like right in tokens and thus applying the law on the transfer of ownership to tokens. The reason given is that tokens, like things, can be individualized and cannot be duplicated.

Under civil law, it is possible to structure the rights by means of general terms and conditions, whereby the effects of a bearer bond under civil law can be achieved. However, it is only in exceptional cases that shareholder rights can be securitized with legal effect. As a rule, securitization is precluded by formal requirements under company law, such as the notarial form in Germany and some other primarily European legal systems.

Thus, the civil law legal nature is a major obstacle to practical usability.

15.3.1.5   Solution de Lege Ferenda

Many legislators have recognized the civil law problem and concluded that, on the one hand, there is a need for electronic issuance of securities and/or electronic securitization of company shares. More and more jurisdictions are therefore creating laws on electronic securities, such as Germany. The example of the (German) law on electronic securities shows how civil law problems can be resolved in this way. Simply put, the electronic securitization act is recognized by law and thus the token is legally granted a deed or security property. In terms of legal structure, this is conceivable in the vast majority of civil law systems. This is because the property of a deed or security can be regulated by simple law.

This accomplishes two things:

- Tokens can be issued in compliance with civil law.
- The ownership of the token is secured and thus the (further) transfer is possible without any problems.

15.4   Conclusions

The issuance of digital securities can significantly simplify corporate financing and increase efficiency. In particular, it gives smaller companies access to the global financial markets.

A key prerequisite for ICOs to become widely usable, for example, is the creation of a legal framework. In this regard, it appears that many legislators have recognized the need for action and are creating appropriate legal regulations.

15.4.1   Advantages of Blockchain Transactions

The Blockchain enables the direct peer-to-peer transfer of securities without the need for an intermediary such as a clearinghouse or custodian. This leads to a significant increase in efficiency, as transactions can be processed in real time without relying on manual processes and paper documents.

By using Blockchain technology, securities transactions can be processed in real time. This eliminates delays and enables the immediate change of ownership of securities. This is particularly beneficial for high-volume trades where fast settlement is critical.

The transparency of the Blockchain provides all parties involved with comprehensive insight into the transaction process. Every step of the securities transaction is recorded on the Blockchain and can be verified by authorized participants. This strengthens trust and reduces the risk of fraud.

The use of Blockchain technology can lead to significant cost savings. By eliminating intermediaries and manual processes, transaction costs can be significantly reduced. In addition, middle, back-office and settlement processes can be automated, resulting in further cost savings.

Blockchain technology can improve the liquidity of the securities market. By providing a global marketplace, investors worldwide can directly access securities and complete trades quickly and efficiently. This can lead to better price discovery and higher trading volumes.

Stock exchanges and capital management companies are increasingly recognizing these advantages and are launching initial projects (a first project was successfully implemented in Germany by LBBW, for example, as part of a bond issue for Daimler AG, (LBBW, 2017))

15.4.2   Challenges in Implementing Blockchain Transactions

Challenges in implementing securities transactions over the Blockchain initially consist of regulatory requirements. Implementing securities transactions over the Blockchain requires consideration of and compliance with regulatory requirements. It is important that Blockchain platforms comply with applicable securities laws and ensure investor protection.

The scalability of Blockchain technology is also a challenge, especially when it comes to processing a large number of securities transactions. The Blockchain must be able to efficiently process a high number of transactions in order to meet the demands of the market.

The integration of Blockchain into existing securities infrastructures requires the creation of interoperability standards and collaboration between different market participants. It is important to ensure that securities can be transferred seamlessly between different platforms to improve market liquidity and efficiency.

15.4.3 Conclusions on Blockchain in Securities

The use of Blockchain technology for securities transactions offers a promising solution to improve the efficiency, transparency and liquidity of securities trading. Despite the challenges associated with the adoption of Blockchain-based systems, the potential for significant benefits in terms of cost, speed and security of securities transactions is enormous. Blockchain technology is expected to play an increasingly important role in the financial industry in the future.

15.4.4 Further Conclusion

The use of Blockchain technology can and will become more widespread in the financial industry in the coming years. The reasons are clear: it enables closer peer-to-peer transactions. "Banking is necessary, banks are not". This phrase, attributed to Bill Gates, will become increasingly important in the future. After all, the development of payment transactions shows a clear tendency towards non-cash payments and, at the same time, providers who want to bring "virtual currencies" to market maturity are increasingly appearing alongside payment service providers. Central banks have also recognized the need for action, not least because of the existing or impending competition,

This applies even more strongly to the area of securities. Here, many Blockchain-based applications have already been successfully tested in practice. The technology is particularly popular with the key players, issuers, or the accompanying banks, and also stock exchanges.

The main reasons for this are the lack of legal regulations. But here, too, legislators have recognized the need for action and are creating the necessary legal framework. Three core areas of application can be identified:

1. Stable coins are likely to be increasingly used in payment transactions to serve as a means of payment in cross-border payment transactions and also as a uniform means of payment within groups or product families. The basic idea of Facebook's Libra is likely to prevail in a similar form. In contrast, CBDCs could possibly raise the question of whether they will come too late, namely, represent a solution to a problem that has long since been solved.
2. In the area of the security, it is foreseeable that tokens will be used in corporate financing, especially for smaller issues. By increasing efficiency, this would give significantly more companies easier refinancing conditions.
3. Finally, the use of Blockchains just lends itself to the field of commerce to make trading much easier and more efficient.

References

BaFin. (n.d.). *Bitcoin, ether et al.: The risks of investing in crypto assets.* BaFin Federal Financial Supervisory Authority. Retrieved July 5, 2023, from www.bafin.de/EN/Verbraucher/ Aktuelles/verbraucher_kryptowerte_en.html.

Birne, S., & Omlor, A. (2020). Digitales Zentralbankgeld im Euroraum [Digital central bank money in the euro area]. *Recht Digital, 1,* 1–10.

Council of the EU. (2022, June 30). *Digital finance: Agreement reached on European crypto-assets regulation (MiCA).* www.consilium.europa.eu/en/press/press-releases/2022/06/ 30/digital-finance-agreement-reached-on-european-crypto-assets-regulation-mica/.

Eurogroup. (2023). *Update on the digital euro project.* www.ecb.europa.eu/paym/digital_e uro/investigation/governance/shared/files/ecb.degov230615_Updateonthedigitaleuro. de.pdf?9af2064f07cbcf772dbdfcb66634f500.

European Central Bank. (2020). *Report on a digital euro.* www.ecb.europa.eu/pub/pdf/other/ Report_on_a_digital_euro~4d7268b458.en.pdf.

Frank-Fahle, C., Sauter, B., & Schmidt, J. (2019). *Regulatory Framework on ICO in the USA, UAE, Germany and Japan* [IWRZ 2019, 122]. https://beck-online. beck.de/Dokument?vpath=bibdata%2Fzeits%2Fiwrz%2F2019%2Fcont%2Fi wrz.2019.122.1.htm&pos=12.

Kaulartz, M., & Matzke, R. (2019). *Die Tokenisierung des Rechts [The tokenisation of law]* [NJW 2018, 3278]. https://beck-online.beck.de/DokumentMarkieren/261467303.

LBBW. (2017, June 28). *Daimler and LBBW successfully utilize Blockchain technology for launch of corporate Schuldschein.* www.lbbw.de/articlepage/press-release/daimler-and-lbbw-successfully-utilize-blockchain-technology-for-launch-of-corporate-schuldsch ein_8zvetwhio_e.html.

Maume, P. (2022a). Die Verordnung über Märkte für Kryptowerte (MiCAR) Teil 1 [The Markets in Crypto Assets Regulation (MiCAR) Part 1]. *Recht Digital, 461.* https:// beck-online.beck.de/Default.aspx?typ=reference&y=300&Z=RDi&B=2022&S=461.

Maume, P. (2022b). Die Verordnung über Märkte für Kryptowerte (MiCAR) Teil 2 [The Markets in Crypto Assets Regulation (MiCAR) Part 2]. *Recht Digital, 497.* https:// beck-online.beck.de/Default.aspx?typ=reference&y=300&Z=RDi&B=2022&S=461.

Mertten, L. (2023, January 12). Was sind Stablecoins?–Definition, Erklärung und Übersicht [What are stablecoins?–Definition, explanation and overview]. *Blockchainwelt.* https:// blockchainwelt.de/stablecoins-sind-preisstabile-kryptowaehrungen-moeglich/.

Möslein, F., & Omlor, S. (Eds.). (2021). *FinTech-Handbuch: Digitalisierung, Recht, Finanzen* (2. Auflage). C.H.Beck.

Nathmann, M. (2019). *Token in der Unternehmensfinanzierung [Tokens in Corporate Finance]* [BKR 540]. https://beck-online.beck.de/DokumentMarkieren/269325011.

Patz, A. (2021). *Überblick über die Regulierung von Kryptowerten und Kryptowertedienstleistern [Overview of the regulation of cryptocurrencies and crypto service providers]* [BKR 2021, 725]. https://beck-online.beck.de/Dokument?vpath=bibdata%2Fze its%2Fbkr%2F2021%2Fcont%2Fbkr.2021.725.1.htm&pos=15.

Index

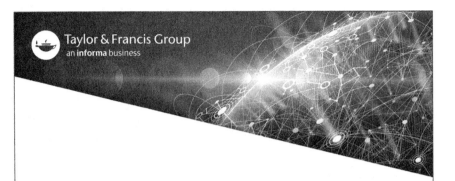

Printed in the United States
by Baker & Taylor Publisher Services